INBORN REALIZATION

A Commentary on His Holiness Dudjom Rinpoche's *Mountain Retreat Instructions*

by KHENPO TSEWANG DONGYAL RINPOCHE

INBORN REALIZATION

A Commentary on
His Holiness Dudjom Rinpoche's
Mountain Retreat Instructions

by KHENPO TSEWANG DONGYAL RINPOCHE

edited by the Samye Translation Group
Richard Steinberg

Inborn Realization:
A Commentary on His Holiness Dudjom Rinpoche's
Mountain Retreat Instructions

Published by Dharma Samudra

Padma Samye Ling
618 Buddha Highway
Sidney Center, NY 13839
(607) 865-8068
padmasambhava.org

ISBN-13: 978-0-9834074-5-4

DEDICATION

Dedicated in honor and memory of His Holiness Dudjom Rinpoche, Venerable Khenchen Palden Sherab Rinpoche, Lama Chimed Namgyal, and all the lineage holders of these secret teachings, as well as all the devoted practitioners of the past, present, and future.

CONTENTS

PREFACE

The Buddha gave a variety of teachings from the age of thirty-five until age eighty-one. As the Great Acharya Vasubandhu said, "The Teacher's teaching can be divided into the two groups of scripture (*lung*) and realization (*togpa*). The only way to uphold the teaching is by reading or studying, and practicing." Academic teachings of scripture are studied and contemplated, and practice instructions are applied to bring realization. These two lineages of scripture and realization are essential for everyone who follows the teachings of the Buddha.

The *Mountain Retreat*, or *Richo* teaching, is particularly designed as a set of practice instructions that bring realization. When the Buddha gave teachings, he didn't say only to study—what you learn intellectually should be absorbed into your heart through practice. Based on the firm foundation of intellectual study and contemplation, *Richo* is an instruction manual that brings forth vivid realization, making the results more tangible in your experience. These teachings directly usher the realization of loving-kindness, compassion, and respect, while going beyond all ego-clinging and grasping.

Throughout Buddhist history—including when Buddhism came to Tibet from the Holy Land of India—combining intellectual study with meditation was the essential practice. In particular, *Richo* was very openly used in all the Practice Lineages of Tibetan Buddhism, especially the Nyingma and Kagyu schools. The teachings always mention that individuals should spend time in hermitages and go to the mountains until they stabilize their realization because there are fewer distractions. Mountain retreat means "hermitage"—it is one of the best places to make yourself strong so you are not disturbed by all the fears and habitual patterns that are not healthy for anyone. Practicing in a hermitage makes it easier for the old habitual patterns that prevent our realization and disturb our peace of mind to subside. That is why the Buddha and Guru Padmasambhava always recommended practicing in mountain retreat.

Among all the types of hermitages, practicing in mountains is very important. For example, all of the twenty-four disciples of Guru Rinpoche preferred to remain in mountain retreat, where they studied and learned until they themselves *became* the teachings. They didn't keep the Dharma outside of themselves. Throughout Tibet, there are so many mountain hermitages where people have practiced to achieve realization. Milarepa chose to stay in mountain retreat, which he named as his "castle," and so many other masters in all the lineages did this as well, including Longchenpa and Jigme Lingpa. This is why *Richo* teachings are very popular.

Many teachers gave *Richo* teachings, and among them, these *Mountain Retreat* instructions were taught by His Holiness Dudjom Rinpoche, one of the great masters of the 20th century. His Holiness Dudjom Rinpoche was predicted by Guru Padmasambhava, and just as he predicted, His Holiness was born in southern Tibet. The moment he was born there was a remarkable sign indicating that this was a great emanation being who would restrengthen the teachings and bring peace and harmony to all beings. As he grew up, His Holiness continued expanding these activities, reaching out to all fortunate disciples and practitioners. He studied and practiced according to the teachings, learning from his tutors in monasteries. Outwardly he achieved realization by his ongoing study and meditation, while inwardly he emanated with the inborn realization of his previous incarnation, the great terton Dudjom Lingpa. His Holiness Dudjom Rinpoche didn't just leave the Dharma as intellectual study—he became an expert of *both* study and practice and was respected by all the masters of the Nyingma school, as well as the masters of all schools of Tibetan Buddhism.

His Holiness Dudjom Rinpoche gave many teachings, but among all of them, *Mountain Retreat* is one of the great teachings for practitioners who want to absorb the teachings deeply into their hearts and minds. I had the great opportunity to receive these teachings directly from His Holiness Dudjom Rinpoche himself, as well as from Ven. Khenchen Palden Sherab Rinpoche, and my father, bhikshu Lama Chimed Namgyal.

I gave this commentary at the beautiful retreat land of Padma Samye Ling in the United States of America in 2011. In the presence and light of these great masters, I wish and pray that these *Richo* teachings will ignite the full potential and inner wisdom of everyone's buddha-nature, now and long into the future, so that we all become great wisdom beings on this Earth, fulfilling our own benefit as well as the benefits of all others, and bringing peace to this world.

I thank everyone who supported and helped with this book, including all of the transcribers, the editors Richard Steinberg, Lama Pema Dragpa, and Toy-Fung Tung, as well as Christa Schoenbrodt, who completed the design and layout. I also thank Lama Jomo Lorraine and Lama Laia Pema Tsultrim for their ongoing support of the Padmasambhava Buddhist Center.

Khenpo Tsewang Dongyal Rinpoche
March 18, 2016
10th day of Guru Padmasambhava as Guru Loden Chokse
Palden Padma Samye Ling

EDITOR'S INTRODUCTION

Embodiment of
Infinite relaxation,
Infinite creativity, and
Infinite love and understanding,
You inspire all beings to realize
The Great Perfection of all that is.
Spiritual Grandfather,
Immortal Dudjom Rinpoche,
I pay homage to you!

His Holiness Dudjom Rinpoche was the single reincarnation of many realized beings, as well as both the regent and mind emanation of Guru Padmasambhava. During a time of mounting political tension, when Tibetan civilization as a whole and Nyingma Dharma in particular was under siege, all the Nyingma masters in a single voice selected him to be the leader of their school, and he ably served in that capacity until his mahaparnirvana in 1987. His Holiness was an indestructible source of inspiration for the Tibetan people before, during, and after their homeland was overrun. In addition to being a superlative spiritual guide who intuitively understood the hearts of beings and how to guide them to spiritual awakening, he discovered termas—many of which are widely practiced today—and wrote many important books, including the definitive history of the Nyingma tradition. He was honored as a perfect master throughout his life, and his spiritual powers were unequalled. At the same time he was the most humble and unassuming of men. After the Tibetan diaspora, he traveled widely, taught freely, and founded centers around the world. He was and is renowned as the teacher of teachers. Indeed, almost every Nyingma master alive today, particularly those who live and teach outside of Tibet, once sat at his feet. In these ways, His Holiness Dudjom Rinpoche contributed mightily to the spiritual evolution of millions of people, and insured that the Nyingma tradition would not only be preserved, but also flourish.

His Holiness was also regarded as one of the supreme Dzogchen adepts of all time. Great lamas sent their most advanced students to him in order to receive the definitive mind-to-mind transmission of ultimate awareness. His Holiness so deeply and perfectly embodied this state that even ordinary people and novice practitioners would feel it simply by being near him, seeing his photo, or hearing his name. Although he left his body twenty-seven years ago, many persons continue to receive his blessings in dreams and visions. Many more do so by sitting at the feet and imbibing the nectar instructions of great masters such as Khenchen Palden Sherab Rinpoche and Khenpo Tsewang Dongyal Rinpoche, who were once his students and who are now his lineage holders.

Khenchen Palden Sherab Rinpoche, like His Holiness, was an unparalled scholar and writer, siddha and Dzogchen adept, and a sublime and selfless being who tremendously enhanced the lives of everyone who met him—as well as those who did not. He completely embodied the Nyingma Dharma, and dedicated his life to upholding and spreading it. And he is as spiritually potent today as he was when he graced us with the beauty of his physical form.

Khenpo Tsewang Dongyal Rinpoche's conduct is pure and he is always casual and relaxed. He is kind, gentle, and charismatic. To be in his presence is to experience the complete dissolution of the conceptual mind and the absolute freedom of the natural state. And while his spiritual power is immense and awe-inspiring, his humility is even more so.

In these and other ways, the Khenpo Rinpoches as well as the great masters who were once His Holiness' students uphold and transmit the Dudjom lineage to fortunate beings in the 21st century. Although the full range and subtlety of the Dudjom lineage is beyond words, we can safely say that it includes infinite concern for the spiritual well-being of others, united with the infinite power to accomplish it. It also includes simplicity, gentleness, and naturalness; and a mind which gives birth to, supports, and dissolves the universe and all the phenomena within it—the Dzogchen state, the Great Perfection—along with great reverence for all beings endowed with nondual wisdom and unconditional compassion. Such is the legacy, at least in part, of His Holiness Dudjom Rinpoche.

One of His Holiness's most renowned and influential texts is *Extracting the Quintessence of Accomplishment: Oral Instructions for the Practice of Mountain Retreat, Expounded Simply and Directly in their Essential Nakedness*. The heart of this text is how to ascertain the Dzogchen state and continuously abide in it, aided by devotion to the spiritual master and the cultivation of unconditional love and compassion for all beings. From late March through April, 2011 Khenpo Tsewang Dongyal Rinpoche gave extensive teachings on this great text to his students during the annual spring retreat at Padma Samye Ling. These teachings were recorded, transcribed, and edited—and just like that, a book was born. Although several great masters have given seminars on His Holiness' *Mountain Retreat* in the past, this may be the first time an extensive commentary on this great teaching has been published.

I thank everyone who participated in the transcription process, including Ani Joanie Andras, Linda Bland, Deana Bodnar, Reneé Cosgrove, Karen Johnson, Cynthia Friend, Patty Ibur, and Kirk Lawson. I appreciate Christa Schoenbrodt's wonderful help with layout. I would also like to thank Dr. Toy-Fung Tung, a scholar and devoted Vajrayana student, for her editorial advice.

Finally, I thank my spiritual father, Khenpo Tsewang Dongyal Rinpoche for more that can be expressed in words.

Through this good work may everyone everywhere enjoy long life, health, and prosperity, the swift fulfillment of all good wishes, and infinite relaxation of body, speech, and mind.

On behalf of the team of Samye Translation editors
Richard Steinberg (Padma Chodrak)
May 12, 2014
New York City

༄༅། རི་ཆོས་བསླབ་བྱ་ཉམས་ལེན་དམ་པ་
ཁྲིད་གོ་བདེར་བརྗོད་པ་
གྲུབ་པའི་བཅུད་ལེན་ཞེས་བྱ་བ་བཞུགས་སོ།

Extracting the Quintessence of Accomplishment

Oral Instructions
for the Practice of Mountain Retreat
Expounded Simply and Directly
in their Essential Nakedness

By

His Holiness Dudjom Rinpoche

Dharma Samudra

༄༅། །བཀའ་དྲིན་མཚུངས་མེད་དཔལ་ལྡན་བླ་མ་དམ་པའི་ཞབས་ལ་གུས་པས་ཕྱག་འཚལ་
ཞིང་སྐྱབས་སུ་མཆིའོ། བདག་དང་བདག་གི་རྗེས་འཇུག་རྣམས་ཀྱི་རྒྱུད་ལ་ཟབ་ལམ་གྱི་རྟོགས་
པ་ཕྱིན་ཅི་མ་ལོག་པ་མྱུར་དུ་སྐྱེས་ནས་ཚེ་འདི་ཉིད་ལ་གདོད་མའི་བཙན་ས་ཟིན་པར་བྱིན་གྱིས་
བརླབ་ཏུ་གསོལ། །དེ་ལ་འདིར་སྔོན་གྱི་སློན་ལམ་ལས་འཕྲོ་རྣམ་པར་དག་པས་མཚམས་སྦྱར་
ཏེ་ཟབ་གསང་རྫོགས་པ་ཆེན་པོའི་ཆོས་དང་དེ་སྟོན་པའི་བླ་མ་ལ་སྙིང་ནས་བློ་ཁེལ་ཞིང་ཉམས་
ལེན་མཐར་སྐྱོལ་བར་འདོད་པའི་གང་ཟག་སྐལ་པ་ཅན་རྣམས་ཀྱི་འཇུག་སྒོར་རི་ཆོས་གནད་ཀྱི་
བསླབ་བྱ་ཡང་གསང་རྫོགས་པ་ཆེན་པོའི་ཉམས་ལེན་དམར་ཁྲིད་ལག་བཅངས་སུ་གོ་བདེ་བར་
འཆད་ལ། སྤྱི་དོན་རྣམ་པ་གསུམ་གྱི་སྒོ་ནས་ཤེས་པར་བྱ་སྟེ། སྦྱོར་བ་ཆགས་ཞེན་གྱི་འཕྲི་བ་
བཅད་ནས་བློ་ཆོས་ཕྱོགས་སུ་བསྒོལ་ཏེ་རྒྱུད་སྦྱོང་ཚུལ། དངོས་གཞི་ལྟ་སྒོམ་སྤྱོད་པའི་སྒྲོ་
འདོགས་བཅད་དེ་སྒྲུབ་པ་ཉམས་ལེན་གྱི་སྲང་དུ་ཞུག་ཚུལ། རྗེས་ཐོབ་དམ་ཚིག་སྡོམ་པ་
བསྲུང་ཞིང་ཚེ་འདིའི་ལས་གཞུག་ཆོས་ཀྱིས་བསྡུ་ཚུལ་ལོ། དེ་ལས་དང་པོའི་དོན་ཅུང་ཟད་སྨྲ་
བར་བྱའོ། །ཀྱེ་མ་འོ་སྐལ་རྣམས་ཀྱི་སེམས་ཞེས་བྱ་བའི་རིག་རིག་ཙུར་ཙུར་པོ་འདི་ཀུན་ཏུ་
བཟང་པོ་དང་དུས་མཉམ་དུ་དང་པོ་ཉིད་ནས་བྱུང་བ་ཡིན་ཀྱང་། །ཀུན་ཏུ་བཟང་པོས་རང་དུ་
མཁྱེན་པས་གྲོལ། རང་རེ་སེམས་ཅན་རྣམས་ཀྱིས་ངོ་མ་ཤེས་པས་འཁོར་བར་མཐའ་མེད་དུ་
འཁྱམས། རིགས་དྲུག་གི་ལུས་གྲངས་ལས་འདས་པ་ཞིག་བླངས། བྱས་པ་ཐམས་ཅད་དོན་
མེད་དུ་སོང་། ད་རེས་མི་ལུས་བརྒྱ་ལ་ཡན་གཅིག་ཐོབ་པའི་དུས་འདིར་འཁོར་བ་ངན་སོང་དུ་
མི་སྐྱེ་བའི་ཐབས་ཤིག་མ་འགྲུབ་ན། ཤི་ནས་གར་སྐྱེ་ངེས་པ་མེད་ཅིང་། འགྲོ་བ་རིགས་དྲུག་

I bow down respectfully and take refuge at the feet of the Glorious and supreme Guru, incomparable in kindness. May we – my followers and I – be blessed so that, the realization of the profound path being born quickly in our nature without the slightest error, we may attain the Primordial Citadel[1] in this very life.

For those who, through the reunion of their perfectly pure past aspirations and potential karma, have heart-felt confidence in the Dharma of the profound and secret Great Perfection and in the Guru who reveals it, and who wish to go through the practice to its ultimate end, for all these fortunate beings here is an entrance door: the vital instructions for mountain retreat, expounding in its essential nakedness the practice of the most secret Great Perfection, put into our hands in a form that is easy to understand.

This should be understood under three main topics:

1. **The Preparation** – having cut the ties of grasping and clinging, how to purify one's mind stream by keeping the mind turned towards the Dharma.

2. **The Main Practice** – having cut misconceptions about view, meditation, and action, how to accurately engage in the practice.

3. **Post-Meditation** – how to keep the samaya and vows, and complete all the subsequent actions of this life with Dharma.

1. The Preparation

Now I will say a little about the first topic. *Alas!* Our mind – that is to say, that which is sometimes clear awareness, sometimes gloomy turmoil – arose at the very beginning simultaneously with Samantabhadra. Samantabhadra, recognizing mind in itself, is free. We sentient beings, through not recognizing this, have wandered endlessly in samsara. Countless times we have taken different forms in the six realms, but all that we have done has been meaningless. Now, for once out of hundreds of times, we have obtained a human body. Unless we put into

༄༅། གང་དུ་སྐྱེས་ཀྱང་སྡུག་བསྔལ་ཁོ་ན་ལས་མ་འདས། མི་ལུས་འདི་ཡང་ ཐོབ་པས་མི་ཆོག་སྟེ་ནམ་འཆི་ཆ་མེད་པས་ད་ལྟ་ཉིད་དུ་ཆོས་གཤའ་མ་ཞིག་བྱེད་དགོས། དེ་ཡང་འཆི་ཁར་མི་འགྱོད་ཅིང་རང་གིས་རང་ལ་མི་ཁྲེལ་བ་རྗེ་བཙུན་མི་ལ་ལྟ་བུ་ཞིག་དགོས་ཏེ། ང་མི་ལ་རས་པའི་ཆོས་ལུགས་ལ། །རང་གིས་རང་ལ་མ་ཁྲེལ་བ། །ཞེས་གསུངས། ཆོས་ལམ་དུ་འཇུག་པ་ལའང་ཆོས་གཟུགས་མཁན་སྐྱི་འགྲེས་ནི་མི་ཆོག་སྟེ། ཚེ་འདིར་ལྟོས་ཀྱི་བྱ་བཞག་འདོད་ཡོན་གྱི་འཁྲི་བ་ཐམས་ཅད་གཅོད་དགོས། དེ་མ་ཆོད་པར་བློ་སབ་སོབ་ཙམ་གྱིས་ཆོས་སྒོར་ལན་གཅིག་ཞུགས་ཀྱང་། ཕ་ཡུལ་ནོར་རྫས་གཉེན་བཤེས་མཛའ་གྲོགས་སོགས་ལ་ཆགས་ན། ཆགས་སེམས་དེས་རྒྱུ་དང་། ཆགས་ཡུལ་དེས་རྐྱེན་བྱས། མཚམས་སྦྱོར་བར་ཆད་བདུད་ཀྱིས་བྱས་ཏེ། སླར་ཡང་འཇིག་རྟེན་ཐ་མལ་པ་དང་འདྲེས་ནས་ལས་མཐའ་ལོག་པར་འགྱུར་པ་ཡིན། དེས་ན་སྒྲོང་ལྷོ་གོས་གཏམ་གསུམ་ལ་བསྐྱུར་ནས་འཇིག་རྟེན་ཆོས་བརྒྱད་ལ་མ་ཆགས་པར་རྩེ་གཅིག་ཏུ་ཆོས་ལ་བློ་སྒྲིལ་བར་བྱ་སྟེ། འཆི་བ་སྙིང་ཟུག་གི་དཔེན་གནས་སུ། །ཞེན་པ་གཏིང་ལོག་གི་སྒྲུབ་པ་པོ། །ཚེ་འདི་བློས་བཏང་གི་སྐུ་མཚམས་བཅད། །སེམས་ཆོས་བརྒྱད་ཀྱི་མི་དང་མཇལ་འཕྲད་མེད། །ཅེས་རྒྱལ་བ་ཡང་དགོན་པ་ལྟ་བུ་ཞིག་བྱེད་དགོས། དེ་མིན་ཆོས་བརྒྱད་དང་འདྲེས་པའི་ཆོས་དེ་དུག་དང་འདྲེས་པའི་ཁ་ཟས་བཟའ་བ་དང་མཚུངས་པས་ཕུང་ཚབ་ཤིན་ཏུ་ཆེ། ཆོས་བརྒྱད་དེའང་བསྡུ་ན་རེ་དོགས་གཉིས་སུ་འདུ་ལ་དེ་ཀ་དོན་ལ་ཆགས་སྡང་གཉིས་པོ་ཡིན། ནང་གི་ཆགས་སྡང་ཕྱི་རོལ་རྒྱལ་བསེན་གཉིས་སུ་བརྫུ་བས་བློ་ཆགས་སྡང་དང་མ་བྲལ་གྱི་རིང་ལ་རྒྱལ་བསེན་དང་མི་འབྲལ་བས་བར་ཆད་ལ་ཟད་པ་མི་འོང་། དེས་

action the means for avoiding rebirth in the inferior realms of samsara, once dead, where we will be reborn is uncertain; and wherever we might take birth in the six classes of beings there is nothing but suffering. To have obtained a human body is not enough by itself. Since the time of death is uncertain, we must practice Dharma genuinely right now. At the time of death we should, like Jetsun Mila, feel no regret or self-reproach. As he said,

"The Dharma tradition of myself, Milarepa,
is not to be ashamed of myself."

To enter the path of Dharma, it is not enough to adopt its outer appearances. We have to sever all ties to desirable things and to activities limited to this life. Without severing these ties, we may enter the door of Dharma with an inconsistent mind, retaining some attachment towards our native land, property, intimates, relatives, friends, and so on; but then, this mind of attachment, creating the root cause, and the objects of attachment, providing the conditions, will be joined together by Mara as the obstacles. Becoming involved once again with common worldliness, our progress will be reversed.

Therefore, giving less importance to food, clothing, and mere talk, without clinging to the eight worldly concerns,[2] we should one-pointedly focus our mind on Dharma.

"In the solitary place The-Thought-of-Death-Fixed-in-the-Heart
The hermit Deeply-Disgusted-with-Attachments
Draws the boundaries of his retreat by renouncing the thoughts of this life,
And does not meet those known as the Eight Worldly Dharmas."

We should act like Gyalwa Yang Gönpa. Otherwise, Dharma mixed with the eight worldly concerns is extremely dangerous and wasteful, like food mixed with poison. The eight worldly dharmas can be condensed into hope and fear, which mean attachment and aversion. Internal attachment and aversion take the outward disguise of Senmo and Gyalpo. As long as you are not free from attachment and aversion, you

༄༅། ན་ཞེ་ཕྱུག་ཏུ་ཆོས་བརྒྱད་ཚེ་འདིའི་རློམ་ཞེན་ཕེ་འདུག་རང་གིས་རང་ལ་ཡང་ཡང་བརྟག་ནས་སྐྱོན་དེ་འདོར་བ་ལ་ནན་ཏན་བྱ། ཆོས་བརྒྱད་ཞེ་ལ་བཅངས་ནས་ལྷར་སྣང་ཆོས་ལྷར་བཅོས་ཏེ་གཡོ་སྒྱུས་བསླུབས་པའི་ཡོ་བྱད་ཀྱང་ལོག་པའི་འཚོ་བ་ཡིན། ཕ་ཡུལ་སྤྲངས་པས་ཆོས་ཕྱེད་གྲུབ་ཟེར་བ་ལྟར་ཕ་ཡུལ་རྒྱབ་ཏུ་བསྐྱུར་ནས་ཆ་མེད་ཀྱི་རྒྱལ་ཁམས་འགྲིམ། གཉེན་གཤེས་དང་བཟང་འབྲལ་བྱས་ཏེ་ཆོས་ཀྱི་བཤོལ་འདེབས་ལ་མི་ཉན། ནོར་རྫས་སྦྱིན་པར་བཏང་ནས་འཚོ་བ་བསོད་སྙོམས་གང་བྱུང་ལ་བརྟེན། འདོད་ཡོན་མཐའ་དག་ལང་ཤོར་གྱི་བར་ཆད་དུ་ཤེས་པར་བྱས་ལ་མི་འདོད་པའི་བློ་བསྐྱེད། ནོར་རྫས་ལྟ་བུ་ལའང་བག་ཙམ་གྱིས་ཆོག་ཤེས་པར་མ་བྱས་ན་གཅིག་བྱུང་གཉིས་དགོས་ཀྱི་རིང་ལ་འདོད་ཡོན་བསླུ་བྲིད་ཀྱི་བདུད་འཇུག་པ་ལ་ཚོགས་མེད། གཏམས་བཟང་ངན་གང་ལའང་བདེན་འཛིན་རེ་དོགས་དགག་བསྒྲུབ་མི་བྱེད་པར་མི་ཤེ་བའི་ཤུལ་གྱི་གཏམ་བཞིན་ཅི་ལབ་རུང་ལབ་ཏུ་ཆུག །མཚན་ལྡན་གྱི་བླ་མ་མ་གཏོགས་བསླབ་བྱ་དྲང་པོར་བཤད་མཁན་ཕ་མ་ཡིན་ཀྱང་མི་ཡོང་བས་ཚོད་རང་གིས་བཟུང་སྟེ་སྣ་ཐག་མི་ལ་མ་ཤོར་བྱ། རྣམ་པ་ཙམ་དུ་དང་རྒྱུད་རིང་བའི་སྒོ་ནས་ཀུན་གྱི་སྣ་མི་བསྲེག་པར་མཐུན་པས་འགྲོགས་ཤེས་པ་དང་། དོན་ལ་སྒྲུབ་པའི་གེགས་སུ་འགྲོ་ན་དྲག་ཞན་སུས་ཀྱང་བསླུ་ལ་མི་ནུས་པ་ལྷུགས་ཀྱི་ཕ་བོང་ལ་དར་ཡུག་བཏགས་པ་འདྲ་ཞིག་དགོས། ཀླུང་གང་ནས་རྒྱབ་རྒྱབ་ལ་མགོ་གུག་གུག་བྱེད་པ་ལ་ཁའི་འཇགས་མ་འདྲ་བའི་མི་གཞི་སླ་མོ་དེས་མི་ཡོང་། སྒྲུབ་པ་ཉམས་ལེན་གང་ཡང་ཐོག་མར་བརྩམས་པ་ནས་མཐར་མ་ཕྱིན་གྱི་བར་དུ། སྙིང་ནས་ཐོག་བབས། འོག་ནས་མཚོ་བརྡོལ། ལོགས་ནས་བྲག་རལ། འཆི་བ་སློག་ལ་བབས་ཀྱང་དམ་བཅའ

cannot get away from Senmo and Gyalpo, and obstacles will not cease.

So, is there any conceited attachment to the things of this life and to the eight worldly concerns in your innermost thoughts? Examining yourself again and again, you should be diligent in giving up these defects. To get anything by deceitfully adopting an artificial Dharma appearance while retaining the eight worldly concerns is a wrong way of life.

It is said: *"By giving up your homeland, half of the Dharma is accomplished."* So, leaving your homeland behind, wander through many unknown countries. Parting from your friends and relatives in a pleasant way, ignore those who try to dissuade you from practicing the Dharma. Giving away your possessions, rely on whatever alms come your way. Understanding all desirable things to be the obstacles linked with bad habits, develop a disinterested mind. If you don't know how to be contented with just a few possessions and so on, once you've got one you'll want two, and it won't be difficult for the deceiving devil of the desirable objects to enter.

Whatever good or bad things people might say, don't take them as true; have no hope or fear, acceptance or rejection. Let them say whatever they will, as though they were talking about someone dead and buried. No one but a qualified guru – not even your father or mother – can give correct advice. Therefore keeping control over your own actions, do not hand your nose-rope to others.

Outwardly good-natured, you should know how to get along harmoniously with everyone without "burning their noses." But in fact, if anyone – superior or inferior – comes to hinder your sadhana practice, you should be unshakable, like an iron boulder pulled by a silk scarf. It won't do to be a weak character whose head bends in whichever direction the wind blows, like grass on a mountain pass.

For any practice, from the moment you begin it until you reach its ultimate end – whether lightning falls from above, a lake springs from below, or rocks fall from all sides – having sworn not to break your

༄༅། གཤིག་རེ་སྐམ་དུ་ཞེ་མནའ་བོར་ལ་དེ་ཀ་བཞིན་དུ་མཐའ་ཐོན་པའང་བྱེད། ཐུན་ཚོད། གཉིད་ཚོད། ཐ་ན་ཁམས་གསེང་ཟས་ཀྱི་ཚོད་སོགས་དང་པོ་རང་ནས་ལང་ཤོར་ལ་མ་བཏང་བར་རིམ་པས་སྦྱོལ་དུ་ཚུད་པར་བྱ། ལྷག་པར་སྤྲོས་བཅས་སྤྲོས་མེད་ཀྱི་དགེ་སྦྱོར་གང་ལའང་རེས་འཛོག་སྐབས་ལ་ས་སྟོང་ཐ་མལ་དུ་དར་གཅིག་ཀྱང་མ་ལུས་པའི་ཉམས་ལེན་བསྐུར་རྐང་སྐྱོམས་པར་བྱེད། མཚམས་ཀྱི་ཚེ་སྒྲུབ་སྒོ་འདག་སྦྱར་རམ་མིན་ཀྱང་གཞན་དང་གདོང་མི་འཕྲད། ངག་མི་གཏོང་། བྱ་ར་མི་བྱེད། སེམས་ཅན་ཚུབ་ཀྱི་རྣམ་གཡེང་ཐམས་ཅད་ཅམ་གྱི་བཞག་ནས། ལྷུང་རོ་དོར། ལུས་གནད་ལེགས་པར་བཅའ། ཡིད་དྲན་རིག་གི་ཐོག་ཏུ་སྤྱང་ལ་བེ་ཕུར་བཏབ་པ་ལྟར་སྐད་ཅིག་ཀྱང་གཡོ་མེད་དུ་སྡོད་ཚུགས་པ་ཞིག་དགོས་ཏེ། ཕྱི་ནང་གསང་བའི་མཚམས་དམ་པ་ལས་རྟགས་དང་ཡོན་ཏན་ཐམས་ཅད་མྱུར་དུ་འབྱུང་བ་ཡིན། ད་རེས་ཁག་ཆེ་བས་ཁོང་དང་འཕྲད། ངག་ཀྱང་བཏང་། དེ་ཕྱིན་ནས་དམ་པོ་བྱའོ་སྙམ་པས་དེ་ལྟར་ཐལ་ན་སྒྲུབ་པའི་གཡང་ཤོར་ནས་ཇེ་ལྷོད་ཇེ་ལྷོད་ལ་འགྲོ། དེས་ན་ཐོག་མ་ཉིད་ནས་སྡོད་ཐག་ཐད་ཀྱིས་བཅད་ན་ཇེ་དམ་ཇེ་དམ་ལ་འགྲོ་ཞིང་སྒྲུབ་པ་བར་ཆད་ཀྱིས་མི་ཁྱེར་བ་ཡིན། གནས་ཀྱི་ཁྱད་པར་མཚན་ཉིད་བརྟག་ཐབས་མང་དུ་འབྱུང་ཡང་སྤྱིར་བཏང་གྲུ་རུ་རིན་པོ་ཆེ་སོགས་གྲུབ་ཐོབ་གོང་མའི་བྱིན་གྱིས་བརླབས་ཤིང་དམ་སེལ་ཅན་གྱིས་མ་བརྟེན་པ་དང་། ཤིན་ཏུ་དབེན་ཅིང་མཐུན་རྐྱེན་འཛོམ་སླ་བ་སོགས་རང་རང་གི་ཁམས་དང་བསྟུན་པ་འཐད། དུར་ཁྲོད་དང་གཉན་ཁྲོད་སོགས་གཞི་བདག་གདུག་པ་ཅན་གནས་པ་རྣམས་སུ་ཕྱི་ནང་གི་རྟེན་འབྲེལ་འགྲིགས་པ་མྱུར་བས་ནུས་པའི་རྒྱལ་གྱིས་ཆུན་ན་སྒོམ་ལ་བོགས་དེ་རང་ཆེ། མ་ཆུན་ན་བར་ཆད་ཀྱང་མང་།

promise even at the cost of your life, you should persevere until the end. From the very beginning, you should come progressively to an established schedule of periods for practice, sleep, meals, and breaks, allowing no bad habits. Whether your practice is elaborate or simple, you should make it even and regular, never sporadic, and not even for an instant should you allow any room for the ordinary.

During retreat, the entryway should be sealed with mud; if not, you must not speak, not spy, and not come face to face with others. Having completely discarded the wanderings of the restless mind, expel the stale breath and correctly assume the essential elements of body posture. The mind should rest upon clear awareness without wavering even for the time of a finger snap, like a peg driven into solid ground. A strict outer, inner, and secret retreat will quickly give rise to all the signs and qualities.[3]

If for some important reason you meet and talk to someone, thinking, "After this I shall be very strict," after this transgression the prosperity of your practice will fade and everything will become slacker and slacker. If at the very start you make a resolute, clear-cut decision to remain seated, making your retreat progressively stricter, your practice won't be swept away by obstacles.

There are many descriptions of particular qualifications and topography of places, but in general a place blessed by Guru Rinpoche and the great siddhas of the past which is not presently in the hands of people of dissenting samaya is suitable; or according to your preference, any utterly solitary place where favorable conditions – food and other necessities – are easily available.

If you have the ability to control the swift evolution of outer and inner causal links in cemeteries and other frightening places, abodes of the cruel demons of the locality, your meditation will be greatly improved; if not, you will have even more obstacles. When your realization becomes vast as space, all adverse conditions arise as friends; it is then excellent to perform secret practices in graveyards and such places. Always forsaking outer and inner entertainments, to dwell in non-

༄༅། རྟོགས་པ་གློང་དུ་གྲུར་ཆེ་འགལ་རྐྱེན་ཐམས་ཅད་གྲོགས་སུ་འཆར་བ་ཡིན་པས་དེ་དུས་
དུར་ཁྲོད་སོགས་སུ་གསང་སྤྱོད་བྱས་ན་ལྷག་པར་བཟང་། རྒྱུན་དུ་ཕྱི་ནང་གི་འདུ་འཛིའི་བྱ་བ་
ཐམས་ཅད་བཏང་སྟེ་བྱར་མེད་དུ་གནས་པ་དོན་གྱི་དབེན་གནས་ཡིན། རྒྱུད་སྦྱོང་བ་དངོས་ལ།
ཐུན་མོང་དུ་བློ་ལྡོག་རྣམ་པ་བཞི་དང་། ཐུན་མིན་སྐྱབས་སེམས་སྒྲིབ་སྦྱོང་ཚོགས་བསགས་
རྣམས་ཁྲིད་ཡིག་བཞིན་རེ་རེ་ནས་ཉམས་ཀྱི་མྱོང་བ་ཐོན་ཐོན་གྱི་བར་དུ་འབད་ཅིང་། ཁྱད་པར་
བླ་མའི་རྣལ་འབྱོར་ལ་ཉམས་ལེན་གྱི་སྲོག་ཏུ་བཟུང་ནས་བརྩོན་དགོས། དེ་མ་བྱས་ན་བསྒོམ་
སྐྱེ་བ་བུལ། ཅུང་ཟད་སྐྱེས་ཀྱང་གེགས་སྟང་། རྟོགས་པ་གཤའ་མ་རྒྱུད་ལ་སྐྱེར་མི་བཏུབ་པས་
བཙོས་མིན་གྱི་མོས་གུས་དྲག་པོས་གསོལ་བ་བཏབ་པས། ཇི་ཞིག་ནས་ཐུགས་རྒྱུད་ཀྱི་དགོངས་
པ་འཕོས་ཏེ་རྟོགས་པ་ཁྱད་པར་ཅན་ཚིག་གིས་བརྗོད་དུ་མི་ནུས་པ་རང་གི་ནང་ནས་སྐྱེ་བར་ངེས་
ཏེ། བླ་མ་ཞང་རིན་པོ་ཆེས། གནས་པ་བསྐྱང་བ། ཉམས་མྱོང་བསྐྱང་བ། ཏིང་ངེ་འཛིན་
བསྐྱང་བ་ལ་སོགས་པ་མང་བར་གདའ་སྟེ། མོས་གུས་ཀྱི་སྟོབས་ལས་བླ་མའི་བྱིན་རླབས་ཀྱིས་
རྟོགས་པ་ནང་ནས་སྐྱེ་བ་འདི་དཀོན་པར་གདའ། ཞེས་གསུངས། དེས་ན་རྫོགས་པ་ཆེན་པོའི་
དོན་རྒྱུད་ལ་སྐྱེ་བ་སྔོན་འགྲོ་ལ་རག་ལས་པ་ཡིན་པས། རྗེ་འབྲི་གུང་པས། ཆོས་གཞན་དངོས་
གཞི་ཟབ་པར་བྱེད་དེ། ངེད་འདིར་སྔོན་འགྲོ་ཟབ་པར་བྱེད། ཅེས་གསུངས་པའི་དགོངས་
པའང་དེ་ལྟར་ཡིན་པར་གདའ་འོ། །གཉིས་པ་དངོས་གཞི་ལྟ་སྒོམ་སྤྱོད་པའི་སྒྲོ་འདོགས་
བཅད་དེ་སྒྲུབ་པ་ཉམས་ལེན་གྱི་སྲང་དུ་གཞུག་ཚུལ་ནི། ཐོག་མར་ཡིན་ལུགས་ཤེས་པའི་ལྟ་བ་
ལ། འདི་ལྟར་རང་གི་སེམས་ཉིད་དོན་དམ་གཤིས་ཀྱི་གནས་ལུགས་དེ་ཐ་སྙད་བློས་བཟོ་བཅོས་

action is to dwell in the true solitary place.

As for the actual purification of your mind, the ordinary aspects are the four thoughts that turn the mind away from samsara; the extraordinary ones are refuge, generation of bodhichitta, purification of obscurations, and the two accumulations. Having practiced each of these assiduously according to the commentaries until you have truly experienced them, you should then consider the most extraordinary guru yoga as the vital essence of practice, and persevere in it. If you do not, growth of your meditation will be tardy; and even if it grows a little it will be very vulnerable to obstacles, and genuine understanding will not be able to take birth in your being. So, if you pray with simple and very fervent devotion, after some time, through the transfer of the heart-mind realization of the Guru, an extraordinary understanding, inexpressible in words, will certainly take birth within. As Lama Shang Rinpoche said:

> *"To nurture stillness, experiences, and deep concentration –*
> *these are common things.*
> *But very rare is the realization born from within through the*
> *Guru's blessings, which arises by the power of devotion."*

Whether the meaning of the Great Perfection will be born in your mind depends on the preliminary practices. Therefore, with this in mind, the Lord Drikung said,

> *"Other teachings consider the main practice profound, but here it*
> *is the preliminary practices that we consider profound."*

2. The Main Practice

Second, the main practice consists in how, having cut through the misconceptions concerning view, meditation, and action, one accurately engages in the practice.

༄༅། ཀྱི་མཚན་མ་ཐམས་ཅད་དང་བྲལ་བར་རིག་ཐོག་ཏུ་གཏན་ལ་ཕབ་པས། རིག་པ་རང་
བྱུང་གི་ཡེ་ཤེས་སུ་ཧྲེན་པར་ཤར་བ་ལ། ཚིག་གིས་བརྗོད་དུ་མེད། དཔེས་མཚོན་དུ་མེད།
འཁོར་བ་ན་ངན་དུ་མ་སོང་། འདས་པ་ན་བཟང་དུ་མ་སོང་། སྐྱེ་མ་མྱོང་། འགགས་མ་མྱོང་།
གྲོལ་མ་མྱོང་། འཁྲུལ་མ་མྱོང་། ཡོད་མ་མྱོང་། མེད་མ་མྱོང་། རྒྱ་གར་ཡང་མ་ཆད། ཕྱོགས་
གང་དུའང་མ་ལྷུང་། མདོར་ན་ཡེ་ནས་དངོས་པོ་སྤྲོས་པའི་མཚན་མ་ཅན་དུ་ནམ་ཡང་གྲུབ་མ་མྱོང་
བས་ངོ་བོ་ཀ་དག་སྟོང་ཉིད་བརྡལ་ཁྱབ་ཆེན་པོ། སྟོང་པའི་མདངས་མ་འགགས་པར་འཁོར་
འདས་ཀྱི་ཆོས་ཁམས་རྒྱ་མཚོ་ཉི་མ་དང་ཉི་མའི་ཟེར་བཞིན་རང་སྣང་བས་ན་ཅང་མེད་ཕྱུང་ཆད་དུ་
སྟོང་མ་མྱོང་བས་རང་བཞིན་ཡེ་ཤེས་ཡོན་ཏན་ལྷུན་གྲུབ་ཆེན་པོ། དེ་ལྟར་སྣང་སྟོང་ཟུང་དུ་འཇུག་
པའི་རིག་པ་སྐུ་གསུམ་གྱི་བདག་ཉིད་གདོད་མ་གཤིས་ཀྱི་གནས་ལུགས་འདི་གཞི་ཡིན་ལུགས་
ཇི་ལྟ་བ་བཞིན་ངོ་ཤེས་པ་ལ་བློ་འདས་རྫོགས་པ་ཆེན་པོའི་ལྟ་བ་ཟེར། སློབ་དཔོན་ཆེན་པོས།
བློ་འདས་ཆོས་སྐུ་དེ་བཞིན་ཉིད། ཅེས་གསུངས། འོ་སྐོལ་རྣམས་ཀུན་ཏུ་བཟང་པོའི་དགོངས་
པ་ལ་མངོན་སུམ་དུ་སྤྲར་འཛིན་བྱེད་པ་ལགས་ཏེ་ཨ་རེ་དགའ་ན། རྒྱལ་བས་ཆོས་ཀྱི་ཕུང་
པོ་སྟོང་ཕྲག་བརྒྱད་ཅུ་རྩ་བཞིར་ཕྱེ་བ་ཐམས་ཅད་ཀྱི་མཐར་ཐུག་རྫོགས་ཆེན་རྒྱུད་འབུམ་ཕྲག་
དྲུག་ཅུ་རྩ་བཞིའི་སྙིང་པོ་དེ་འདི་རང་ཡིན། འདི་ལས་འགྲོ་ས་སྐར་མ་གང་མེད། འདིའི་
ཐོག་ཏུ་ཆོས་ཐམས་ཅད་ཀྱི་སླར་ཐག་གཅོད་དགོས་པ་ཡིན་ནོ། །ད་དེ་ལྟ་བུའི་ལྟ་བ་ལ་ཐེ་
ཚོམ་དང་སྒྲོ་འདོགས་ནང་ནས་ཆོད་པར་བྱས་ཏེ་དེའི་རྒྱུན་སྐྱོང་བ་ལ་སྒོམ་པ་ཟེར་བ་ཡིན།
གཞན་གཏད་སོ་དང་བཅས་པའི་སྒོམ་པ་ཐམས་ཅད་བློས་བྱས་ཀྱི་རྟོག་སྒོམ་ཡིན་པས་ང་ཅག་དེ་

a. The View

First, as for the view that recognizes the true nature, our own mind itself is the nature of absolute reality. Divested of all conditional and artificial characteristics fabricated by the intellect, this nature is established with certainty as awareness. Awareness arises naked as the self-originated primordial wisdom. This awareness cannot be expressed in words, nor shown by examples. It is neither corrupted in samsara, nor improved in nirvana; neither born, nor ceases to be; neither liberated, nor confused; neither existent, nor non-existent; neither delimited, nor falling to either side. In brief, from the beginning awareness has never existed as a substantial entity with elaborated characteristics: its nature is primordially pure, empty, vast, and all-pervasive. As the radiance of emptiness is unobstructed, the ocean of phenomena of samsara and nirvana appears spontaneously, like the sun and its rays. Neither is awareness a blank nothingness, totally void, for its natural expression is primordial wisdom, the qualities of which are vast and spontaneously accomplished.

Thus awareness, in which appearances and emptiness are inseparably united, is the natural sovereign of the three kayas, and the nature of primordial reality. To recognize exactly what it is constitutes the view of the Great Perfection. As the Great Master, Guru Padmasambhava said,

> *"The dharmakaya, beyond mind, is suchness."*

What a wonder it is thus to behold directly Samantabhadra's mind!

This is the very heart of the 6,400,000 Tantras of the Great Perfection, which are themselves the ultimate point of the 84,000 sections of the whole of Lord Buddha's teachings. There is not even an inch to go beyond this. The ultimate elucidation of all phenomena should be achieved according to this.

༄༅། འདུ་མི་བྱེད། སྔར་གྱི་ལྟ་བ་དེ་ཀ་ཚུགས་མ་ཤོར་བའི་ངང་ལ་སྒོ་ལྔའི་ཤེས་པ་ཐམས་ཅད་རང་བབས་སུ་གློད་ནས་ལྷུག་པར་བཞག །འདི་འོ་ཞེས་ཆེད་དུ་མི་བསྒོམ། བསྒོམ་ན་བློ་ཡིན་པས་བསྒོམ་རྒྱུ་ཅི་ཡང་མེད། ཡེངས་སུ་སྐད་ཅིག་ཀྱང་མི་འཛུག །རང་ཐོག་ཏུ་འཛོག་པ་དེ་ལས་ཡེངས་ན་འཁྲུལ་པ་དངོས་ཡིན་པས་མ་ཡེངས་པར་བྱ། རྟོག་པ་ཅི་ཤར་ཡང་འཆར་དུ་བཅུག་ལ། དེའི་རྗེས་སུ་ཡང་མི་འབྲང་། བཀག་ཀྱང་མི་བཀག །འོ་ན་ཇི་ལྟར་བྱ་ཞེ་ན། ཡུལ་གྱི་སྣང་བ་ཅི་ཤར་ཅིར་སྣང་ཐམས་ཅད་བུ་ཆུང་ལྷ་ཁང་ལ་བལྟ་བ་ལྟར་སྣང་ཆ་ལ་འཛིན་པ་མ་ཞུགས་པར་སོ་མར་བཞག་པས་ཆོས་ཐམས་ཅད་རང་སར་རང་སན་བཟོ་མ་ཉམས། མདོག་མ་འགྱུར། བཀྲག་མ་ཡལ་བར་སྣང་ཡང་དེ་ལ་ཞེན་འཛིན་གྱི་རྟོག་པས་མ་བསླད་པས་སྣང་རིག་ཐམས་ཅད་གསལ་སྟོང་གི་ཡེ་ཤེས་རྗེན་པར་འཆར་བ་ཡིན་ནོ། །ཡར་ཆོས་ཟབ་ཟབ་དང་རྒྱ་ཆེ་ཆེའི་མིང་བཏགས་མང་པོ་ཞིག་གིས་བློ་དམན་ཀུན་མགོ་འཁོར་ཞིང་འདུག་པས། དོན་ཛོག་ཛོག་ཧྲིལ་ཧྲིལ་མཛུབ་ཚུགས་ཏུ་བསྟན་ན། རྟོག་པ་སྔ་མ་འགགས། ཕྱི་མ་མ་ཤར་བའི་བར་དེར། ད་ལྟའི་ཤེས་པ་སོ་མ་བསྒྱུར་བཀོད་སྤྲུ་ཙམ་མ་སོང་བའི་གསལ་རིག་རྗེན་ནེ་བ་ཞིག་མི་འདུག་གེའོ་དེ་ཀ་རིག་པ་རང་གི་བཞུགས་ཚུལ་ཡིན། ཡང་རྟག་པར་དེ་ཁོ་ནའི་ངང་དུ་མི་གནས་པར་རྣམ་རྟོག་ཅིག་ཐོལ་གྱིས་འཆར་གྱི་མི་འདུག་གེ །དེ་རིག་པ་དེའི་རང་རྩལ་ཡིན། འོན་ཀྱང་དེ་ལྟར་ཤར་མ་ཐག་ནས་ངོ་མ་ཤེས་པར་རྣམ་རྟོག་རང་རྒྱུད་པར་འཕྱུམས་ན་འཁྲུལ་པ་ལུ་གུ་རྒྱུད་ཅེས་འཁོར་བའི་རྩ་བ་ཡིན། ཤར་མ་ཐག་ཏུ་ངོ་ཤེས་ཙམ་གྱིས་རྗེས་མཐུད་མེད་པར་རང་ཐོག་ཏུ་གློད་དེ་བཞག་ན་རྣམ་རྟོག་གང་ཤར་ཐམས་ཅད་རིག་པ་ཆོས་སྐུའི་གློང་དུ་ཕྱམ་ཕྱམ་གྲོལ་བ་འདི་

b. The Meditation

Having thus cut from within all doubts and misconceptions about the view, to experience this view continuously is called "meditation." Apart from this, all meditations with targets are intellectual meditations devised by thought; we do nothing like that. Without straying from the firmness of the view, remain free, releasing all the perceptions of the five sense-doors in their natural state. Do not meditate thinking, "This is it." If you "meditate," that is the intellect. There is nothing to be meditated upon. Do not let yourself be distracted even for an instant. If you wander from dwelling in awareness itself, that is the real delusion, so do not be distracted. Whatever thoughts arise let them arise. Do not follow them, do not obstruct them.

You may ask, "Then what should be done?" Whatever manifestations of the phenomenal world may arise, remain in a state of natural freshness without grasping at them, like a small child looking inside a temple. If you do so, all phenomena remain in their own place, their aspect is not modified, their color does not change, their luster does not vanish. Although the phenomenal world is present, if you do not contaminate it by wanting and clinging, all appearances and thoughts will arise as the naked, primordial wisdom of radiant emptiness.

The great number of teachings that are said to be very profound and vast puzzle people of narrow intellect. If we were to point a finger at the essential meaning which emerges out of them all, one would say: when past thoughts have ceased, and future thoughts have not arisen, in the interval is there not a perception of nowness, a virgin, pristine, clear, awake and bare freshness which has never changed even by a hair? Ho! This is the abiding mode awareness (*rigpa*). Now, one does not remain forever in that state; doesn't a thought suddenly arise? This is the self-radiance of that awareness. But if you do not recognize it as such the very moment it arises, this thought will spread out into ordinary thoughts. This is called the "chain of delusion." It is the root of samsara. If you simply recognize the nature of the thoughts immediately as they arise, without extending them, leaving them freely to themselves, then whatever thoughts arise are all spontaneously liberated in the expanse

༄༅། ག་འབྲིགས་ཆོད་ཀྱི་ལྷ་སྒོམ་གཅིག་ཏུ་དྲིལ་བའི་ཉམས་ལེན་དངོས་གཞི་ཡིན། དགའ་རབ་རྡོ་རྗེས། གདོད་ནས་དག་པ་དབྱིངས་ཀྱི་ངང་ཉིད་ལས། །རིག་པ་ཐོལ་སྐྱེས་སྐད་ཅིག་དྲན་པ་དེ། །རྒྱ་མཚོའི་གཏིང་ནས་ནོར་བུ་རྙེད་པ་འདྲ། །སུས་ཀྱང་མ་བཅོས་མ་བྱས་ཆོས་ཀྱི་སྐུ། །ཞེས་གསུངས། འདི་ལ་རྡོ་རྗེ་རུས་གདུགས་ཏེ་ཉིན་མཚན་ཡེངས་མེད་དུ་བསྒོམ་དགོས་པས་སྟོང་ཉིད་གོ་ཡུལ་དུ་མ་ལུས་པར་ཏིག་ཐོག་རང་དུ་སྤྲུངས་ཤིག །ད་ནི་སྒོམ་པ་དེ་ལ་སྤྱོད་པས་བོགས་འབྱུང་ཞིང་ཉམས་ལེན་གྱི་སྲང་དུ་གཞུག་ཚུལ་ལ། གཙོ་བོར་སྔར་བཤད་པ་ལྟར་བླ་མ་ལ་སངས་རྒྱས་དངོས་ཀྱི་འདུ་ཤེས་དང་སྐད་ཅིག་ཀྱང་མ་བྲལ་བས་སྙིང་ནས་གསོལ་བ་ཐུར་ཚུགས་སུ་འདེབས་པ་འདི་མོས་གུས་དཀར་པོ་ཆིག་ཐུབ་ཅེས་བྱ་བ་ཡིན་ཏེ་གེགས་སེལ་བོགས་འདོན་གང་ལས་ཀྱང་འདི་ལྷག །ལམ་ཐམས་ཅད་བཙན་ཆོད་དུ་འགྲོ་བ་ཡིན། སྒོམ་སྐྱོན་བྱིང་ཞིང་རྨུག་ན་རིག་པ་རྟུར་ཕྱུངས། འཕྲོ་ཞིང་རྒོད་ན་ཤེས་པ་ཁོང་གློད། རྒྱུན་དུ་བསྒོམ་མཁན་གྱི་དྲན་རིག་ཏུར་ཏུར་པོ་དེས་ཆེད་དུ་གཟུར་བའི་འཛུར་དྲན་མ་ཡིན་པར་རང་ངོ་རང་ཤེས་མ་བརྗེད་ཙམ་པའི་དྲན་པས་ཟ་ཉལ་འགྲོ་འདུག་སྤྱོད་ལམ་མཉམ་རྗེས་གང་གི་སྐབས་སུའང་རྒྱུན་ཆགས་སུ་སྐྱོང་ཞིང་། བདེ་སྡུག་དང་ཉོན་མོངས་པའི་རྟོག་པ་སོགས་གང་ཤར་ཐམས་ཅད་ལ་རེ་དོགས་སྤྲོང་ལེན་གཉེན་པོས་གཞོམ་པ་སོགས་གཏན་ནས་མི་བྱེད་པར་ཁོ་རང་གི་ངོ་བོ་བདེ་སྡུག་གི་ཚོར་བ་ཇི་ལྟར་འདུག་པ་དེ་ཀ་རྗེན་ནེ། ཧྲིག་གེ །ཡེ་རེ་འཛོག་པ་སྟེ། ཐམས་ཅད་ལ་གནད་གཅིག་ལས་མེད་པས་བསམ་བློ་མང་པོས་མགོ་མ་འཁོར། སྤང་བྱའི་རྣམ་རྟོག་དང་ཉོན་མོངས་ཀྱི་སྟེང་དུ་གཉེན་པོའི་སྟོང་ཉིད་ལོགས་སུ་བསྒོམ་མི་དགོས་ཏེ། སྤང་བྱ་ཁོ་རང་རིག་པས་

of awareness – dharmakaya. This itself is the main practice uniting the view and meditation of Trekchö.

As Garab Dorje said,

> *"When awareness arises abruptly from the natural state of the primordially pure expanse,*
> *This instant recollection is like finding a gem in the depths of the ocean:*
> *This is the dharmakaya which has not been contrived or made by anyone."*

Just like when "stone meets bone," you should experience this with great energy day and night, without distraction. Not allowing emptiness to remain in the domain of theory, bring everything back to awareness itself.

c. Action

Now, about how to improve meditation by putting it into action to accurately engage in the practice, as it was said before, the most important thing is fervent devotion, to pray with ardor from the heart, without ceasing even for an instant to consider the Guru as the real Buddha. This is the one remedy that cures all diseases and is superior to all other ways of dispelling obstacles and making progress. With it, levels and paths will be traversed with great momentum.

If your meditation sinks and becomes dull, revive alert awareness; if it scatters and becomes wild, relax deep inside. Yet, this should not be an intentional and forceful retrieval made by the usual meditating mind keeping watch. Be simply mindful not to forget the recognition of your true nature. Preserving this in all circumstances – while eating, sleeping, walking, sitting, in or out of meditation periods – whatever thoughts arise – happy, painful, or defiled – remain without a trace of hope or doubt, rejection or acceptance, and do not try in any way to destroy them with antidotes. Whatever feelings of happiness or suffering there may be, leave them as they are in their true nature – naked, fresh, clear, vast, and limpid.

༄༅། ངོས་ཟིན་པ་དང་མཉམ་དུ་སྤྲུལ་གྱི་མདུད་པ་ཞིག་པ་ལྟར་རང་གྲོལ་དུ་འགྲོ་བ་ཡིན། འོད་གསལ་རྡོ་རྗེ་སྙིང་པོའི་སྐབས་དོན་གྱི་མཐར་ཐུག་འདི་ལྟ་བུ་ཕལ་ཆེར་གྱིས་ཚིག་ཏུ་སྨྲ་ཤེས་ཀྱང་ཉམས་སུ་བླང་མ་ཤེས་པར་ནི་ཙོའི་ཁ་ཧོན་བཞིན་དུ་སོང་ནས་གདའ། འོ་སྐྱོལ་རྣམས་བསོད་ནམས་ཤིན་ཏུ་ཆེ་བ་ཡིན་ནོ། །ད་དུང་ལེགས་པར་སེམས་དང་གོ་རྒྱུ་ཡོད་དེ། རང་ཅག་ཚོ་རབས་ཐོག་མེད་པ་ནས་ད་ལྟའི་བར་དུ་འཁོར་བར་འཆིང་བྱེད་ཀྱི་དགྲ་མི་ཤ་བོ་དེ་གཟུང་འཛིན་གཉིས་པོ་འདི་ཡིན། ད་རེས་བླ་མའི་བཀའ་དྲིན་ལས་རང་གནས་ཀྱི་ཆོས་སྐུ་ངོ་འཕྲོད་པས་དེ་གཉིས་བྱ་སྤྲུ་མེ་ལ་བསྲེགས་པ་ལྟར་རྗེས་མེད་ཤུལ་མེད་དུ་གཏོང་བ་དེ་སྙིང་ཚིམས་པོ་མིན་ནམ། འདི་ལྟ་བུའི་སྨྱུར་ལམ་གདམས་ངག་ཟབ་མོ་ཐོབ་ནས་ཉམས་སུ་མ་བླངས་ན་ཡིད་བཞིན་གྱི་ནོར་བུ་རོའི་ཁ་ནང་དུ་བཅུག་པ་དང་འདྲ་སྟེ་རེ་ཕང་། སྙིང་མ་རུལ་བར་ཉམས་སུ་ལོངས་ཤིག དེ་ཡང་ལས་དང་པོ་པའི་རིགས་ལ་རྣམ་རྟོག་ནག་པོ་ཁ་འཁྲུམས་ཀྱིས་དྲན་པ་ཡེངས་སུ་བཅུག་ཡོང་བས་རྣམ་རྟོག་བརྟད་འཁྲིལ་མང་ཙམ་འོག་འགྱུར་སོང་རྗེས་སྐབས་ཤིག་ན་དྲན་པ་ཧྲིག་གེ་སླེབས་ནས་ང་ཡེངས་འདུག་སྙམས་པའི་འགྱོད་པ་སྐྱེ་ཡང་། དེ་ཚེ་རྣམ་རྟོག་སྔ་མའི་གཞུག་གཅོད་དང་ཡེངས་པ་ལ་འགྱོད་པ་སོགས་གང་ཡང་མི་བྱ་བར་དྲན་པ་ཧྲིག་གེ་སླེབས་པ་དེ་ཀའི་ཐོག་ཏུ་རང་བབས་ཀྱི་རྒྱུན་བསྐྱང་བ་ཁོ་ནས་ཆོག །རྣམ་རྟོག་ལ་ཆོས་སྐུར་བལྟ་མི་སྲུང་ཟེར་བ་གྲགས་ཆེ་ཡང་ལྷག་མཐོང་གི་རྩལ་མ་རྫོགས་རིང་ཆོས་སྐུ་ཡིན་ལོ་ཙམ་གྱི་དང་ནས་ཞི་གནས་ཧད་པོར་བཞག་ན་ཅི་ཡིན་འདི་ཡིན་མེད་པའི་བཏང་སྙོམས་ལུང་མ་བསྟན་གྱི་སྐབས་སུ་ཚུད་དོགས་ཡོད་པས། དེས་ན་དང་པོའི་རིང་རྣམ་རྟོག་གང་ཤར་ལ་ཅེར་གྱིས་བལྟས་ནས་བརྟག་དཔྱད་བསམ་

Thus, since for all there is nothing but a single point, do not confuse yourself with all sorts of cogitation. There is no need to meditate upon emptiness as an antidote distinct from the undesirable thoughts and obscurations. If you recognize the nature of these undesirable thoughts with awareness, at that very moment they will be liberated by themselves, like a snake untying its knot.

Almost everyone knows how to express this ultimate hidden meaning of the radiant adamantine essence in words, but not how to put it into practice; and so it has become just like a parrot's litanies. We who practice it are so greatly fortunate!

Now, there is more to be understood which we must consider carefully. The two deadly enemies which have bound us to samsara since beginningless time until now are the grasper and the grasped. Now that by the grace of the guru we have been introduced to the dharmakaya nature residing in ourselves, these two are burnt up like feathers, leaving neither trace nor residue. Isn't that delectable!

Having received the profound instructions of such a swift path, if you do not put them into practice, they will be just like a wish-fulfilling gem put in the mouth of a corpse – a miserable loss! Don't let your heart rot; take up the practice.

Beginners will find that the mind, completely invaded by black thoughts, will stray into distraction. Even more tiny thoughts will proliferate unnoticed, until a lucid mindfulness comes back and you will think sadly, "I have wandered." At that moment, do not do anything like interrupting the course of the thoughts, feeling regret about your wandering, and so on; simply remain in this clear mindfulness, and keep on experiencing the natural state. This by itself is enough.

> *"Do not reject the thoughts: see them as dharmakaya."*

So goes a well-known saying. However, until your experience of vipashyana has been perfected, merely to think, "This is dharmakaya," and remain in blank shamatha involves the risk of being caught in an

༄༅། གཞིག་ཅིར་ཡང་མི་བྱ་བར་རྣམ་རྟོག་ངོ་ཤེས་མཁན་རང་གི་ཐོག་ཏུ་མི་གནན་གྱིས་བྱིས་པའི་རྩེད་མོ་ལ་བལྟ་བ་ལྟར་སྣང་མེད་རྩིས་མེད་གཡས་ཀུང་དུ་འཇོག །དེ་ལྟར་བཞག་པ་ན་རྟོག་མེད་རང་བབས་སུ་གནས་བདེ་བའི་ཆ་དེའང་གློ་བུར་ཐོལ་བྱུང་དུ་བཤིག་པས་སྐད་ཅིག་མ་དེར་སེམས་ལས་འདས་པའི་ཡེ་ཤེས་རྗེན་ལྷང་ངེར་འཆར་བ་ཡིན། ལམ་གྱི་སྐབས་སུ་བདེ་གསལ་མི་རྟོག་གསུམ་གང་རུང་གི་ཉམས་དང་མ་འདྲེས་པ་ཞིག་མི་འོང་ཀྱང་མཆོག་འཛིན་ཞེན་རློམ་རེ་དོགས་སྤྱི་ཙམ་མེད་པར་བཞག་ན་གོལ་ས་དེས་ཆོད། རྒྱུན་དུ་གཡེང་བར་སྤྲང་སྔེ་དྲན་འདུན་རྩེ་གཅིག་པས་བསྒོམ་པ་གལ་ཆེ། རེས་འཇོག་དང་གོ་ཡུལ་ལ་འབྱམས་ནས་ཞི་གནས་ཕྱོགས་མགོ་ཙམ་ལ་རང་མཐོང་སྐྱེས་ཏེ་ཉམས་མྱོང་ལ་གདར་ཤ་མ་ཆོད་པར་ཁ་ཕྱིར་ལ་མཁས་པ་ཙམ་གྱིས་མི་ཕན་ཏེ། རྫོགས་ཆེན་ལས། གོ་བ་ལྷན་པ་འདྲ་སྟེ་གོག་ནས་འགྲོ། །ཞེས་དང་། ཉམས་ན་བུན་འདྲ་སྟེ་ཡལ་ནས་འགྲོ། །ཞེས་པ་ལྟར་ཡུལ་གྱི་རྐྱེན་བཟང་ངན་ཕྲན་བུ་རེས་ཀྱང་སྒོམ་ཆེན་པ་བསླུས་ནས་རྐྱེན་ཐོག་ཏུ་འཚོལ་བ་མང་། སྒོམ་རྒྱུད་ལ་ཐེབས་ཀྱང་རྒྱུན་དུ་མ་བསྒོམ་ན་གདམས་ངག་ཟབ་མོ་དཔེ་ཆའི་ལོགས་ལ་ལུས་ཏེ་བློ་དྲེད་ཆོས་དྲེད་ཉམས་ལེན་དྲེད་ནས་སྒོམ་གཤའ་མ་སྐྱེ་དུས་མི་ཡོང་། སྒོམ་ཆེན་སྙིང་པ་ཉམས་ལེན་གསར་པའི་དང་ནས་མགོ་བོ་བ་སྤུ་ཁ་ལེར་གུམ་ཉེན་ཡོད་པས་ཤིན་ཏུ་གཟབ་དགོས་སོ། །དེ་ལྟར་རྒྱུན་རིང་བར་གོམས་པས་ཇི་ཞིག་ན་མོས་གུས་སོགས་རྐྱེན་གང་ཡང་རུང་བ་ཞིག་གིས་ཉམས་མྱོང་དེ་རྟོགས་པར་ན་འཕར་ནས་རིག་པ་རྗེན་ལྷག་གེར་མཐོང་། མགོ་ཤུབ་ཕུད་པ་བཞིན་གྱི་ཡངས་ཕྱུ་ལེར་འགྲོ། དེ་ནི་མ་མཐོང་བ་མཐོང་བའི་མཆོག་ཅེས་པ་ཡིན། འདི་ནས་རྣམ་རྟོག་སྒོམ་ལ་ཤར་ཏེ་གནས་འགྱུ་

amorphous equanimity devoid of any characteristic whatsoever. So, to begin with, whatever thoughts arise just stare at them without analyzing or pondering, and rest upon the "recognizer" of the thoughts, without caring about them or giving them any importance, like an old man watching children at play. Remaining like this you will settle into a kind of stagnation in the natural state devoid of thoughts. When this is suddenly destroyed, instantly a wisdom transcending the mind will arise, naked, fresh, vivid, and lofty.

On the path, there cannot but be some mixing with experiences of bliss, clarity, and thoughtlessness; but if you remain without even a hair of feeling satisfied about yourself, conceited attachment, hope or doubt, this will prevent you from going astray. It is very important that, always discarding distraction, you practice with one-pointed vigilant mindfulness. If you stray into sporadic practice and theoretical knowledge, you will become conceited about a vague tranquility, and without having thoroughly clarified your experiences, you will only be verbally clever. This will bring no benefit at all. As it is said in the Great Perfection,

> *"Theory is like a patch, it will fall away,"*
> and,
> *"Experiences are like mist, they will vanish."*

This is how many great meditators are led astray by good or bad minor circumstances, and get lost in them. Even when meditation has penetrated your mind, you need to cultivate it continuously, otherwise the deep instructions will be left on the pages of the books, and your mind, the Dharma, and your practice will become impervious so that the birth of genuine meditation will never come. You old meditators, still novices in practice, watch out – there is a danger that you may die with your head encrusted with salt.

After you have practiced continuously over a long period, a time will come, when through fervent devotion or some other circumstance, experiences will turn into realization, and awareness will be seen naked and resplendent. It is like taking a cloth off your head: Such a happy

༄༅། མཉམ་གྲོལ་དུ་འགྲོ་སྟེ། དེ་ཡང་དང་པོ་རྣམ་རྟོག་ངོ་ཤེས་པས་གྲོལ་བ་སྔར་འདྲིས་ཀྱི་མི་དང་འཕྲད་ལྟ་བུ། བར་དུ་རྣམ་རྟོག་རང་གིས་རང་གྲོལ་བ་སྦྲུལ་གྱིས་མདུད་པ་ཞིག་པ་ལྟ་བུ། ཐ་མ་རྣམ་རྟོག་ཕན་མེད་གནོད་མེད་དུ་གྲོལ་བ་ཁང་སྟོང་གི་རྐུན་མ་ལྟ་བུ་རྣམས་རིམ་པར་འབྱུང་ཞིང་། ཆོས་ཐམས་ཅད་རང་རིག་གཅིག་པུའི་ཆོ་འཕྲུལ་དུ་ཐག་ཆོད་པའི་ཡིད་ཆེས་དྲག་པོ་ཞིག་ནང་ནས་སྐྱེ། སྟོང་ཉིད་སྙིང་རྗེའི་རྩ་ཀློང་འཁྲུགས། འཁོར་འདས་གཉིས་ལས་འདམ་ཁ་ཟད། སངས་རྒྱས་དང་སེམས་ཅན་བཟང་ངན་མེད་པར་རྟོགས། ཇི་ལྟར་བས་ཀྱང་བློ་བདེ་ཆོས་ཉིད་ཀྱི་ངང་ཁོ་ན་ལས་གཡོ་མི་ཤེས་པས་ཉིན་མཚན་བར་མེད་དུ་འབྱམས་ཀླས་པས་ན། རྫོགས་ཆེན་ནས། རྟོགས་པ་ནམ་མཁའ་འདྲ་སྟེ་འགྱུར་བ་མེད། །ཅེས་པ་ལྟར་རྣལ་འབྱོར་པ་དེ་ལུས་ཐ་མལ་མི་རུ་སྣང་ཡང་སེམས་ཆོས་སྐུ་བྱ་རྩོལ་དང་བྲལ་བའི་དགོངས་པ་ལ་བཞུགས་པས་ས་ལམ་ཐམས་ཅད་བྱར་མེད་དུ་བགྲོད། མཐར་བློ་ཟད་ཆོས་ཟད་བུམ་པ་ཆག་པའི་ནམ་མཁའ་ལྟར་ལུས་རྡུལ་ཕྲན་དུ་དེངས། སེམས་ཆོས་ཉིད་དུ་དེངས། གདོད་མའི་གཞི་དབྱིངས་ནང་གསལ་གཞོན་ནུ་བུམ་པ་སྐུར་འཁྱིལ་བ་ཞེས་བྱ་བ་ཞིག་ཡོང་རྒྱུ་རེད་པ། འོ་དེ་ནི་ལྟ་སྒོམ་སྤྱོད་པ་མཐར་ཕྱིན་པས་ཐོབ་ཏུ་མེད་པའི་འབྲས་བུ་མངོན་དུ་གྱུར་པ་ཞེས་བྱ་བ་ཡིན། ཉམས་དང་རྟོགས་པའི་སོ་མཚམས་དེ་དག་ཀྱང་གོ་རིམ་ཅན་དང་། གོ་རིམ་དང་བྲལ་བ་དང་། གཅིག་ཅར་ཉིད་དུ་སྐྱེ་བའང་འབྱུང་བ་ནི་གང་ཟག་གི་དབང་པོའི་ཁྱད་པར་གྱིས་ཡིན་ཀྱང་འབྲས་བུའི་དུས་སུ་རྣམ་དབྱེར་མ་མཆིས་སོ། །སྤྱི་དོན་གསུམ་པ་རྗེས་ཐོབ་དམ་ཚིག་སྡོམ་པ་བསྲུང་ཞིང་ཚེ་འདིའི་ལས་གཞུག་ཆོས་ཀྱིས་བསྡུ་ཚུལ་ནི། དེ་ལྟར་ལྟ་སྒོམ་སྤྱོད་པའི་ཉམས་ལེན་ལ་འབད་དུ་ཟིན་

relief! It is the supreme seeing of that which was not seen. From then on, thoughts will arise as meditation. The still and moving (aspects of the mind) will be liberated simultaneously.

At first, liberation of thoughts through their recognition is like meeting someone you already know. In the middle, self-liberation of thoughts is like the undoing of a snake's knot. Finally, liberation of thoughts, which cause neither benefit nor harm, is like a thief in an empty house. These three will happen progressively. A strong and total conviction that all phenomena are the display of your own awareness will take birth from within. Waves of emptiness–compassion will surge forth. Preferences between samsara and nirvana will cease. One will realize that buddhas and beings are not good or bad. Whatever one does, day and night in a vast and perfect continuity, one will never move from the total satisfaction of the absolute nature. As it is said in the Great Perfection,

> *"Realization is unchanging like the sky."*

Although a yogi like this has the appearance of an ordinary person, his mind dwells in the effortless vision of dharmakaya, and without action he traverses all the levels and paths. Finally, his intellect exhausted, phenomena exhausted, like space in a breaking vase, his body dissolves into minute atoms and his mind dissolves into reality (*dharmatā*). This is called "dwelling in the space of the primordial ground," the "inner radiating youthful vase body." So it will be.

This is the ultimate completion of view, meditation, and action. Therefore it is called the "actualization of the fruit which is without attainment." The stages of experience and realization may appear either progressively, or without any particular order, or all at once, according to the capacities of different individuals. But at the time of the fruit, there are no differences.

3. The Post-Meditation

Third, as for the post-meditation, preserving samaya and vows, and the

༄༅། ཀྱང་རྗེས་ཐོབ་སྤྱོད་ལམ་ལ་ཐབས་མི་མཁས་པས་སྡོམ་པ་དང་དམ་ཚིག་ལས་ཉམས་པར་གྱུར་ན། གནས་སྐབས་སུ་ས་ལམ་གྱི་གེགས་དང་བར་ཆད་དུ་འགྱུར་ཞིང་མཐར་ཐུག་མནར་མེད་པའི་དམྱལ་བར་ལྟུང་ངེས་པའི་ཕྱིར་རྟག་ཏུ་དྲན་ཤེས་ཀྱི་བྱ་ར་དང་མ་བྲལ་བས་སྲུང་བླང་ཕྱིན་ཅི་མ་ལོག་པ་ཞིག་ཅི་ནས་གལ་ཆེ་སྟེ། སློབ་དཔོན་ཆེན་པོས། ལར་ལྟ་བ་ནམ་མཁའ་བས་ཀྱང་མཐོ། །ལས་རྒྱུ་འབྲས་བག་ཕྱེ་བས་ཀྱང་ཞིབ། །ཅེས་གསུངས། དེས་ན་རྒད་པོའི་བློ་རྩིངས་སྤྲངས་ལ་རྒྱུ་འབྲས་ལ་ཞིབ་པར་སྤྱད། དམ་ཚིག་བཅས་སྡོམ་ཕྲ་ཞི་ཕྲ་བ་ཡང་མ་ཉམས་པར་བསྲུང་ཞིང་ཉེས་ལྟུང་གི་དྲི་མས་མ་གོས་པར་བྱ། གསང་སྔགས་ཀྱི་དམ་ཚིག་ལ་རྣམ་གྲངས་མང་ཡང་བསྡུ་ན་རྩ་བའི་བླ་མའི་སྐུ་གསུང་ཐུགས་ཡི་དམ་ཚིག་ཏུ་འདུ། བླ་མ་ལ་མིའི་འདུ་ཤེས་སྐད་ཅིག་ཙམ་སྐྱེས་པས་ཀྱང་དངོས་གྲུབ་ལོ་ཟླར་འགྱུར་བར་གསུངས། དེ་ཅིའི་ཕྱིར་ཞེན་ཡུལ་གཉན་པའི་གནད་ཀྱིས་ཏེ།། གང་ཕྱིར་རྡོ་རྗེ་འཛིན་པ་ཡིས། །དངོས་གྲུབ་སློབ་དཔོན་རྗེས་འབྲང་གསུངས། །ཞེས་སོ། །དེས་ན་གང་སུ་ཡང་རུང་སྟེ་དང་པོར་བླ་མར་མ་བཟུང་བར་དུ་ནི་རང་ཉིད་ལ་རང་དབང་ཡོད་ལ། བླ་མར་བསྟེན་ནས་དབང་དང་གདམས་ངག་གི་འབྲེལ་ཕན་ཆད་དམ་ཚིག་མི་བསྲུང་བའི་དབང་མེ་དེ། དབང་བཞིའི་མཇུག་ཏུ་བླ་མ་དཀྱིལ་འཁོར་གྱི་གཙོ་བོའི་མདུན་དུ་བཏུད་དེ། དེང་ནས་བརྩམས་ཏེ་བདག་བྲན་དུ། །ཁྱེད་ལ་བདག་ནི་འབུལ་ལགས་ན། །ཁྱེད་ཀྱི་སློབ་མར་བཟུང་བ་དང་། །ཆ་ཤས་ཀུན་ནི་སྤྱོད་དུ་གསོལ། །ཅེས་ཁས་བླངས་པ་འདིས་རང་ཉིད་ཇི་ལྟར་ཆེ་ཞིང་བཙན་རུང་བླ་མ་ལ་གཉའ་ཤོར་ཟིན་པ་མ་ཡིན་ནམ། དེ་བཞིན་དུ། གཙོ་བོས་ཇི་ལྟར་བཀའ་སྩལ་པ། །དེ་དག་ཐམས་ཅད་བདག་གི་

way to complete the subsequent actions of this life with Dharma, if you persevere with diligence in the experience of view, meditation, and practice, yet are unskillful in the methods of the path of action of post-meditation, so that your vows and samayas degenerate, then for the present there will be interruptions and obstacles on the levels and paths, and ultimately you will certainly fall into the "hell without intermission." Therefore, it is very important to always be vigilant and mindful, never confusing what must be rejected with what must be adopted. As the Great Master, Guru Padmasambhava said,

> *"Though my view is higher than the sky,*
> *My conduct regarding cause and effect is finer than barley flour."*

So, giving up the hasty gross mind, you should act very carefully regarding cause and effect. Keeping intact the samayas and precepts, even the smallest of them, you should remain unstained by faults and downfalls. All the samayas of the Secret Mantra vehicle, as many as can be enumerated, are gathered into the samaya of the Guru's body, speech, and mind. If, even for a fraction of an instant, you think of the Guru as an ordinary person, accomplishment is months and years away. You may ask why. As it has been said,

> *"For Vajra holders, accomplishment follows after the Master."*

This the vital point.

So, at first, whoever you may be, as long as you are not linked to the guru, you depend on yourself alone. But once you are relying on the guru and have become linked with him by initiations and instructions, from then on you have no power to not keep the samaya. At the end of the four initiations, you bow in front of the Guru, the main figure of the mandala, and say,

> *"From now on I offer myself as a servant.*
> *Accept me as your disciple and use even the minutest part of me."*

In giving such consent, however great or powerful you are, have you

༄༅། བགྱི། །ཞེས་དམ་བཅས་ནས་དེ་ཕན་ཆད་གང་གསུངས་མི་བསྒྲུབ་པའི་དབང་ཨེ་ཡོད།
རང་གིས་དམ་བཅས་པ་དེ་མ་བསྒྲུབ་ན་མིང་མ་སྨན་ཀྱང་དམ་ཉམས་ཟེར་བ་ལས་འོས་མ་མཆིས།
།གཞན་ཡང་བླ་ཆེན་འཁོར་མང་བ། ནོར་ཕྱུག་པ། དབང་བཙན་པ། ཁ་ཐབས་བཟང་བ་
རྣམས་ལ་དམ་ཚིག་ལྷག་པོར་བསྲུང་། དམན་ཆ་བཟུང་བའི་བླ་ཆུང་སྤྲང་པོའི་བརྟུལ་ཞུགས་
ཅན་རྣམས་ལ་དམ་ཚིག་བསྲུང་མི་དགོས་པར་བཤད་པའང་མེད། གང་ལའང་ཁེ་ཉན་གྱི་གནད་
ཀ་གོ་བ་ཞིག་དགོས་པ་ལས་ཧ་ཀན་འཐོམ་ལངས་པ་བཞིན་བསྡད་པས་ཡོང་བ་མིན། དེ་ལྟར་
དམ་ཚིག་བསྲུང་དགོས་པ་དེའང་བླ་མའི་དོན་དུ་འདུག་གམ་རང་གི་དོན་དུ་འདུག་སེམས་རྣལ་
དུ་ཕེབ་ལ་བསམ་མནོ་སྣོན་འཐག་འཐག་ཐོངས། བླ་མའི་དོན་དུ་འདུག་ན་དེ་རིང་རང་ལ་ཅམ་
གྱིས་བཞག་པས་ཆོག་སྟེ་དེ་མིན་རང་མགོར་རང་གིས་ཐལ་བ་འདེབས་མི་རིགས། མཆེད་
གྲོགས་ཀྱི་དམ་ཚིག་སྤྱིར་བཏང་དུ་སངས་རྒྱས་ཀྱི་བསྟན་པའི་སྒོར་ཞུགས་སོ་ཅོག་ལ་བཟང་པོར་
བལྟ་ཞིང་དག་སྣང་བྱར། གྲུབ་མཐའི་ཕྱོགས་ཁྱེར་དང་སྐྱུར་འདེབས་སོགས་སྤང་། ཁྱེ་བྲག་
ཏུ་བླ་མ་གཅིག་དང་དཀྱིལ་འཁོར་གཅིག་གིས་བསྐུས་ཚད་རྡོ་རྗེའི་སྤུན་གྲོགས་ཡིན་པས་བརྩེས་
བཅོས་འགྲན་སེམས་ཕྲག་དོག་གཡོ་སྒྱུ་སོགས་སྤངས་ཏེ་སྙིང་ནས་མཛའ་ཞིང་གཅུག་པར་བྱ།
སེམས་ཅན་ཐམས་ཅད་བདག་གི་ཕ་མ་དྲིན་ཅན་ཤ་སྟག་ཏུ་འདུག་པ་ལ་ཨ་ཙ་མ། འདི་རྣམས་
འཁོར་བ་ཐར་མེད་ཀྱི་སྡུག་བསྔལ་དྲག་པོས་གཟིར་བ་ལས་བདག་གིས་མ་བསྒྲུབ་ན་སུ་ཡིས་
སྐྱོབ་སྙམ་དུ་ཤས་མི་བཟོད་པས་སྙིང་རྗེ་སྒོམ་ལ་བློ་སྦྱོང་། སྒོ་གསུམ་ཅི་ནུས་ཀྱིས་ཕན་པ་འབའ་
ཞིག་སྒྲུབ་ཅིང་དགེ་བ་ཐམས་ཅད་གཞན་དོན་དུ་བསྔོ། རྒྱུན་དུ་བསམ་དགོས་རྒྱུ་ཆོས་དང་བླ་

not presented your bowed head to the Guru? You also say,

> *"Whatever the main [deity] asks, I will do."*

Once you have sworn in this way, have you the power to ignore anything he says? Not to accomplish your own promise does not deserve to be called anything other than breaking the samaya, however this may sound. It has never been said that you have to keep the samaya perfectly with important gurus who have many attendants, who are very rich, powerful, and prosperous, but that there is no need to keep it with modest gurus, who take a humble position, the beggar-like yogis. Whichever the case, you must understand the crucial points of advantages and risks, since to remain as dull as an old horse won't work. This need to keep the samaya, is it for the Guru's benefit or your own? Deeply recollect yourself, and think this over carefully, as when grinding medicine. If it is for the Guru's benefit, then you can forget it right away. But if it's not, then there is no point in throwing ashes on your own head.

In general, the samaya with your Dharma brothers and sisters comprises holding all those who have entered the door of Lord Buddha's teachings in high esteem, and of training yourself in seeing everything as pure. You should abandon all criticism and partisan discrimination between philosophical schools. More particularly, all those who have the same guru and the same mandala are vajra brothers and sisters, so renounce contempt, rivalry, jealousy, and deceit, and from your heart consider them as intimates.

All sentient beings without exception have been our own kind parents. Alas! The fierce suffering of samsara, which has no release, harasses all of them. If I do not protect them, who else will? Unable to bear this thought, train yourself in sustaining compassion. Whatever you might be able to accomplish with your three doors, do only that which is truly beneficial to others, and dedicate all merit to them.

At all times, there are only three things to be considered: the Dharma, the Guru, and sentient beings. Do not contradict your intentions by

༄༅། མ། སེམས་ཅན་གསུམ་ལས་མེད་པས་བསམ་པ་དང་ལག་ལེན་མ་འཆོལ། རྟགས་དང་མིང་གི་རྟོགས་ལྡན་དང་གྲྭ་པ་རྣམས་ལ་མ་འགྲན་པར་མ་མགལ། ཁ་རྡུ་ཆུག་ལ་རང་སེམས་ཆུན། འདི་ག་གལ་ཆེ་ཤོས་ཞིག་ཡིན་པས་སྐྱུག་བརྫུས་མ་འདེབས། གཞི་ནས་རང་དོན་ཆོ་ཕྱི་མ་ཁོ་ནར་བསམ་ན་ཆོས་ཟེར་བ་དེ་རང་གིས་བྱས་པ་ཞིག་དགོས་རྒྱུ་ལས། ཤི་ཚར་རྗེང་གཞན་གྱིས་བསྒྲུབས་པའི་དགེ་རྩ་ལ་རེ་དགོས་བྱུང་ན་ཕན་པ་དཀའ་བར་མཆིས་སོ། །དེས་ན་བློ་ཁ་ནང་དུ་བཀུག་སྟེ་སྦྱོར་བ་སྙིང་ནས་ངེས་པར་འབྱུང་བའི་བློས་ཆོ་དང་སྒྲུབ་པ་མཉམ་པའི་དྲན་འདུན་བརྩོན་འགྲུས་དྲག་པོས་གཞི་བཟུང་། དངོས་གཞི་ལྷ་སྒོམ་ཟབ་མོའི་ཉམས་ལེན་ལ་གནད་དུ་བསྣུན་ཏེ། རྗེས་ཐོབ་དམ་ཚིག་བསླབ་སྡོམ་གྱི་ཚུལ་ལས་སྤང་བླང་འགལ་མེད་དུ་སྤྱོད་པའི་ལག་རྗེས་སུ་ཡོན་ཏན་རང་དབང་མེད་པར་ནང་ནས་སྐྱེ་ཏེ། རྫོགས་པ་ཆེན་པོ་ནི་སྡིག་ཅན་བཙན་ཐབས་སུ་འཚང་རྒྱ་བའི་ལམ་ཡིན་པའི་ཕྱིར་རོ། །དེ་ལ་ཟབ་དྲག་པའི་དབང་གིས་བར་ཆད་ཀྱང་ཡོད་པས་ཁེ་ཆེ་སར་ཉེན་ཆེ་བ་དང་འདྲ། དེའི་རྒྱུ་མཚན་རང་གི་སྔོན་བསགས་ཀྱི་ལས་ངན་ཐམས་ཅད་གདམས་ངག་གི་ནུས་པས་སློང་བའི་རྟགས་སུ་ཕྱིར་རོལ་དུ་བདུད་ཀྱི་བར་ཆད་ཆོ་འཕྲུལ་འབྱུང་བའང་། སྒྲུབ་གནས་དེར་ལྷ་འདྲེས་གཟུགས་སྟོན་པ་དང་། མིང་ནས་འབོད་པ་དང་། བླ་མར་བརྫུས་ནས་ལུང་སྟོན་པ་དང་། འཇིགས་སྐྲག་གི་ཆོ་འཕྲུལ་སྣ་ཚོགས་ཉམས་སམ་རྨི་ལམ་དུ་འབྱུང་བའང་། དངོས་སུའང་གཞན་གྱིས་བརྡེག་བཙོག་ཧག་རྐྱེན་ན་ཚ་སོགས་མ་ངེས་པར་འབྱུང་བ་དང་། སེམས་ཐོག་ཏུ་དོན་མེད་པར་སྡུག་བསྔལ་དྲག་པོ་མྱོང་བ་དང་། སྐྱོ་ཞིང་དུ་སྙིང་འདོད་པ་དང་། ཉོན་མོངས་དྲག་པོ་སྐྱེ་བ་དང་། མོས་གུས་བྱང་སེམས་སྙིང་རྗེ་

your actions. Do not compete with those who bear the trappings or names of yogis or monks. Bite your lip, control your mind. This is extremely important – do not play the fool.

If, for your own real good, you think only of future lives, it is clear that Dharma is something that has to be done by yourself. You might put your hope in virtuous actions performed by others after your death, but it may well prove difficult to derive any benefit from them. So, turn your mind inward; lay the foundation by having complete disgust for worldly activities and firm resolution to make your life and your practice one. Erect the main construction by hitting the vital point through the practice of the profound view and meditation. After completion, act without confusing what has to be rejected with what has to be adopted in the application of the samayas, precepts, and vows. As a result, the qualities will have no choice but to flourish from within. That is why the Great Perfection is the path for sinners to swiftly become buddhas.

The great profundity of this Dharma carries obstacles with it in the same way that great profit goes together with great risk.The reason for this is that all the accumulated bad karma of your past lives will, by the power of the instructions, arise outwardly as the obstacles and apparitions of Mara. At the place where you practice, spirits will show their forms and call you by name. Taking the guise of the Guru, they will make predictions. Various frightful hallucinations will arise in your inner experience, thoughts, and dreams. In reality, you might be subject to attacks, quarrels, thieves, robbers, diseases, and other unexpected hazards. In your mind, for no reason at all, you will experience intense suffering and sadness, which will make you want to cry. Strong defiled thoughts will develop, while fervent devotion, aspiration to enlightenment, and compassion will decline. Thoughts in which you see hostility everywhere will drive you nearly mad. Beneficial words will be misinterpreted. You won't feel like staying in retreat, and you will be tempted to annul your promise. Inverted views regarding the Guru will develop. You will feel doubt about the Dharma. You will be falsely accused even though innocent, you will acquire a bad reputation, close friends will turn into enemies, and so on. Various

༄༅། །ཁྲི་བ་དང་། རྣམ་རྟོག་དགྲར་ལངས་ཏེ་སྨྱོ་གྲབ་བྱེད་པ་དང་། ཕན་གཏམ་ལོག་པར་གོ་བ་དང་། རི་ཁྲོད་དུ་སྡོད་སྙིང་མི་འདོད་པར་དམ་བཅའ་གཏོང་སྙིང་འདོད་པ་དང་། བླ་མ་ལ་ལོག་ལྟ་སྐྱེ་བ་དང་། ཆོས་ལ་ཐེ་ཚོམ་ཟ་བ་སོགས་དང་། གཞན་ཡང་མ་ཉེས་ཁ་ཡོག་དང་། གྲགས་པ་ངན་པ་དང་། མཛའ་བོ་དགྲར་ལངས་པ་སོགས་ཕྱི་ནང་གི་རྐྱེན་མི་འདོད་པ་སྣ་ཚོགས་འབྱུང་བ་སྲིད། འོ་དེ་ཚོ་ཀློངས་ཚད་ཡིན་པས་ངོ་ཤེས་པར་གྱིས་ཤིག །ཁེ་ཉེན་གྱི་སོ་མཚམས་འདི་ན་ཡོད། བར་ཆད་དེའང་གནད་ཀྱིས་ཟིན་ན་དངོས་གྲུབ་ཏུ་འགྱུར། དབང་དུ་སོང་ན་གེགས་སུ་འགྱུར། འདི་ལ་དམ་ཚིག་དག་ཅིང་མོས་གུས་ལྷེམ་བརྒྱུད་མེད་པའི་སྙིང་རུས་ཅན་གྱིས་བླ་མ་ལ་བློ་གཏད། སྙིང་བཅོལ། ཅི་མཛད་ཁྱེད་ཤེས་ཀྱིས་གསོལ་བ་ཕུར་ཚུགས་སུ་གཏབ། རྐྱེན་ངན་དེ་འདོད་ཐོག་ཏུ་ཁྱེར་ཏེ་ཉམས་ལེན་ལ་དྲག་ཏུ་འབད་པས། ཇི་ཞིག་ན་རྐྱེན་ཁོའི་ཕོ་ཚུགས་རང་ཞིག་ལ་སོང་ནས་ཉམས་ལེན་ལ་བོགས་ཐོན། སྣང་བ་བན་མ་བུན་དུ་འགྲོ། བླ་མ་དང་གདམས་ངག་ལ་སྦྱར་བས་ཀྱང་ཡིད་ཆེས་སྐྱེ། ད་ཕྱིན་ཀློངས་བྱུང་ཡང་ཨའུ་ཙེ་སྙམ་པའི་བློ་གདིང་རྙེད་དེ་འོང་། འོ་དེ་ནི་ཚར་ཚད་ཡིན་ཏེ་རྐྱེན་ལམ་དུ་ལོངས་པས་ཚར་ཀློངས་འགྲིགས་པ་ཡིན། ཨ་ལ་ལ། ཕ་རྒན་ང་རང་ཚོ་ལ་དགོས་རྒྱུ་ནི་དེ་རང་རེད། ཁ་ཟ་འདོད་ལ་སྐྱིད་པ་འདར་ཕྲིལ་ཕྲིལ་ལྷ་མི་རོ་ལ་འཛབ་པ་ལྟར་མ་བྱེད་པར་བློ་སྟོབས་བསྐྱེད་ཅིག །ཡང་གང་ཟག་བསགས་རྒྱབ་དམན་པ། དམ་སྡོམ་ཀློད་པ། ལོག་ལྟ་ཆེ་བ། ཐེ་ཚོམ་མང་བ། ཁས་ལེན་མཐོ་ལ་ཉམས་ལེན་ཞན་པའི་སྙིང་ལ་རྟུག་དྲི་ཁ་བ་ཆོས་བླ་མའི་གདམས་ངག་དཔེ་ཁྲིའི་སྟེང་དུ་བཞུགས་སུ་གསོལ། རྐྱེན་ངན་དེ་ལ་ཤི་སྐྱར་འཐམ་ནས་རྗེས་སུ་འབྲངས་པས

undesirable circumstances may well arise, outside and inside.

Ho! These are critical points of eruption. You must recognize them. Here is the frontier between benefit and danger. If you handle these obstacles with the key means, they will turn into accomplishments. If you fall under their power, they will become hindrances. So, with pure samaya and persistent unwavering devotion, give your faith and heart to the Guru, praying ardently with complete confidence in whatever he may do. If you take these difficult circumstances as something desirable and persevere resolutely in the practice, after some time the solidity of these conditions will collapse by itself and your practice will progress.

Appearances will become insubstantial like mist. Confidence in the Guru and his instructions will grow as never before. Even when these happenings occur again, you will find a firm assurance, thinking, "That's all right." Ho! This is the point of solution. By bringing these circumstances on the path, the critical points have been settled. A la la! This is exactly what we old fathers want. So, don't be like a jackal approaching a man's corpse, longing to eat it, but its haunches shaking with fear. Develop a strong mind.

Those whose accumulation of merit is meager, whose samaya and vows are lax, whose wrong views are great, whose doubts are many, who are high in promises and low in practice – such people, whose hearts smell like farts, request the Guru's teaching to remain on their bookshelves. Clutching unfavorable circumstances tightly by the hand, they follow them. Having easily found their weak points, the devil will be able to drag them down the path to inferior realms. Alas! Pray to the Guru that this does not happen.

༄༅། བདུད་ཀྱིས་གླག་རྙེད་དེ་ངན་འགྲོའི་ལམ་དུ་ཁྲིད་པ་མཆི། ཨ་ཁ་ཁ། དེ་འདྲ་མི་འབྱུང་བར་བླ་མ་ལ་གསོལ་བ་ཐོབ། དེ་ཡང་ངན་རྐྱེན་ལམ་དུ་སློངས་པ་ནི་ཅུང་ཟད་སླ་མོད། བཟང་རྐྱེན་ལམ་དུ་སློངས་པ་འདི་ཤིན་ཏུ་དཀའ་བས་རྟོགས་པ་མཐོན་པོར་རློམ་པ་དག་ཀྱང་ཚེ་འདིའི་ཆེ་ཐབས་འབའ་ཞིག་ལྷུར་ལེན་པ་རྣམ་གཡེང་ལྷའི་བུའི་བདུད་ཀྱི་འབབས་སུ་བཀོལ་དོགས་ཡོད་པས་ཤིན་ཏུ་གཟབ་དགོས། ཡར་འགྲོ་མར་འགྲོའི་ས་མཚམས་སྒོམ་ཆེན་སྲང་ལ་འདེགས་ས་འདི་ན་ཡོད་པས་གོ་བར་གྱིས། ནང་གི་རྟོགས་པའི་ཡོན་ཏན་གྱི་རྩལ་ཁ་མ་རྫོགས་པར་དུ་ཉམས་གྲོང་གི་ལོ་རྒྱུས་གང་ཐོད་ཐོད་ལ་བཤད་དུ་མི་རུང་བས་ཁ་ཚུམ། གཞན་ཡང་ལོ་མཚམས་ཟླ་མཚམས་ཀྱི་སྡུག་ཡུས་མ་འདྲེན་པར་མི་ཚེ་ཁོ་ན་ལ་ཚད་བཙུགས་ནས་ཉམས་ལེན་ལ་འབུང་། སྟོང་ཉིད་ཁ་ཕྱེར་གྱིས་བློ་ཁྲིད་ནས་ཀུན་རྫོབ་རྒྱུ་འབྲས་ཀྱི་དགེ་སྦྱོར་ཁྱད་དུ་མ་གསོད། གྲོང་ཆོག་འདྲི་འདུ་ལ་སོགས་ལྟོ་ཕྱིར་གྲོང་ཡུལ་དུ་ཡུན་རིང་མ་སྡོད། དོན་མེད་ཀྱི་ལས། དགོས་མེད་ཀྱི་གཏམ། ཕན་མེད་ཀྱི་བསམ་མནོ་རྣམས་ཆུང་དུ་ཆུག །ཟོག་དང་གཡོ་སྒྱུ་སོགས་ཆོས་འགལ་གྱིས་མི་མགོ་མ་བསྐོར། འདོད་ཡོན་ལ་ཞེན་པས་གཞོག་སློང་དང་ཁ་གསགས་སོགས་ཀྱིས་ལོག་འཚོ་མ་སྒྲུབ། ལྟ་སྤྱོད་མི་མཐུན་པ་དང་སྡིག་པའི་གྲོགས་མ་བསྟེན། རང་སྐྱོན་རང་གིས་ཐོན། གཞན་གྱི་སྐྱོན་མཚང་མ་བརྗོད། ཐ་མ་ཁའི་རིགས་ཐམས་ཅད་དམ་སྲིའི་འཕྲུལ་དུ་གསུངས་པས་སྙིང་ནས་སྤོངས། ཆང་འདི་དམ་རྫས་སུ་བརྟེན་བྱ་ཡིན་ཀྱང་ར་རོ་བ་ཙམ་དུ་བག་མེད་པར་མ་འཐུང་། དད་ཅན་གྱིས་བཀུར་སྟི་བསྒྲུབ་པ་དང་། དད་མེད་ཀྱིས་སྐུར་འདེབས་ངན་གཞོམ་སོགས་བཟང་འབྲེལ་ངན་འབྲེལ་གང་ཡང་ཁྱད་མེད་དུ་ལམ་དུ་ཁྱེར་ལ་སློན་

If bad circumstances that arise on the path are relatively easy to deal with, good circumstances present much greater difficulties. There is a danger, that supported by the belief that you have attained a high level of realization, you devote yourself to ways of achieving greatness in this life, and become the servant of the distracting Devaputra devil. You must be very careful. You must know that this is the crossroads where you can go up or down; the point where great meditators are put to the test. Until the expression of the qualities of your inner understanding has reached perfection, it is wrong to recount your experiences to everyone; so keep your mouth shut. Furthermore, don't boast about your years or months of retreat, but practice earnestly for the duration of your entire human life. Do not belittle the gaining of merit through the cause and effect relationships of relative truth, deceiving yourself with mere words about emptiness.

Village ceremonies for the taming of demons and so on are performed in order to get food, so don't stay long in populated places. Meaningless action, unnecessary talk, and unprofitable thoughts must all be reduced. Don't fool others by pretense and deceit, which will contradict the Dharma. Don't practice wrong livelihood by making indirect requests and uttering flatteries because of your longing for desirable things. Don't associate with negative people or with those whose views and actions are not in harmony with yours. Disclose your own defects, and don't speak of the hidden faults of others.

All kinds of smoking are considered the tricks of the oath-breaking demons, so reject them from the heart. Alcohol should be taken as an element of samaya, but not drunk without control to the point of intoxication.

༄༅། ལམ་དག་པས་རྗེས་ས་བཟུངས། དུས་ཀུན་ནང་དུ་རིག་པ་དཔའ་མ་ཞུམ་པར་གཟིངས་མཐོ་བའི་ངང་ནས་ཕྱིའི་སྤྱོད་ལམ་དམན་པའི་ཟ་བཟུང་། རྒྱལ་པོའི་གོས་གྱོན། བཟང་ངན་འབྲིང་གསུམ་ཐམས་ཅད་གོང་དུ་ཁུར། འཚོ་བ་ངན་ངོན་ལ་བརྟེན་ནས་རི་ཁྲོད་དུ་སྡོད་ཚུགས་ཟུངས། བློ་རྩེ་སྙིང་པོ་ལ་གཏོད། གྲུབ་ཐོབ་གོང་མའི་རྣམ་ཐར་ལ་ཡར་དཔེ་གྱིས། སྨོན་ལས་ལ་ཁག་མ་འགེལ་བར་ཆོས་མགོ་གཙང་སིང་ངེ་ཐོན་པ་རེ་གྱིས། འཕྲུལ་རྐྱེན་ལ་ཁག་མ་འགེལ་བར་རྐྱེན་གང་བྱུང་གི་ཐོག་ཏུ་ཚུགས་ཐུབ་པ་རེ་གྱིས། མདོར་ན་རང་སེམས་དབང་པོར་བཞག་ནས་མི་ཚེ་ཆོས་ལ་དྲིལ་ཏེ་འཆི་དུས་བློ་ལྷག་མེད་པར་རང་གིས་རང་ལ་མ་ཁྲེལ་བ་ཞིག་གྱིས། ཉམས་ལེན་ཐམས་ཅད་ཀྱི་གནད་ཀ་དེ་ན་ཡོད་དོ། །ནམ་ཞིག་འཆི་བའི་དུས་ལ་བབས་ཚེ་ནོར་རྫས་ཅི་ཡོད་སྤྱོད་དག་བྱས་ལ་ཁབ་གཅིག་ཙམ་ལའང་ཆགས་ཞེན་མེད་པར་བྱ། དེ་ཡང་རབ་འཆི་ཁར་བྲོད་པ་སྐྱེ་བ། ཐ་མ་ཤི་ཡང་མི་འགྱོད་པ་བྱ་ཡིན་པས། རྟོགས་པའི་འོད་གསལ་ཉིན་མཚན་ཁོར་ཡུག་ཏུ་སོང་ན་བར་དོ་མེད་དེ་ལུས་རྒྱུ་ཞིག་པ་ཙམ་ཡིན། དེ་མིན་བར་དོར་གྲོལ་བའི་བློ་གདིང་འདུག་ན་གང་ལྟར་བྱས་ཀྱང་རུང་། དེ་ལྟར་མེད་ན་སྔར་ནས་འཕོ་བ་ཉམས་ལོག་ཏུ་ཚུད་པར་སྦྱངས་ཏེ་དུས་ལ་བབས་པའི་ཚེ་ལས་ལ་སྦྱར་བས་གང་དུ་མོས་པའི་ཞིང་ཁམས་སུ་འཕོས་ནས་དེ་རང་ས་ལམ་གྱི་ལྷག་མ་བགྲོད་དེ་འཚང་རྒྱ་བར་འགྱུར་རོ། །དེས་ན་རང་རེའི་བརྒྱུད་པ་རིན་པོ་ཆེ་འདི་ལ་སྨོན་བྱུང་གི་ལོ་རྒྱུས་རྙིང་པ་ཙམ་མ་ཡིན་པར། དེང་སང་ཡང་ཁྲིགས་ཆོད་དང་ཐོད་རྒལ་གྱི་ལམ་ལས་རྟོགས་པ་མཐར་ཕྱིན་ཏེ་གདོས་བཅས་འཇའ་ལུས་འོད་ཀྱི་ཕུང་པོར་དེངས་བཞིན་པ་འདི་ག་ལྟར་ལ། ནོར་བུ་པོར་ནས་འཆིང་བུ་མི་འཚོལ་བར་གདམས་ཟབ་

You should take along the path all connections, both with people who hold you in good esteem and treat you well, and with people who dislike you and treat you badly; good or bad, without caring at all, accept them with pure and good wishes. At all times, inwardly keep your spirits high without losing courage, and outwardly, on the path of action, remain humble. Wear worn-out clothes. Consider everyone - good, bad, or neutral - above yourself.

Live frugally and remain steadily in mountain hermitages. Fix your ambition on the condition of a beggar. Follow the example of the lives and perfect liberation of the siddhas of the past. Not blaming your past karma, practice Dharma flawlessly and perfectly. Not blaming circumstances, whatever they may be, remain steadfast. In brief, taking your own mind as witness, pledge this life to Dharma. At the time of death, free of thoughts about things left undone, you should not be ashamed of yourself. The vital point of all practices is here.

When the time of death is due, give away whatever possessions you have without being attached to even a needle. At the moment of death, the highest practitioners will be cheerful, middling practitioners will be without apprehension, and ordinary practitioners will feel no regret. If the radiating light of realization shines continually by both day and night, then there is no bardo, and death is nothing more than the destruction of the body. If not this, then if you have confidence that you will be liberated during the bardo, whichever way you do it is fine. If not even that, then, having previously trained and become experienced in the practice of transference, put it into action when the time comes, towards whichever pure land you desire – the rest of the paths and levels will be traversed there, and you will attain buddhahood.

In our precious lineage, this is not at all some old story from the past. Nowadays also, just in the same way, through the paths of Trekchö and Tögal, realization reaches its ultimate fruition and the gross body dissolves into rainbow light. If you throw away this precious gem, don't search for a lesser one. We are extremely fortunate to find these deep instructions, which are like the heart and blood of the dakinis! So,

༄༅། མཁའ་འགྲོའི་སྙིང་ཁྲག་འདི་ལྟ་བུ་དང་འཕྲད་པ་ནི་ཤིན་ཏུ་སྐལ་པ་བཟང་བ་ཡིན་པས་སེམས་ཀྱི་དཔང་བསྟོད་དེ་སྤྲོ་བ་བསྐྱེད་ལ་སྒོམས་ཤིག །དཔེ་འདིའང་རྗེས་འཇུག་རྣམས་ཀྱི་སྙིང་ནོར་དུ་ཟུངས་ཤིག་དང་ཕན་པ་ཆེན་པོ་འབྱུང་བར་སྲིད་དོ། །ཞེས་པའང་འོག་མིན་པདྨ་འོད་གླིང་གི་སྒོམ་གྲྭ་པ་རྣམས་ཀྱི་རི་ཆོས་ཉམས་ལེན་དུ་དམིགས་པའི་རྒྱུ་བྱས། མི་ཕྱེད་པའི་དད་གུས་ཀྱི་ནོར་ལྡན་སྒྲུབ་བརྩོན་རིག་བཟང་རྡོ་རྗེས་བསྐུལ་བའི་རྐྱེན་བྱས་ཏེ། འཇིགས་བྲལ་ཡེ་ཤེས་རྡོ་རྗེས་སྙིང་གཏམ་བསླབ་བྱ་དམར་ཁྲིད་ཀྱི་ཚུལ་དུ་བརྗོད་པ་སྐལ་ལྡན་རྣམས་ཀྱི་རྒྱུད་ལ་རྟོགས་པའི་ཡེ་ཤེས་བཙན་ཐབས་སུ་སྐྱེ་བའི་རྒྱུར་གྱུར་ཅིག །

elevate your mind and meditate with joy. Disciples, treasure this book in your heart and great benefits may ensue.

For the benefit of the retreat practice of all the meditators of Ogmin Pema Ö Ling (hence the root cause) and at the request of the industrious practitioner Rigsang Dorje, possessor of the jewel of immutable, respectful faith (hence the pretext), this was spoken from the heart by Jigdral Yeshe Dorje (Fearless Adamantine Wisdom) in the form of naked oral advice. May the wisdom of realization be born instantaneously and mightily in the nature of all fortunate beings.

Dedicated to all practitioners of the past, present, and future, and to world peace.

Translated according to the golden explanations of Tulku Thondup Rinpoche, Dungsey Trinley Norbu Rinpoche, and Taklung Tsetrul Rinpoche, and with the kind assistance of many vajra brothers and sisters.

Originally published in 1979 by Orgyan Kunsang Chökhorling, 54 Gandhi Road, Darjeeling, India. Reprinted in 1998 by Vajrayana Foundation, 2013 Eureka Canyon Road, Corralitos, CA 95076 USA.

Reedited with corrections by Philippe Turenne and Pema Dragpa during the Miracle Month in 2011 at Padma Samye Ling.

If there is any merit in this publication,
May it be dedicated to the long life of the Teaching and of the Great Gurus,
So that sentient beings may be helped ceaselessly.

Notes

[1] The Absolute Paradise of the Primordial Buddha, Kuntuzangpo (*Skt. Samantabhadra*), the Ever-Excellent One.

[2] The eight worldly considerations or dharmas are: gain and loss; pleasure and pain; fame and obscurity; praise and blame.

[3] Outer retreat means to remain within the limits of the hermitage, not to speak, not to spy outside, etc. Inner retreat is to practice according to the modalities of the practice one has undertaken without distraction of body, speech, and mind. Secret retreat is to remain in awareness.

The Three Kaya Copper-Colored Mountain Temple at Palden Padma Samye Ling

His Holiness Dudjom Rinpoche

CHAPTER 1

THE MOUNTAIN RETREAT, GRATITUDE, AND DEVOTION

Welcome to our annual one-month Dzogchen retreat. I am very grateful that we have gathered together, and thank all of you for being here. During this time, we will be studying, contemplating, and most importantly practicing the teachings of the great master, His Holiness Dudjom Rinpoche. As His Holiness himself said, these are simple, essential instructions for everyone who desires to swiftly and directly experience the true nature and glory of their mind.

Many of us had the good fortune to encounter the precious living body of His Holiness Dudjom Rinpoche. Those of us who did not have this opportunity are still connected to his dharmakaya mind, and have unlimited access to his wisdom, love, and power. Thus, if you have a connection to his dharmakaya mind, it is the same as meeting him in person.

His Holiness was one of the greatest Tibetan Buddhist masters of the twentieth century, and ample information is available regarding his life and work. One example is the small biography he inspired and indirectly instructed me to write, entitled *Light of*

Fearless Indestructible Wisdom: The Life and Legacy of His Holiness Dudjom Rinpoche. Interested people can consult that book, as well as other sources. According to the lineage instructions, all public discourses of a great master's teachings ought to include a brief biography of that master. Therefore, at the end of this retreat, I will say something about the life of His Holiness. But for now I will go directly to the teaching itself, which is called *Extracting the Quintessence of Accomplishment: Oral Instructions for the Practice of Mountain Retreat, Expounded Simply and Directly in their Essential Nakedness*. It is also known simply as *Mountain Retreat*.

What is a "mountain retreat?" On the external level, a mountain retreat is any physical location that is ideal for spiritual practice. It is synonymous with "hermitage." Buddha Shakyamuni discussed the importance of the hermitage at all levels of his teachings, and he lived and taught in various hermitages throughout his life. For example, about five kilometers from the city of Shravasti there is a hermitage known as Jetavan Grove, which we have had the good fortune to visit during our trips to India. The Buddha gave many teachings in Jetavan Grove.

The hermitage is needed because there are many distractions where we live and work. Family members, friends, neighbors, colleagues, and our various responsibilities demand a great deal of attention and time, while also often evoking and reinforcing strong emotional and intellectual patterns. We may have a deep yearning for sustained spiritual practice, but our lives as they are presently constituted do not allow it. Facing such a predicament, many people in India and Tibet chose to leave their homes and jobs. They renounced everything and went to a hermitage.

As the Vinaya tells, the most likely hermitage spot for Indian people in ancient times would be a forest. But the hermitage can be any place that is totally removed from everyday distractions, that is safe, secure, and free from wild animals, robbers, and other dangers. In Tibet there are not many forests, so most people who wanted to devote themselves to spiritual practice retreated to the mountains. This is why many practice manuals composed by Tibetan masters have the word 'mountain' in the title. For example, the great master Karma Chagme gave extensive instructions in a famous text recently translated as *Karma Chagme's Mountain Dharma*.

With regard to Holiness Dudjom Rinpoche's *Mountain Retreat* teaching, it begins with the following homage: "I bow down respectfully and take refuge at the feet of the glorious and supreme guru, incomparable in kindness. May we—my followers and I—be blessed so that with realization of the profound path, arising quickly in our nature without the slightest error, we may attain the primordial citadel in this very life."

It is important to reflect on the kindness of the lineage masters—in particular our root teachers—before we begin any spiritual activity. Since the Buddha's appearance in this world 2,600 years ago, the teachings have been practiced, actualized, and preserved by countless noble beings. A chain of great light has been forged, the essence of which is boundless love, compassion, and wisdom. For lifetimes, we have been blind to these beautiful qualities; they have been like a treasure buried deep within the recesses of our hearts. Today, at long last, we can see the treasure—the treasure that we are—and have the means to excavate and make brilliant use of it. We ourselves are now part of that chain of great light. Our good fortune is in large measure due to the lineage masters who preceded us, because their immense devotion, generosity, and forethought insured that this great light would continue to shine long after they left their bodies.

I received these *Mountain Retreat* teachings many times from His Holiness, and also quite a few times from Khenchen Palden

Sherab Rinpoche. His Holiness and Khen Rinpoche were like great spiritual chefs, spontaneously and effortlessly creating wonderful Dharma feasts in accordance with the needs and tastes of their students. In other words, His Holiness and Khen Rinpoche customized the teachings for individuals. They gave us the spiritual sustenance we needed, in the right amount, and in a manner we could understand. They were always perfectly attuned to our progress; their instruction changed as we changed, and often anticipated our changes. For this and for many other reasons I pay homage to the incomparable kindness of these two great masters.

The term "incomparable kindness" is a term of praise reserved for the root teacher, the one who nurtures your development like a spiritual father or mother. The teachings refer to "three kindnesses:" teaching, empowerment, and pith instruction. Through these, and through the power of his or her sheer presence, which is beyond birth and death, the root teacher continuously and selflessly leads you toward your truest, deepest self—enlightenment itself.

The first sentence of the *Mountain Retreat* is very important, and it bears repeating: "I bow down respectfully and take refuge at the feet of the glorious and supreme guru." This is an expression of unwavering faith and confidence in the root teacher, in the teachings he or she bestows upon you, and in your own potential. If you continually cultivate this kind of devotion, your spiritual roots will grow wide and deep. You will make continuous progress on the path, and you will ultimately attain enlightenment. If you are without it, even if you receive the most profound Dzogchen or Mahamudra pith instructions, they will not help you very much. The teachings say that when you plant a seed in desert sand, nothing grows, but when you plant a seed in rich soil, in an area where there is ample sun and rainfall, the seed will germinate and there will be fruit. Devotion fulfills in that manner.

CHAPTER 2

BODHICHITTA, HUMILITY, AND REALIZATION

Whenever we begin a formal practice session we take refuge and generate bodhichitta. The essence of refuge is devotion. The essence of bodhichitta is unlimited, impartial love and compassion for all sentient beings. We have already spoken briefly of how important devotion is to spiritual develoment. Bodhichitta is equally important.

We share the world with others. If we are indifferent, judgmental, or antagonistic to any of them, we limit ourselves and sow seeds of bitterness and discord. Conversely, if we open our hearts and minds and learn to recognize the intrinsic value of everyone, if we cultivate the desire and ability to help others, our relationships will become harmonious and inspiring, and our spiritual horizons will continuously expand.

Devotion and bodhichitta are supreme catalysts to spiritual development. If they are lacking, meditation becomes a chore, and we will be tempted to give it up. But the more we arouse these beautiful qualities, the easier and more enjoyable meditation becomes. Our ability to apply the essence of practice in daily life increases, and our realization of the true nature blooms.

The sincere practice of devotion and bodhichitta also enables us to let go of ego, which is, along with the negative emotions that support it, the chief impediment to spiritual progress. The ego is the idea of being a unique and special individual, separate from and more important than others. The great masters have always urged us to abandon this limited and limiting idea and reawaken to the boundlessness and all-inclusiveness that we truly are.

From ancient times until now, when practitioners bow to the master or to the shrine, they prostrate themselves completely on the ground. They place the highest part of their bodies—their heads—towards the lowest part of the object of refuge, which are the feet. Many of us who have visited India have seen young people bowing before their elders and touching their feet. These gestures are physical manifestations of devotion. They signify the desire to submit to the guidance of a higher authority, and the willingness to surrender the ego.

The unchecked ego defends and promotes itself, all the while belittling others. It may for a time become convinced of its sovereignty. This is known as arrogance. The teachings say that when you reach this stage your mind is like an iron ball, solid and impermeable. Even if an ocean's worth of water is poured on it, not a drop will sink in. At this time the example and guidance of realized beings has no impact. All possibility of spiritual growth is precluded, since arrogance has closed the mind.

The opposite of arrogance is humility. Humility is the realization that you are not more important than others, that you have a lot to learn, and that you need help. Humility means surrendering the ego to the master, to the teaching, and to the path.

The fullest expression of humility is the awakened mind, all embracing and free from judgments. This is the full apprehension that your own mind and the infinite universe are inseparable and perfect. It is Dzogchen realization, synonymous with boundless love, compassion, and wisdom. The paradox is that although this state is innate and ever-present within yourself, it is extremely difficult to access without preparation. According to the mahasiddha Saraha and other great masters, preparation involves accumulating merit and receiving the blessings of the master. Through these, realization is attained.

Thus far, we have been discussing the qualities of gratitude, devotion, bodhichitta, and humility. We have just begun to reawaken these qualities within ourselves, and they are fragile, while ego is still strong. But as long as we remain steadfast on the path, they will blossom and ultimately overwhelm the ego. When that happens, Dzogchen realization is ours. Realization can come unexpectedly, in surprising ways, but whenever it comes, it is unmistakable.

We need both patience and courage, because the path to full realization takes time and is not easy. Many challenges await us, both psychological and physical. The biographies of the great masters tell of the great hardships they endured, often for long periods. But they never stopped practicing. Session after session, day after day, year after year they cultivated gratitude, devotion, bodhichitta, and humility. They accepted challenges, using them as fuel for the journey. Then suddenly realization burst within them, and they became sky yogis.

The sky yogi's realization is like the brilliant sun in the clear autumn sky. Free of clouds, mist, and pollution, it is shines gloriously, its rays extending to the farthest reaches of space and time. When we attain this state we are peaceful, happy, and confident. Our kindness, compassion, and wisdom blaze. We become the equals of Buddha Samamtabhadra, Buddha Shakyamuni, Guru Padmasambhava, and all the great masters.

His Holiness calls Dzogchen realization a "primordial citadel." Primordial means original, as well as timeless; citadel signifies that which is impregnable and indestructible. The primordial citadel is your own mind, unbound by ideas and emotions. When you attain this state, should all the buddhas of the three times and ten directions suddenly appear before you, you would have nothing to ask them. Should millions of enemies suddenly surround you, you would be undaunted. You are free from hope, fear, and fixation. This is the absolute state, your essence and birthright. Through diligent spiritual practice, you bring it to life.

CHAPTER 3

THIS PRECIOUS AND IMPERMANENT LIFE

His Holiness writes, "For those who, through the reunion of their perfectly pure past aspiration and potential karma, have heartfelt confidence in the Dharma of the profound and secret Great Perfection and in the Guru who reveals it, and who wish to go through the practice to its ultimate end; for all those fortunate beings here is an entrance door, the vital instructions for mountain retreat, expounded in their essential nakedness. This is the practice of the most secret Great Perfection put into our hands in a form that is easy to understand." With these words, His Holiness gives is an overview of the entire teaching.

The beginning of this overview acknowledges that our current situation is extremely positive. It has not come about by accident, nor is it some random occurrence; it is the direct result of our past deeds, and a manifestation of our good karma. Every one of us is a beautiful, intelligent human being with vast spiritual potential. We live in a democratic country, and enjoy many freedoms and luxuries. We are very fortunate. Look around the world—how many people in other countries have what we have?

We often forget our good fortune. The ego likes to focus on what it does not have. When this happens, we lose connection to our own beauty, as well as to the beauty that surrounds us. Ego also likes to focus on difficulties. And it is true—we often undergo great trials in life. But no matter what we are going through, there is always a bright side. Our great spiritual potential and power is never compromised by circumstances, no matter how difficult they might be. Our inner beauty remains intact no matter what we lose or what we gain, for that matter. This is not to say that we should ignore or belittle difficulties. We must address and work through them. Whenever possible, we should use them as catalysts for our spiritual growth. But difficulties are not the whole of our experience. Even in the midst of the greatest darkness, there always will be light.

Let us therefore appreciate what we have and build upon it. The opportunity will not last, and we cannot know when, or if, we will ever find it again. His Holiness writes, "We sentient beings…have wandered endlessly in samsara. Countless times, we have taken different forms in the six realms, but all that we have done has been meaningless. Now, for once out of hundreds of times, we have obtained a human body….To have obtained a human body is not enough by itself. Since the time of death is uncertain, we must practice Dharma genuinely right now. At the time of death, we should, like Jetsun Mila, feel no regret or self-reproach. As he said, 'The Dharma tradition of myself, Milarepa, is not to be ashamed of myself.'"

Samsara is the path of ego, of hope and fear, of regimented thinking, and the five negative emotions. Actions motivated by these states, even if they yield enormous wealth, fame, and power, never result in enduring peace and happiness. On the contrary, they often result in disillusionment and despair. And worldly success alone, no matter how great, cannot help us cope with death.

Enduring peace and happiness is achieved by practicing Dharma. When we practice Dharma, we are reconnecting to unconditional love, compassion, and wisdom, which are aspects of the true nature of our minds. Indestructible bliss is inherent is this state, and so is the ability to enhance the lives of others. Whoever attains this state has great confidence at the time of death, and can say with utter truthfulness, "I have made the most of my life, and I am ready for what follows. All is good. I will maintain this view as I leave this physical form."

In the modern age, most of us cannot devote all our time to formal spiritual practice. We must work and earn income, take care of our health and homes. In many cases we are responsible for the well-being of others. There is nothing wrong with any of this. However, without a sense of boundary and proportion, worldly activity becomes all consuming and never-ending. When this occurs we may stop attending to our spiritual progress, and any gains we have made will wither away. We should definitely try to avoid this, and strive to balance the worldly and spiritual dimensions of our lives. We should find time for formal practice and apply the teachings at every moment.

The present moment is crucial. Just as what we have done in the past has led us to the present, whatever we do right now will determine our future. We have the power and resources to direct our future in a positive direction. At the same time, the present moment is not going to last—it is impermanent. Impermanence is an ever-present force in our lives. We are getting older, not younger. Death is getting closer, not farther away. So it is very important to start taking advantage of all that we have right now.

The great master Karma Chagme taught that the human body is borrowed from the five elements: space, wind, fire, water, and earth. That which is borrowed is not ours to keep; sooner or later we will have to give it back. As long as we are occupying a body, he continues, we ought to use it for spiritual purposes. We should use our hands to prostrate to images of the Buddha, Dharma, and Sangha. We should use our feet to circumambulate stupas, temples, and other sacred sites. We should use our tongue to recite prayers and mantras. And we should use our hearts and minds to cultivate loving-kindness and compassion for all beings. Karma Chagme teaches that if we use our bodies in these beautiful ways, when the time comes to leave them we will have no regrets.

Tibet is mountainous. Its climate is quite harsh, and wild animals and bandits roam the countryside. Particularly in ancient times, there were very few serviceable roads. Even so, Karma Chagme taught his students that when the opportunity for pilgrimage presented itself, they should take it—it may never come again. The great master used travel as a metaphor for the spiritual path.

Once we are on the path, we should not allow ourselves to be interrupted by what is not particularly important, or what does not require immediate attention. Many times, just before we are about to do a formal meditation session, we think, "I should check my email again," or "this is a good time to re-organize my bookshelves." If we take these thoughts seriously, enact them, and put off practice, what is this but procrastination? If we want, we can always find tasks to keep ourselves busy. But to what end? The teachings say that constant busy-ness is like a kitten chasing its tail. Even if it catches its tail, what does it gain?

We are beginning a one-month retreat. We have come here on our own volition. We are staying in a beautiful hermitage that is very conducive to spiritual practice, in order to study and practice the teachings of the great master, His Holiness Dudjom Rinpoche. Everything is in our favor.

"The Dharma tradition of myself is not to be ashamed of myself," said Milarepa, as he was nearing death. In a humble, understated way, he was saying, "I have made the most of my precious human life." Many great masters through the centuries have expressed sentiments to that effect upon their passing. During the last few moments of his life, my father said, "I have no regrets." Khen Rinpoche said something similar. We should strive to achieve the same level of contentment, serenity, and fearlessness as these great masters. Let us attend to our spiritual progress without delay, and bring it to completion while we still have time.

QUESTION: *How does delusion arise from dharmakaya mind?*

ANSWER: *Dharmakaya mind is open and free, like the sky. Just as there is wind energy within the sky, there is wind energy within the mind. When the wind energy of the mind stirs, a thought arises. If we remain aware of dharmakaya, the thought just passes through. If we forget dharmakaya, the thought seems real and we take it seriously as an object. In the next moment the subject—the ego or "I"—appears. Then there is a chain reaction. The process grows increasingly intense and complex, delusion arises, and negative emotions begin to manifest. All of this is vividly described in the* Prayer of Kuntuzangpo.

Every master says that we should not grasp the thought, but look to the mind itself. The moment we look to the mind itself we do not see anything specific. Everything is open and free. That means we have returned to dharmakaya. Once we have returned to dharmakaya, we should remain there, and let the mind do what it likes to do. When the wind energy of mind stirs, when the mind moves and a thought arises, we should not grasp it. What comes will go; what comes and goes is never binding. This is true of the thoughts which appear within our minds; it is equally true of all external phenomena. Growing accustomed to this is the basis of Dzogchen meditation. Therefore, we should identify dharmakaya mind and abide in that state with mindfulness. At the same time, with regard to thoughts and external phenomena, we should cultivate non-grasping and let go.

QUESTION: *There seems to be some compatibility between the Buddhist view of the nature of reality and that of certain branches of modern science. What do you think?*

ANSWER: *The Buddhist view is that the universe and all that it contains—time, space, worlds, beings, and every transformation—is a manifestation of mind. There are no boundaries between mind and phenomena, and mind itself is inconceivable. I am far from being an expert, but it seems to me that modern science has not reached a consensus on the nature of reality.*

In the early days of quantum physics, some scientists noticed that simply by observing subatomic particles they were changing the behavior of those particles. They inferred that mind and phenomena, at least on the subatomic level, were more intimately connected than what was previously believed. This insight is in line with the Buddhist view. However, it remained conceptual.

Scientists have made astounding discoveries, many of which have greatly improved the lives of beings. Whatever helps beings is always compatible with Buddhism. But science operates solely within the domain of conceptuality, and conceptuality can only go so far. You must transcend concepts—as well as all searching and striving, however refined—in order to ascertain the nature of reality. But please remember that the person who is saying this is a Buddhist practitioner and not a scientist.

CHAPTER 4

THE PREPARATION

As His Holiness himself says, his *Mountain Retreat* text is the essence of the complete nine yana teachings of Buddha Shakyamuni, put in a condensed form that is simple and easy to practice. It contains all the necessary guidelines and tips for a devoted practitioner. If you go on retreat with this text, relying upon it and practicing it with full faith, that along with the oral instructions of your root teacher will be sufficient to activate your realization. So this *Mountain Retreat* is very special.

His Holiness divided his teaching into three topics. In his own words, the first is "The Preparation—having cut the ties of the grasping and clinging, how to purity one's own mind stream by keeping the mind turned towards the Dharma."

What does it mean, to "keep the mind turned towards the Dharma?" It means to directly ascertain the true nature of our minds, and to dedicate ourselves to the temporal and spiritual happiness of all beings. This cannot be accomplished without strong commitment and discipline.

There are twenty-four hours in a day. During that time we

must work and sleep. We must obtain, prepare, and eat food. We have responsibilities to loved ones. All of this is important—but there is so much else that is not. If we want to progress spiritually, we must eliminate or reduce our involvement with that which is inessential or trivial. We must prioritize spiritual practice, otherwise we will not grow. Neurotic states of mind based on ignorance, attachment, and anger will arise and sweep us away, just as they always have. We will be unable to accomplish our own benefit, much less the benefit of others.

Spiritual practice includes study, meditation, and reciting prayers and mantras. But what is the root of all of this? It is loving-kindness and compassion, along with gratitude, devotion, and humility. It is patience and gentleness. It is opening the mind so that it becomes as vast and all encompassing as space. If we want a single word that encompasses all of these beautiful qualities, that word is bodhichitta.

Keeping the mind towards the Dharma begins by arousing bodhichitta, and it continues with contemplating death. Death is not alien or strange, but simply a part of the magical display of this world. Countless beings before us have died, and we will be joining them before long. It is said that in this life death is the one certainty. It is even more certain than tomorrow.

What is the link between arousing bodhichitta and contemplating death? When you arouse bodhichitta, your heart becomes tender, your mind opens, and life is increasingly smooth, joyful, and dreamlike. When you contemplate death, you learn to treasure and make the most of each and every moment, and you also become unattached and fearless. When you are transformed in these ways, death is nothing to worry about. In fact, you will be quite eager and excited to experience what the transition is all about. This was the state attained by many great masters, one of whom, as I just mentioned, is Milarepa.

Milarepa's life story is well known. But what about the actual name, *Milarepa*? That story begins with Milarepa's grandfather, who was a great and well-known ngakpa. Once, an invisible demon was creating disturbances for many people. Through his meditation power, Milarepa's grandfather squeezed the demon very tightly. The demon cried "*Mila! Mila!*" which means, "Oh man, oh man!" This was a declaration of submission and defeat. Many people heard the demon's cry. To honor Milarepa's grandfather and his triumph over the demon they started calling him *Mila*. In this way, *Mila* became the family's last name.

When Milarepa was a young boy he had a wonderful singing voice. It is said that his renditions of Tibetan folk songs elicited tears of joy in those who heard them. At this time, the people called him *Mila Tupaka*, "Mila, Whose Voice Brings Happiness." Years later, after Milarepa mastered Tummo practice, he no longer needed to wear heavy woolen clothing. He wore only thin cotton, even during the coldest parts of the year. It was extremely unusual for a Tibetan to dress that way, so the people renamed him *Milarepa*, "Mila, Who Wears Cotton." Even after he became known as Milarepa he continued to sing, but now he sang songs of spiritual instruction. Many of these songs were written down by his students. In modern times they have been translated into many languages, including English. So the beautiful voice of Milarepa is still being heard.

Venerable Khenchen Palden Sherab Rinpoche

CHAPTER 5

ROOTING THE PRACTICE

His Holiness writes, "To enter the path of Dharma, it is not enough to adopt its outer appearances. We have to sever all ties to desirable things and to activities limited to this life." This means that we must be dedicated to the path, and not allow ourselves to get sidetracked by distractions. It is also important to remember that a superficial or even casual attitude toward practice will not help us very much. We need real passion and commitment, otherwise we might easily become Dharma tourists.

A tourist visits a place, enjoys the sights and sounds for a while, then leaves. Years ago, I had the opportunity to visit Disney World for a short time along with my father and Khen Rinpoche. We saw some wonderful things, but looking back I have to wonder, did this really help us? What did we gain from that visit, except a few nice memories?

The Dharma has come to the West. Texts have been translated and are readily available, while qualified teachers are giving teachings and empowerments. There are Dharma movies and museums, and there is plenty of information available for free on the internet. If we like, we can tour one site after another and entertain ourselves quite well. On one level this is good—the Buddha and Guru Padmasambhava said that any exposure to the teachings, even if it is fleeting or superficial, will ultimately take root and blossom. But that is for the future. If we want results now, we need to be Dharma residents, not tourists.

As tourists, we seek a break from the routine and difficulty of everyday life. We go to places that have bright sunshine, cool breezes, and other people to make our beds. Dharma practice is not like that. Beautiful experiences will arise, but so will hardship. If we believe that the spiritual path should always be sunny and warm, we will reject and even run away from storms. We might blame the teaching, the teacher, and our spiritual brothers and sisters. Eventually, we may even give up our practice. This has happened to practitioners many times in the past. It could happen to us.

Difficulties will arise on the spiritual journey. We might be tempted to escape them, but no matter how fast and far we go, the same difficulties will be waiting for us. Difficulties are an inevitable and necessary part of the spiritual journey. As Dharma practitioners, we have no choice but to meet them head-on.

For inspiration, we should read the life stories of the great masters. Every great master was a great practitioner first. A great practitioner is one who is determined and courageous, rooted like a healthy tree. When a healthy tree encounters powerful wind and rain, it bends but never breaks. The more it endures, the stronger and more lush it becomes. This ability is fully present within each and every one of us, but it must be recognized, valued, and utilized. In the beginning stages of practice, when difficulties arise, we will do well simply to endure them. With a little experience, we can use difficulties to purify and transform ourselves. Later, when our Dzogchen meditation becomes strong, difficulties will be seen as part of the natural display of reality itself, and neither good nor bad.

In addition to accepting and making use of difficulties, it is also important that we do not fixate on the sensational and spectacular aspects of Dharma. Khen Rinpoche always said that if you keep looking at the sky while you are walking, you can trip and break your neck. This is a message not to get caught up in so-called higher states of consciousness, or in miracles and wonders. While it is true that many great masters have spiritual powers, their abilities arose naturally because of their disciplined, well-rounded practice. They valued the ground as much as the sky, and we should do the same. In fact, at the beginning stages of our spiritual evolution, the ground is even more important.

His Holiness continues, "We have to sever all ties to desirable things and to activities limited to this life." Desire is natural. But when your desire is strong, it preoccupies you, and you forget and neglect what you already have. Then, as you pursue your desire, you consume enormous time and energy. You also create considerable anxiety. Will I get what I want? When will I get it? Even if you obtain the object of your desire, anxieties continue. Can I keep it? Can I have more? For this reason, the Buddha taught, "Less desire and more contentment—that is noble." Why is this? Because with less desire and more contentment your mind is peaceful. You will better appreciate, enjoy, and build on what you already have. And you will have much more time and energy for spiritual practice.

In a previous life, the Buddha was born as the universal king known as Nahlay Nu, and he ruled all four continents of the world. The teachings speak of four types of universal kings. The most powerful of these bears the golden wheel, the second most powerful bears the silver wheel, and the third and fourth bear the copper wheel and the iron wheel, respectively. Nahlay Nu bore the golden wheel; he was therefore the highest of the high. By contrast, the King of Shambhala is the fourth type.

The great master Vasubandhu wrote in the *Abhidharmakosha* that whenever a universal king marches his armies to another country, the inhabitants of that country are never afraid and actually welcome him. In this way, Nahlay Nu commanded unprecedented power and respect around the world.

Still, Nahlay Nu was unsatisfied. He wanted to expand his dominion. In particular, he wanted to be king of the god realms. Nahlay Nu focused his attention on the heights of Mount Sumeru, the abode of the gods. Bearing his golden wheel, he swiftly arrived there, followed by his armies and entourage. Indra, the king of the gods, immediately received and honored him and arranged a big reception. Now, Indra had accumulated a great deal of positive merit in previous lifetimes, which was how he became king of the gods. His merit equaled Nahlay Nu's. Thus, Nahlay Nu could not take the power from Indra, he could only share it. He had to sit on the same throne as Indra, and he was not happy. He thought, "I wish Indra would disappear!" At that moment Nahlay Nu fell back to earth. The moment he landed, everything changed. Nobody recognized him. He had become totally ordinary. He became deeply depressed, and remained like that until the end of his life.

The message of this story is not that desire is evil or wrong, but rather that if we do not know when to put the breaks on it, we can crash. The teachings warn that the six senses can be insatiable. The eyes, ears, nose, tongue, and skin adore beautiful objects, and the mind loves its thoughts. We must apply our intelligent awareness to discipline our senses, because our senses will never discipline themselves.

There are many examples in the teachings which show the consequences of undisciplined desire. Moths are drawn to the light of candles and are burned in their flames. Deer are attracted to pleasant sounds. Hunters know this, and can draw them from their safe havens by playing beautiful melodies on their flutes. Bees enjoy the smell of pollen, but when they linger too long inside of flowers they become trapped. When fish are lured by the taste of bait on a fisherman's hook, they are easily snared. Elephants like to roll around in the mud to cool off from the hot sun and also to ward off mosquitoes. They are powerful beings, but if they spend too much time in the mud they can get stuck there, and become easy prey for hunters. And human beings, like Nahlay Nu, who already have everything they need and more, can end up with nothing in the insatiable pursuit for what is out of reach.

As practitioners, our goal with regard to desire should be balance. To achieve balance, we need mindfulness, alertness, and conscientiousness. These are powerful assistants who help keep us free from extreme states which derail us from our spiritual goals. For this reason, balancing desire should not be thought of as a burden, but as a blessing. We can still enjoy the objects of the six senses, but in moderation, and without compulsion and obsession. At the same time, we will have more time and energy for Dharma practice. In this way, even though we are not cutting out desire as completely as did Buddha Shakyamuni, Milarepa, and other great masters, we are at least not under its control.

At the same time, we should continually renew and deepen our commitment to our spiritual goals. By practicing Dharma we will improve our lives and be increasingly able to help others. We will be free from our intellectual and emotional delusions and perceive the purity and perfection of the entire universe. We should strive to realize this; at the same time, we should not expect immediate results. Why? Because our intellectual and emotional patterns are ingrained and resilient. Our self-involvement is strong, our concern for others wavers, and desire is still a powerful force. All this can and will be transformed, but only over time. This means that in the beginning we need faith. We must believe in the possibility of spiritual growth and in our own potential. Then, as we practice with devotion and joyful effort, we will experience the truth of the teachings. Our hearts and minds will open. Our faith will yield compassion and wisdom. This will inspire us to further discoveries, and ultimately to enlightenment itself. Enthusiastic, short-term practice cannot achieve this effect. It is like hay-fire—explosive, sudden, and quickly gone.

CHAPTER 6

ASANGA

There are many stories about devoted beings who manifested extraordinary perseverance on their spiritual journeys. One of these concerns Asanga. Asanga became one of the most famous masters in Buddhist history. To understand his contribution, we should briefly review the history of Buddhism. Then I will tell his remarkable story.

According to tradition, the Buddha turned the wheel of Dharma four times. The first three are widely known, while the fourth—the Vajrayana—is secret. The second turning of the wheel of Dharma is known as *Prajnaparamita*, or "Perfection of Wisdom." There are many Prajnaparamita sutras of various lengths—100,000 lines, 25,000 lines, 18,000 lines, and there is even a single syllable version. The root teaching of the Prajnaparamita sutras is emptiness. Emptiness has both an outer and inner meaning.

Regarding the outer meaning, the Prajnaparamita says that everything that we see, hear, smell, taste, touch, and think is empty. The entire universe and each and every sentient being is empty. Confusion and spiritual awakening are empty, too. Empty means utterly open and free—ungraspable, beyond the reach and range of the intellect.

The great master Nagarjuna, in his Madhyamaka teachings, used logical analysis to explore and reveal all the philosophical implications of emptiness. His work is renowned as being the greatest exposition of the Buddha's Prajnaparamita teachings, from the perspective of the outer meaning.

What is the inner meaning of the Prajnaparamita? It is to directly realize the empty nature of all phenomena. This generally includes studying and comprehending the outer meaning, but ultimately going beyond it. Realizing emptiness is not an intellectual achievement. It is continuously to experience the living truth of the emptiness of all phenomena. In his Prajnaparamita teachings, the Buddha showed how to accomplish this inner meaning. He also articulated the levels or stages of progress, known as the paths and bhumis. But he did not do so explicitly. And this brings us to Asanga.

The histories tell that Asanga studied the Prajnaparamita literature and was fascinated by it. He entered Nalanda Monastic University to broaden his knowledge and became quite accomplished intellectually. But he began to see that there was a deeper level of understanding of the Prajnaparamita that went beyond the intellect, and to realize this understanding became the driving force of his life. Asanga visited many masters, pleading to be taught the inner meaning of the Prajnaparamita, but none could do so. One master said that there was only one being in the universe who could teach him what he wanted to know: the Future Buddha, Maitreya. Asanga asked, "Where is Maitreya?" He was told that Maitreya resided in Tushita Heaven. "How can I get there to meet him?" "You cannot meet him as you would a regular person. You have to meditate and pray."

"How do I do that?" So the master gave him all the necessary empowerments and instructions for practicing on Maitreya, and then Asanga departed for the mountain known as *Riwo Chaking*.

Riwo is Tibetan for "mountain." *Chaking* means "chicken feet." Scholars hold varying opinions as to its location. Some place it as far away as China. Khen Rinpoche, however, said that Chicken Feet Mountain is in the range of mountains that stretch between Nalanda and Bodhgaya, although he could not identify the precise one. Citing a number of Buddhist histories, Khen Rinpoche said that there had long been a deep connection between this mountain and Maitreya, thus making it the ideal place for Asanga's practice. The story of that connection begins with Kashyapa, one of the Buddha's greatest disciples.

Kashyapa was born into a very wealthy family and lived on a grand estate. He was drawn to the spiritual life, but it was his parents' wish that he remain with them. As Kashyapa was very devoted to them, he complied. When his parents passed away, he decided to leave the family estate. All he took were the clothes on his back, which were made of a very special fabric. He gave everything else to his servants.

Kashyapa was in his thirties when he first met the Buddha. The histories say that the moment he laid eyes upon the Buddha, he said, "You are my teacher." And the Buddha replied, "Yes, and you are my student." At that instant Kashyapa attained full arhat realization. Then he offered his clothes to the Buddha.

Later on, as the Buddha moved closer to mahaparanirvana, he gave his robes to Kashyapa, which was an indirect message that he had selected Kashyapa to be his regent. From that moment until his own mahaparanirvana, Kashyapa always placed the Buddha's robes on his lap when he meditated.

After Kashyapa became regent, Prince Ajatasatru, the son of King Bimbisara, approached him. At an earlier time, Prince

Ajatasatru did not have much interest in the Dharma, but that had changed. Ajatasatru said, "The Buddha entered mahaparanirvana before I could meet him. Before you enter mahaparanirvana, I want to receive teachings from you." Kashyapa agreed. Shortly afterwards Ajatasatru heard a voice in his dream saying, "Your uncle is gone." He awoke with a start and thought, "Kashyapa has entered mahaparanirvana." He quickly went to see Ananda, who said, "Kashyapa is within Chicken Feet Mountain." Ananda and Ajatasatru went there right away. Through his meditation power, Ananda opened the mountain so that they could see Kashyapa. Kashyapa was in the middle of the mountain, sitting in meditation posture, with the Buddha's robes on his lap. He had indeed entered mahaparanirvana.

According to the teachings, Kashyapa will remain in this position until the coming of the Future Buddha, the fifth buddha of this Fortunate Aeon, Maitreya. After Maitreya appears on this earth and attains enlightenment, he will gather all of his old students. For his first teaching, he will take them to Chicken Feet Mountain, and will lead them to Kashyapa. He will pick up Kashyapa's arm and say, "This is the regent of the Fourth Buddha. His name is Kashyapa. Among the Buddha's students, he achieved the greatest mastery of the twelve ascetic practices and the highest degree of contentment." Then Maitreya will pick up the robes from Kashyapa's lap, display them to his students, and say, "These are the very robes worn by the Buddha." At that moment, according to the teachings, Kashyapa will self-emanate fire. The flames will consume all his physical aggregates and his body will dissolve into the true nature of the five elements. This will inspire Maitreya's students very deeply so that many of them will attain arhathood on the spot.

Asanga meditated at that very place for three years. But he received no signs from Maitreya during that time, and became very sad. "All of this effort, and not a single sign. It is best I leave." So Asanga left. On the way down the mountain he noticed a hole in the rock face. Suddenly a bird emerged from the hole and flew away. Asanga looked inside and saw imprints of flapping wings on the rock. "A bird's wings are so soft and delicate," thought Asanga, "Yet by brushing this rock again and again they have left their mark. This is a sign that I need to be more persevering." With that thought Asanga resumed his retreat.

Another three years passed. Asanga meditated strongly, but once again there were no signs from Maitreya. He was very upset and decided to end his retreat. On his way down the mountain he noticed a huge boulder on the ground with a large, deep crack. High above the boulder was an over-hanging cliff. Asanga saw a tiny drop of water falling from the cliff and onto the rock. Then, after a while, another drop fell. "One tiny drop of water after another, slowly falling on this huge boulder, eventually caused it to crack," Asanga thought. "This is a sign that I need to be more persevering." And so Asanga went back up the mountain to began his retreat anew.

Yet another three years went by. Asanga put great effort into his practice, but nothing even remotely like a sign occurred. He was very upset and decided that enough was enough. He started to descend the mountain. On the way down he noticed a man rubbing an iron bar with a piece of silk. Asanga asked, "What are you doing?" And the man said, "I am making needles," and he pointed to a pile of needles nearby. "He is doing the impossible," Asanga thought. "This is a sign that if one believes in and works hard towards a goal, it will manifest." Asanga returned to his practice, quite confident that this time he would see Maitreya.

For three more years Asanga practiced with unremitting devotion. But the results were the same as before—no signs. Asanga was crushed. He thought, "Twelve years of my life have passed, and I am no closer to my goal than when I started. I give up. I will go back to Nalanda. No matter what kind of sign I see, I will not return." And so Asanga walked down the mountain, and took the road that led to Nalanda.

After walking for a while, Asanga saw an emaciated female dog lying by the side of the road, writhing in pain, her underbelly infested with maggots. Asanga felt profound compassion for this dog. He picked up a small knife, which was on ground nearby, cut a piece of flesh from his own thigh, and gave it to her to eat. Asanga wanted to remove the maggots from her underbelly. He realized that if he were to use his hands to do this, he would injure the maggots. So he decided that he would remove them with his tongue. He lay down on his stomach, very close to the dog. He was a little repulsed, so he closed his eyes. He extended his tongue towards the maggots, but his tongue fell to the ground. He tried again, and the same thing happened. Asanga opened his eyes. The dog was gone. Standing before him, resplendent and luminous, was Maitreya. Asanga began to weep uncontrollably. He cried, "My Lord, I have been seeking you for so long. Why have you come only now?" And Maitreya replied, "My son, I have always been with you, but your obscurations prevented you from seeing me. Your twelve-year retreat removed many of your obscurations. The great compassion you manifested towards that dog removed the rest." The teachings say that Maitreya took Asanga with him to Tushita Heaven, and for fifty years taught him the inner meaning of the Prajnaparamita.

This story about Asanga beautifully illustrates the power of perseverance. As you travel on the spiritual path, there may be prolonged periods when it seems that you are not progressing. You can become discouraged and may even want to quit. But the truth is that every moment you practice—even if you do not realize it—you are accumulating great stores of energy on the deepest and most subtle levels. One drip of water after another will eventually fill a large bowl, or crack a huge boulder. Perseverance in spiritual practice is even stronger. Trust in this, keep your practice alive, and one day quite unexpectedly you will see the Future Buddha by your side, or even in the mirror.

Guru Padmasambhava

CHAPTER 7

OBSTACLES ARE OPPORTUNITIES

In the next portion of the *Mountain Retreat* teaching, His Holiness Dudjom Rinpoche discusses obstacles. An obstacle is anything that blocks our progress towards our goal. That is how it initially appears, but essentially every obstacle is an opportunity.

The teachings say that dedicated practitioners should know that Buddhas and obstacles are equally kind. How is this? The Buddhas give us teachings and provide inspiration, blessings, and support. They are also perfect role models. Obstacles give us the chance to test and apply what we have learned. During practice sessions, we cultivate loving-kindness and compassion, inner peace and pure vision. While we are seated on our meditation cushion we might believe that we have already aroused and embody these qualities. But it is only when we get up and encounter difficult situations in the dynamic of life that we will know for sure. In similar fashion, warriors may sharpen and perfect their skills in controlled environments, but only when they encounter real enemies on the battlefield will they know the true extent of their strength and bravery.

Obstacles put us on the path in the first place, as the life stories of the great masters plainly show. When Prince Siddhartha closely observed the sufferings of aging, sickness, and death, he was motivated to leave the kingdom and seek liberation. These were the conditions that led to his becoming the Buddha. Guru Padmasambhava was installed at a young age as the Prince of Oddiyana. Some of his actions were misinterpreted. He was prosecuted and then banished from the kingdom. He went to the cemetery to meditate and after igniting his enlightened qualities, he began benefiting beings on an enormous scale. In Tibet, Milarepa became embroiled in family troubles while still young, which led to his becoming a black magician and a mass murderer. All of this turmoil inspired him to seek a spiritual solution. After Milarepa met his teacher, Marpa, he engaged in rigorous practice, purified his negative karma, and became one of the greatest yogis in Buddhist history. Then there is Longchenpa, who experienced a great deal of hardship in his monastery and had to leave. While wandering, he met and received Dzogchen teachings from his root teacher, Rigdzin Kumaradza. Longchenpa practiced and perfected what he was taught, and he wrote many beautiful, deeply influential books on the theory and practice of Dzogchen. In his poetry, Longchenpa often expressed gratitude for the obstacles which led him to the path of Dharma and, in particular, to his root teacher, as these then led to his realization.

Guru Padmasambhava said that obstacles are the royal road to enlightenment. He also said that we should take all six sensory experiences with us on the path. But in the beginning stages of practice this is a difficult undertaking, because we are far too attached to our egos and desires, as well as to the people and events in our lives. For this reason we should do as His Holiness counsels, and sever or at least reduce our ties to the greatest extent possible.

His Holiness specifically mentions giving "less importance to food, clothing, and mere talk." Of course, we need food and clothing, as well as shelter, to remain healthy and strong. The problem is that we often want much more than we need. Shopping, cooking, searching for the best restaurant, redecorating our homes—if we are constantly engaged in these kinds of activities, how much time and energy will we have for practice? The solution is moderation.

"Mere talk" refers in large measure to using speech to promote ourselves and belittle others. This is a major part of ego's insatiable quest for recognition and reputation. We want to be seen by others as special, not ordinary. This creates enormous obstacles not only in our everyday lives, but in our spiritual lives as well. For example, we might have visions or special dreams. Experiences such as these can be true signs of progress, but if we broadcast them to others hoping that they will be impressed, we are moving entirely in the wrong direction.

People who cling to their spiritual experiences can come to believe that they are very powerful, or that they are divine beings with a special purpose. They can attract followers, and become the heads of spiritual communities. The cults in Jonestown and in other places were formed that way. In these instances, the leaders manipulated their followers and led them to tragic ends. Similar stories can be found throughout the history of world religions, not only in the West but in the East, and also within Buddhism.

For this reason, the story of Tharpa Nagpo, also known as Rudra, occupies a very important place in Vajrayana Buddhism. According to the histories, Tharpa Nagpo received higher tantric teachings, practiced them, and acquired considerable spiritual power. But he used this power for totally egotistical purposes, created enormous suffering for others, and in the end had to be subjugated. His story is told to remind us of what can happen when we mishandle the fruits of our practice. The ego is by nature ambitious and tricky. When fueled by spiritual energy, it can be downright dangerous. We need to be vigilant and constantly remind ourselves that the purpose of Dharma is to make us more humble, gentle, and kind.

His Holiness also counsels us give up the eight worldly concerns. The eight worldly concerns can be divided into two groups: the four we want, and the four we want to avoid.

The four we want are:

1) gain
2) pleasure or happiness
3) fame or high status
4) praise or sweet words

The four we want to avoid are:

1) loss
2) pain or suffering
3) obscurity or notoriety
4) blame or harsh words

The eight worldly concerns are also called the "eight worldly dharmas" and the "eight practices of samsara." The great master Longchenpa said that whoever is preoccupied by them is like a sick person in bed—no matter how often he or she changes position, it is impossible to find comfort.

As long as our minds are captivated by thoughts and emotions, it is difficult not to engage in the eight worldly concerns. We are trying to free our minds completely, but this takes time. What should we do until then? We should strive for less attachment. One way to accomplish this is to see all phenomena as dreams, illusion, or magic. Another way is way is to remember impermanence.

Impermanence is a major theme throughout Buddhism. The Buddha said that among all thoughts, the thought of impermanence is supreme. He compared it to an elephant's steps, which leave deeper and wider footprints on the earth than the steps of any other animal. Many important Buddhist texts—for example Patrul Rinpoche's *Words of My Perfect Teacher*—have extensive sections on impermanence. Why is it so emphasized? Because impermanence is the way of nature.

What we want is impermanent, what we get is impermanent, and we ourselves are impermanent. When death comes, everything we have and know, including our self-identities, must be abandoned. If we truly accept this, we will stop wanting so much, and so intently. We will better value what we have and what we are. Our empathy will grow, because we know that all beings are subject to impermanence and death, just as we are. Our self-importance will diminish, because we realize that death can come at any time, and we have no control over it. Overall, our lives will be more peaceful and productive.

In addition to contemplating impermanence and death, we should try to remember that even if we successfully navigate our way around the eight worldly concerns, if have not attained any spiritual stability, we will not secure happiness. We have all heard or read about extraordinarily wealthy, famous, and powerful people who are very unhappy. Some seek relief by going to psychiatrists, drinking heavily, or using drugs. Others fall into criminal activity, or take their own lives. Others grow sad or bitter when old age saps their ability to enjoy the fruits of their success.

His Holiness writes, "The eight worldly dharmas can be condensed into hope and fear, which means attachment and aversion." Hope and attachment refer to what we want. Fear and aversion refer to what we do not want. What we want and do not want are manifestations of our minds. Our minds are infinite and pure. Whenever possible, we should tune into this.

These have been the pinpoint instructions on how to deal with obstacles. If we put them into practice, we will be healthier, happier, and more productive. We will be able to make an ongoing contribution to the world. His Holiness is not imposing dogma or forcing rules down our throats. Rather, he is simply placing a mirror before life, so we can see it as it really is.

QUESTION: *Rinpoche, can you say something about laziness?*

ANSWER: *Laziness is resistance to spiritual practice, and the teachings mention three types. The first is known as "casual laziness," which manifests in thoughts such as "I don't feel like practicing now. I'll do it later, or tomorrow." This is a combination of lethargy, procrastination, and lack of enthusiasm. The second is called "habitual pattern laziness." This refers to the mental, verbal, and physical activities we find familiar, identify with, and most enjoy. Indulging these seems more compelling than practice. The third is "self-deprecating laziness," which includes all mistaken beliefs that we are somehow flawed, inferior, or incapable of spiritual growth. These three types of laziness manifest singly, in pairs, or all together.*

QUESTION: *My habitual patterns are very strong. As you say, they are so compelling and seem impossible to resist. What should I do?*

ANSWER: *Take a stand. Say to yourself, "Every time I have indulged in this behavior, it has been unsatisfying. Enough is enough—I will give in no longer!" Mean what you say and commit to it. You should also pray to the Buddha, Guru Padmasambhava, and the lineage masters, saying, "Please bless me to be free from all habitual patterns." Your own commitment, the earnestness of your prayers, and blessings of the realized beings will unite with your aim and help create the change.*

QUESTION: *People have so many responsibilities in modern times. Even when we eliminate frivolous or inessential activities, there is still so much to do. What is the best way to practice in these circumstances?*

ANSWER: *We should look at what we have to do during the course of a day and find a good time for practice. It may be before we leave for work in the morning, or in the evening after we return. It could even be at mid-day, during a lunch hour. No matter how busy we are, if we truly want to practice, we can find some time. Then, once we have found the time, we must use it the way we intended. It is also very important to learn how to integrate practice into our daily activities. This was the sole method by which some of the eighty-four mahasiddhas attained their high realization.*

The teachings say that even when we have the opportunity to do a solitary retreat, we should also make and keep a schedule, otherwise our practice might get too casual or loose. Traditionally, while on retreat, practitioners divide the day into four, five, or six sessions.

Although we have many responsibilities today, in many ways the responsibilities facing people of earlier times were even more daunting. For example, if we want to write, most of us have immediate and unlimited access to computers, as well as to pens, pencils, and paper. In old Tibet, all writing was done with brushes, ink, and paper, none of which was easy to come by. Obtaining ink was particularly difficult. In monasteries and hermitages, for example, ink had to be made from scratch. The first stage of the process was to place bowls above the butter lamps, in order to gather the dust raised by the flames. Many stages followed; each one was arduous and time consuming. Tibetans used to joke that some people entered the monastery or hermitage to become monks and yogis, and ended up ink-makers instead.

Buddha Shakyamuni

CHAPTER 8

ATTACHMENT AND BEYOND

A garden of beautiful flowers does not spring up by itself. Someone had to plant and nurture it. It is not necessary for us to have seen this. We can know what happened simply by observing what is before us now. The same principle applies when we look at our lives. We may not know who we were or what we did in past lifetimes, but we can infer that it was good. This is because good can only come from good.

Our present good, which is the result of past good, can be the cause of even greater good in the future. The future is hard to predict, but we can certainly aim it in a positive direction by our present actions. On the worldly level, one of the ways people direct their future is by saving and investing their money. On the spiritual level, we do so by developing and expanding our minds through practice and meditation.

As practitioners of the Mahayana, we do not practice and meditate for ourselves alone, but for all sentient beings. We want every one to enjoy boundless peace and happiness, and we direct and dedicate all of our efforts towards that end. This is known as bodhichitta. The Buddha compared an action infused with bodhichitta to a drop of water that merges with the ocean. The positive energy is not confined, limited, or in danger of disappearing; it becomes one with and inseparable from that which is infinite and eternal. It can be drawn upon not only by those who helped generate it, but by anyone who needs it, and there is no expiration date. Actions done with bodhichitta transcend concepts of spiritual and non-spiritual, large and small. The recitation of a single mantra, the giving of a handful of food to an animal, or even opening and closing a door—anything at all, done with a good heart and pure intention, is of real and lasting value for all beings.

At the same time, we should always beware of attachment. Attachment—to anyone and anything—is a real problem for our spiritual development. The first attachment that His Holiness mentions is the one to "our native land." This includes the country, region, and family into which we were born and raised, and also the beliefs, values, and behaviors familiar to us. In ancient times, it was very common for people to remain in one place their entire lives, and to have little or no exposure to other people and ideas. "Where the bush grows, it dies," was a popular saying in Tibet. In such circumstances it was easy to become attached to prescribed ways of life. Furthermore, people were expected to do so. If someone found this to be limiting and wanted to transcend it, he or she would face resistance, even hostility. "Leave your homeland," the teachings say. And many people, facing such a predicament, did just that.

But there is another option. In ancient times, successive generations of Sakya masters stayed with their families in a single location—the Ponpuri Hills, in southern Tibet, near Shigatse. The Sakya masters believed that this stability was conducive to the preservation and strengthening of their Dharma tradition.

There have been other family lineages in other parts of Tibet who did the same. So it is not the case that remaining home and maintaining close personal ties is automatically detrimental to spiritual growth.

In the eighth century, the great master Vimalamitra told King Trisong Deutsen and his sons that he would return to Tibet every century in order to revitalize the Dzogchen teachings. Since that time, many Vimalamitra emanations have appeared, including Longchenpa. In the latter part of the eighteenth century, Vimalamitra emanated again, in the form of the great master Khenpo Ngakchung. Khenpo Ngakchung was born in Kham, in eastern Tibet. His master was Nyoshul Lungtok, who was one of Patrul Rinpoche's foremost disciples. When Khenpo Ngakchung was around fourteen or fifteen, he said to his master, "I want to stay here and receive many teachings from you. But when you pass away, I want to leave, and wander about with no fixed destination." Nyoshul Lungtok replied, "There is no need to wait until I die—you can go wandering now. But remember the saying, 'Whoever leaves home loses all shame.'" Nyoshul Lungtok was reminding Khenpo Ngakchung that people often become undisciplined, reckless, and sometimes wanton in new environments. Khenpo Ngakchung deeply pondered his master's words, and decided to remain where he was.

"By giving up your homeland, half of the Dharma is accomplished." It is true—when staying in your current place prevents your practicing Dharma, you may have no other option but to leave. But as the above examples illustrate, circumstances can vary. Your current situation may be ideal for practice. If it is not, it might become so in the future. Can you be certain that in leaving one set of difficult circumstances, you will not be taking on another that is even worse? To leave your homeland, or to remain—which is better? It all depends on what works best for your spiritual development. But you may not even have to decide. Simply resolve again and again to be free from all ideas and emotions—then you leave your homeland without packing a single suitcase, or taking a single step.

Not only homeland, but also food and clothing can be powerful attachments. We have to eat, and it is certainly enjoyable, but we should not overdo it. Gluttony is detrimental to spiritual practice and so is excessive fasting. It is best to eat fresh, healthy foods in sensible portions. The teachings also say that if possible, we should eat once a day. This was instructed by Buddha Shakyamuni, and it is part of his legacy. Clothing is also necessary, but again we should exercise reason. Adorning ourselves in expensive silks and jewels or in attention-grabbing clothes does not help our spiritual development; neither does dressing in rags.

The point is to avoid the extremes of asceticism and indulgence. Balance and moderation are the best path. This is known in Buddhism as the *Middle Way*. When our conduct follows the *Middle Way* our wind energies and channels become peaceful and relaxed. This revitalizes us physically and leads to more serene, clear, and powerful states of mind.

We should also apply the *Middle Way* in our relationships, and avoid the extremes of perpetual solitude and endless socializing. Our family, friends, and all beings deserve our respect, attention, and assistance. At the same time, we should be strong, and make time for daily practice, and also—when time permits—for extended retreat. If people make unreasonable demands on our time and energy, or if they are resistant or even hostile to our spiritual aims, we should remember our bodhichitta commitment and remain calm and patient. We should pray to the lineage masters for guidance and assistance. These obstacles might transform of their own accord. If they prove intractable, we might have to remove ourselves from the situation—leave our homeland, as it were.

His Holiness says, "Whatever good or bad things people might say, don't take them as true; have no hope or fear, acceptance or rejection. Let them say whatever they will, as though they were talking about someone dead and buried." We want others to say positive things about us. We want to be admired, not disdained, and we certainly do not want to be ignored. We also want to defend ourselves when we are misunderstood and misrepresented. This is the way of the ego. But the way of the practitioner is to disengage from all this. For this reason, we should become like people "who are dead and buried."

The dead and buried neither see, nor hear, nor feel. They cannot react to our admiration, disdain, or indifference. They are perfectly, permanently disengaged. How do we, the living, attain such a state? First, we must want to attain it. Then, we must train in letting go of who and what we think we are. We must be relaxed, natural, and above all patient, because accomplishing this practice is not easy. But if we persevere, the time will come when our self-detachment is complete. At this time, what once were the worst insults are now the purest sounds, and blame is as good as praise.

Aryadeva

CHAPTER 9

THE QUALIFIED GURU AND STUDENT

His Holiness Dudjom Rinpoche stresses the importance of the qualified guru throughout his *Mountain Retreat* teaching. What is the nature of a qualified guru? A simple and profound description was given by the future Buddha Maitreya, in collaboration with his student, the great master Asanga, in their *Mahayanasutralankara*, or the *Ornament of the Mahayana Sutras*. In this teaching, Maitreya and Asanga say that the guru is gentle, peaceful, and content, has a strong and stable mind, possesses excellent knowledge of the scriptures, enthusiastically upholds the teachings, has direct realization of the true nature, and wants to and is capable of helping others. To put this even more succinctly, the guru is one who completely embodies the teachings of the Buddha.

The teachings of the Buddha can be divided into three categories, known as the *Three Baskets*: Vinaya, Sutra, and Abhidharma. The Vinaya pertains to behavior, or morality. The Sutras pertain to mind training, or concentration. The Abhidharma, which includes the Vajrayana, pertains to the true nature of reality, or wisdom. The order is significant. The Vinaya comes first because it deals with that which is most tangible and practical—behavior. The Vinaya teaches which actions to accept and which to reject in order to achieve a state of inner peace. Whoever achieves this has a beneficial effect on others, as the following story from the Vinaya histories beautifully shows.

In ancient times there was a man from Shravasti, named Nesu Tamdzin Tilap, who had seven daughters and a very talkative wife. He was also very poor, but even so, was able to marry off every one of his daughters. One day all seven daughters, along with their husbands, came to his house for a long-term visit. There was not much to eat, so all his daughters and especially his wife began complaining. They blamed and criticized him. Nesu Tamdzin Tilap thought, "This endless nagging—the fires of hell cannot be worse."

A short while later he left his house, as it was time to plow. Nesu Tamdzin Tilap had a small piece of land, but only one ox. Two oxen were necessary to plow the field, so he had to borrow another one from a friend who lived far away. He went to his friend, acquired the second ox, returned to his own land, and plowed for a very long time. By the time night came he was hungry, tired, and wanted to go back to the house. But he thought, "There is no food there, and no peace. What should I do?" He resolved to keep working the field every day until the crops came up—then there would be food for everyone, and an end to the complaining. With that thought, he went home. But the next morning he awoke to discover that the ox he borrowed had escaped. Now he was in big trouble. He dropped to the ground and just sat there, staring into space. He was utterly despondent.

In the distance he saw a monk quietly meditating under a tree. Immediately he began to feel a little better. "Such a beautiful and peaceful person—how fortunate he is. Perhaps I should speak to him." He walked over to the monk and said, "You look so peaceful—are you?" And the monk smiled and said, "Yes, I am." Nesu Tamdzin Tilap felt the rest of his despondency release, and he too felt peace.

The moral of this story is that when we are peaceful, we give peace to others. The gift of peace transforms lives and is the heart of all morality training. We acquire this ability by reducing and ultimately releasing all of our negative behaviors, and by adopting and doing that which is positive. This is the essence of the Vinaya.

While the Vinaya teachings pertain to disciplined behavior, the second of the three baskets—the Sutras—pertain to disciplined mind. As we all know, the undisciplined mind is wild and scattered and creates mischief and chaos. In order to remedy this, the Buddha gave extensive Shamatha teachings throughout the Sutras. Shamatha is concentration practice. It harnesses and catalyzes mind's great power. This great power manifests as love, compassion, and wisdom, and also peace. In this way, Shamatha reinforces, deepens, and expands the work of the Vinaya.

Abhidharma, the third basket, pertains to the true nature of reality, or wisdom. By studying and practicing the Abhidharma teachings, we become free from believing in the intrinsic existence of personal identity and all phenomena. This leads us to the realization that mind by nature is pure, infinite, and all encompassing, just like space. Mind is space, phenomena are space, and space is no other than indestructible, all-pervasive peace. Thus, the work that was begun in the Vinaya and developed in the Sutras is completed in the Abhidharma.

By fully assimilating the three baskets of teachings, the qualified guru embodies, transmits, and understands all the paths that lead to perfect peace and happiness. What then is the nature of a qualified student? The great master Aryadeva, among others, said that a qualified student is someone who is honest, sincere, and passionately committed to his or her spiritual development. These qualities, along with deep devotion to the guru and faith in his or her instructions, propel to us enlightenment.

The teachings say that once the connection between a qualified guru and a qualified student is forged, it is the student's responsibility to maintain and cultivate it. Gurus teach directly, indirectly, mysteriously, and in ways that cannot even be described. Students should therefore continually open and expand their hearts and minds, and be alert at all times—who knows when or in what form an important teaching will be transmitted? To facilitate this, the student should not see the guru as an ordinary person, or even as a bodhisattva, but as a living buddha.

His Holiness says that only a qualified guru can give advice. With regard to anything that is related to the path of spiritual awakening, that is exactly so. We go to doctors to treat our ailments, automobile mechanics to fix our cars, and accountants to prepare our taxes, because these people are experts at what they do. A qualified guru is also an expert, but his or her expertise goes far beyond the objects and concerns of this life. A qualified guru shows us the state of mind that is unborn and undying, beyond past, present, and future. When we connect to the guru deeply and meaningfully in the ways we have just discussed, we will achieve the very same state.

CHAPTER 10

COURAGE, COMMITMENT, AND RETREAT

His Holiness strongly advises us not to hand our nose-ropes over to others. This is of course a metaphor. As is widely known, Tibetan people use yaks—particularly the hornless variety—for riding and also for carrying loads. A ring is put in the nose of each yak, to which ropes are attached. Whoever is riding or leading the yaks uses these ropes to control them. In this way, yaks do not decide for themselves where they are going. Literally and figuratively, their destiny lies in another's hands. The metaphor could not be more clear. We must retain our independence and autonomy, otherwise we might find ourselves forever doing others' bidding, like beasts of burden in human forms.

His Holiness continues, "Outwardly good-natured, you should know how to get along harmoniously with everyone without 'burning their noses.' But in fact if anyone—superior or inferior—comes to hinder your sadhana practice, you should be unshakeable like an iron boulder pulled by a silk scarf. It won't do to be a weak character whose head bends in whichever direction the wind blows, like grass on a mountain pass."

As practitioners, we must be courageous—steadfast on the path and absolutely committed to attaining our goals. If we want to make our own lives meaningful and to contribute that which is of lasting value to the world we must not allow anyone to deter us, regardless of their station. We should hold our ground firmly, but also peacefully and with respect. This is part of the practice of bodhichitta, and it is good for us, as well as for the people with whom we are dealing. The teachings say that strength within and gentleness without is very powerful. There are many stories about practitioners who transformed the hearts of adversaries with simple, kind, and dignified responses, clearing the way so that their spiritual journey could continue.

It is also important that we treasure our practice. Then it is easy to be strong and steadfast. One way to accomplish this is by reflecting on the path that led us to the Dharma, as well as the wealth of opportunities we now possess. "For a long time I have been the slave of strange ideas and negative emotions, which has brought me, as well as those with whom I have been in contact, little satisfaction and a great deal of suffering. At this time I have met a guru. My every observation tells me the guru is not an ordinary person, but sublime. I am quite flawed; nonetheless the guru has accepted me with love and given me teachings and practices that will free my mind. If I do not take these gifts to heart and make them a living reality, I will revert to my old, bad habits, and likely die that way. If, on the other hand, I honor and make ample use of these gifts, I will become similar to the guru—peaceful, happy, and very capable of enhancing the lives of others."

Courage and commitment are essential at all times on the spiritual path. This is particularly true with regard to retreat. The teachings are quite adamant—no matter what obstacles arise, retreat commitments must never be broken or altered. Because obstacles that arise during short retreats are less intense and more manageable, it is highly recommended that beginners as well as more seasoned practitioners do many three-day, one-week, or one-month retreats before attempting longer ones. Slow, steady growth is best.

What is true for retreat is true for every kind of practice, at every stage of the path. For example, if you are a beginning Shamatha practitioner, you select an object and gaze at it one-pointedly. Your goal is to keep your mind quiet and concentrated for one minute. When you are able to do this, you increase the time to two, then three, and eventually to five minutes or longer. When Nowzong Jhamo, the wife of one of King Trisong Deutsen's sons, asked Guru Padmasambhava for meditation instruction just before he was to leave Tibet, he told her to practice meditation the way an old house leaks. In the early stages, the drips are small and intermittent. Then they get bigger and more frequent. The final stage is like a waterfall.

In Tibet, retreatants traditionally keep to a schedule of four, five, or six sessions per day. Each session lasts two to three hours, with breaks lasting an hour or two. Retreatants go to sleep around 9 p.m. and arise at 4 or 5 a.m. Early morning is filled with fresh, powerful spiritual energy—the Buddha attained enlightenment shortly before dawn. Thus, early morning is one of the ideal and most auspicious times for spiritual practice, not only during retreat, but all the time.

In the Vinaya it says, "The sun is rising, the crows are cawing, the farmers are plowing, and the robbers are crying. Don't sleep—practice!" "The sun is rising" of course means early morning; it also refers to the Dharma, and our good fortune to be connected to it. "The crows are cawing" means reciting prayers and mantras. "The farmers are plowing" means cultivating wisdom and compassion. "The robbers" are negative forces—the thoughts and emotions that distract us from the fully awakened state. If we want these robbers to stop stealing from us, we must apply the teachings, "Don't sleep—practice!" This entire passage, particularly the last line, is a reminder that if we want enlightenment, we have to work for it. It is not an instruction to deprive ourselves of sleep, or to neglect our bodies. We need sleep, food, and clothing. If we are ailing, we should seek and apply the remedy. We should always treat our bodies with respect and care, for they are the beautiful vessels by which we cross the ocean of samsara. Not only that, our bodies are the mandala of all the peaceful and wrathful deities, as the Vajrayana teachings proclaim.

While we are on retreat, we should not indulge in anything mundane. Rather, we should be totally absorbed in Dharma. His Holiness writes, "During retreat, the entryway should be sealed with mud; if not, you must not speak, not spy, and not come face to face with others.... A strict outer, inner, and secret retreat will quickly give rise to all the qualities." In Tibet, once the retreat house was prepared and the practitioner was safely inside, he or she had others seal the door with mud. This insured there would be no contact between the practitioner and the outside world for the duration of the retreat. Sealing the door was not necessary if the retreat was taking place in a cave, or in a cabin within a monastic enclave. In these instances, signs with instructions were placed nearby to notify everyone that a retreat was in progress, and the message would be respected. These and any other measures that secure the physical privacy of the retreatant are known as the "outer retreat."

The "inner retreat" means no communication. Today this means no television, no newspapers, no internet, no email, no cell phones, and no texting. All interaction with the outside world must be severed.

The "secret retreat" refers to the mind. We do not invite or indulge in thoughts about family, friends, business dealings, and so forth. We do not recollect the past or plan for the future in any way. Instead, we focus solely on Dharma—unconditional love and compassion for all beings, devotion to the buddhas and lineage masters, and so forth; then, when the time comes for meditation, we release all concepts and abide in the Dzogchen state. Like this, we awaken and glorify the beautiful qualities of our minds that have for so long been hiding under the veil of discursiveness.

His Holiness says that before we begin any formal practice, we should "expel the stale breath and correctly assume the essential elements of body posture." The stale breath refers to the sediments of attachment, anger, and ignorance that are lodged within the channels, winds, and essence elements of our subtle bodies. To expel it, we do the breath purification exercise three or nine times. This is supported and enhanced by good body posture, known as the *Seven Postures of Buddha Vairochana*, the details of which we will discuss below.

Having expelled the stale breath and assumed the right posture, we begin our formal practice, following the oral instructions of our teachers. Session by session, day by day, if we keep practicing with courage and commitment, signs of accomplishment will come. We must not yearn for or expect such signs, or be discouraged with ourselves if they seem slow in coming. We should be free of hope and fear regarding meditative accomplishment. All that is necessary is that we persevere. Success is sure to follow.

Jamgon Kongtrul the Great

CHAPTER 11

REVIVING THE PRACTICE AND THE IMPORTANCE OF PLACE

The recitation of the four renunciation thoughts in His Holiness's *Dudjom Tersar Ngondro* concludes with the prayer, "May my mind turn towards the Dharma." Variations of this prayer appear in many Vajrayana sadhanas, and also in the poems and songs of the great masters. Why is it so important to turn the mind towards the Dharma? Because the mind likes its habits very much and resists change. It needs persistent reminding to let go and to open up, to forsake self-importance and to embrace others. This is true not only for beginners, but for experienced practitioners as well. For the latter, it often happens that after a period of steady progress in meditation, negative or even disturbing thoughts and emotions erupt with great force. The temptation to give in to these thoughts and emotions is very strong at such times. Even great masters have experienced this. But the solution, as these same great masters tell us in their poems and songs, lies in remembering the importance of Dharma and turning the mind to it with more faith and dedication than ever before.

It also sometimes happens that people are enthusiastic about practicing the Dharma at first, but then their enthusiasm grows cold. They make little or no effort to remedy this and eventually quit. In so doing, they never give themselves the opportunity to reap the full rewards of spiritual practice—they are cheating themselves. The great master Jamgon Kongtrul, in his *Calling the Lama from Afar*, metaphorically described this as follows: "The seeds were planted, everything sprouted, the time for harvest had come—then a sudden deluge of rain ruined it all." We must not let this happen. If we lose interest in our practice, there are many ways to revive it. We can pray to the lineage masters and read their life stories. We can contemplate the four renunciation thoughts, engage in meritorious activity, and consult our teachers.

The spiritual journey is not linear; there are many twists and turns. It is important to be aware of this, so that when the unexpected arrives, you will not be intimidated or shaken. Furthermore, since your practice is yours and no one else's, it is ultimately your responsibility to keep it alive and flowing. This is true when you are integrating your practice into a busy modern life, as well as when you are on retreat.

Regarding retreat, one of the most important considerations is place. His Holiness Dudjom Rinpoche says, "There are many descriptions of particular qualifications and topography of places, but in general a place blessed by Guru Rinpoche and the great siddhas of the past, which is not presently in the hands of people of dissenting samaya, is suitable; or according to your preference, any utterly solitary place where favorable supports—food and other necessities—are easily available."

As His Holiness says, anywhere Guru Padmasambhava appeared is a sublime place for retreat. The same is true for the places graced by Longchenpa, Milarepa, and other great masters. In general, it is good to conduct a retreat wherever noble beings have cultivated unconditional love, compassion, and wisdom. These beautiful qualities reverberate in places long after the people who cultivated them are gone. Truly, this is what makes a spot sacred, or a land holy. At the same time, there are many places on this earth that have up to now not been visited by great masters, but which nonetheless are naturally rich with spiritual power.

There are also many sacred places in India associated with Buddha Shakyamuni. The four principal locations are where he was born, where he reached enlightenment, where he gave teachings, and where he entered mahaparanirvana. The Buddha himself advised devotees to visit and practice in these places. Over the centuries, many people have done just that, and the accumulated force of so much positive energy has made these places ideal for retreat.

After the Buddha attained enlightenment under the Bodhi Tree, he did not teach for seven weeks. Some time after the third week, using his miraculous power, he traveled throughout the entire 3000-fold universe and blessed it. According to the teachings, there was not a single spot, not even as small as a horse's hoof that he did not bless. Guru Padmasambhava also blessed the entire universe, particularly all the sacred spots.

The Buddha once visited Mount Kailash, which is in western Tibet, with 500 arhats. He said to the arhats, "You must recount the stories of your former lives." And each one of the arhats complied with the Buddha's request. This was the only place the Buddha visited in Tibet during his lifetime. However, it is said that he left his footprints behind the mountain at Riwoche Monastery in Tibet during the time he was blessing the 3000-fold universe.

The great masters say that although it is highly auspicious to conduct a retreat in one these sacred places, it is not mandatory. Any place which is safe and attractive, which has not been a site of violence and negativity, and which inspires openness of heart and mind is perfectly sufficient. Also, the place we choose should not be too remote, otherwise it might be too difficult to obtain food and other necessities. We do need to be attentive to our material needs while we are on retreat. At the same time, we should avoid extremes. Deprivation will not help us, nor will indulgence.

His Holiness says, "If you have the ability to control the swift evolution of outer and inner causal links in cemeteries and other frightening places, abodes of the cruel demons of your locality, your mediation will be greatly improved. If not, you will have even more obstacles." This instruction is meant for all Vajrayana practitioners—in particular, practitioners of Chod—who, having achieved some degree of meditative stability, can communicate with invisible beings.

The existence of invisible beings is dismissed by some as superstition, but this is perhaps a narrow-minded view. Aided by modern technology, scientists have proven the existence of life forms and world systems on both the micro and macro levels that were not only imperceptible, but also unimaginable centuries ago. The six senses, unaided, are limited—most of what is right in front of our faces escapes our notice. Knowing this, how can we categorically deny the existence of invisible beings simply because we cannot not see them?

According to the teachings, there are six realms of sentient beings, as well as nagas. Among the six realms we can see only humans and animals. Gods, asuras, hungry ghosts, and hell beings are for the most part invisible. As for nagas, they often appear as water snakes or other amphibious creatures, but they are not limited to those forms. Most of the time they cannot be seen.

The teachings say invisible beings will contact us if our hearts and minds are open and our practice is stable. But if we are skeptical and our practice is shaky, even if we do a retreat in cemeteries or in other places where invisible beings dwell, contact will not occur. They will ignore us as if we were stone or wood.

When invisible beings do contact us, it is usually in the form of a test. These tests are usually not easy or pleasant, but they do reveal the true depth of our devotion, bodhichitta, and nonattachment. We swiftly discover how far we have progressed on the spiritual path, or how far we have to go. Many great masters have reported being tested in this way.

It is therefore very good, when we have attained some degree of stability and confidence in our practice, to do retreat where invisible beings dwell, just as His Holiness says. Then, when the test comes, we must not react, but simply witness without hope or fear. If, on the other hand, we are inexperienced or somehow not ready, it is better to stay in a quiet, secure place.

The teachings say that no matter where we do our retreat, every time we reach a new stage of spiritual development, we will be tested. These tests always involve eruptions of one or more of the negative emotions: attachment, anger, arrogance, jealousy, and ignorance. If we believe in, speak, and act on these emotions, greater obstacles than ever will arise. If, on the other hand, we let negative emotions come and go without grasping, we will accomplish a deep and thorough purification, and our realization will deepen.

As we have said, a retreat can be conducted in a cemetery, or at one of the sacred spots in India, Nepal, or Tibet. It can be conducted in a quiet cabin in the woods, a monastery, or in your own home. The choice of place depends on your temperament, needs, and resources. Of course, on the absolute level there is only one place—the place in which you and all beings are dwelling right now. From this perspective, your body is the retreat house and life itself is the retreat.

Buddha Samantabhadra

CHAPTER 12

NGONDRO

Buddha Samantabhadra knows that the entire universe is the display of his own mind. He is eternally enlightened, and has no need of spiritual training. Although we share the same nature as Buddha Samantabhadra, we believe the universe exists outside and independent of us. We are distracted by phenomena, and for lifetime after lifetime we have not been able to find our way home. But now we have established a connection to the lineage. We have met a qualified guru and received instruction. We have both the capacity and time to put this instruction to good use. All the causes and conditions are in place—we have all that we need to become Buddha Samantabhadra.

In order to accomplish this re-awakening, we must purify our minds. As His Holiness instructs, there are two aspects to the purification process: ordinary and extraordinary. The ordinary aspect is contemplating the *Four Thoughts that Turn the Mind from Samsara*. These four thoughts are called "ordinary" because to understand them no great scholarship and no meditative insight is needed. Their meaning, for the most part, is self-evident. The four thoughts are: 1) life is precious; 2) everything is impermanent; 3) actions have consequences; and 4) samsaric existence is very difficult.

The first thought, life is precious, means that each life is unique and irreplaceable. Even accounting for reincarnation, the one-of-a-kind individual that you are right now has never existed before and will never exist again. Considering the infinite array of causes and conditions necessary to bring you into existence, your presence here is wondrous, nothing short of a miracle. And, as long as you are alive, possibilities abound—most importantly, spiritual possibilities. Truly, you have no limits. And what is true for you is true for every single sentient being.

Impermanence, the second thought, means that everything and everyone is constantly changing. Hours, days, and years pass swiftly. We were babies once, then children, then teenagers, and now we are adults. We have seen innumerable sights, heard innumerable sounds, and thought innumerable thoughts. We experienced the alteration of happiness and sorrow many times. People have come into our lives and people have gone. Some who have gone will never return. The day of our own departure is coming—on that day, everything and everyone we know will have to be relinquished.

Change that we can see is known as gross impermanence. Change we cannot see is called subtle impermanence. Regarding the latter, great realization beings and some scientists have long known that the sub-microscopic elements that make up the phenomena of the universe are in constant flux. Even though suns, planets, stars, and our own bodies appear relatively stable, they are not. Nothing remains perfectly still, not even for an instant. Solidity is an illusion. All is motion. At the same time, everything is intimately connected and in perfect harmony. Commenting on this, the great master Mipham Rinpoche said that if one tiny particle in the universe—be it as small, or smaller than an atom—were to suddenly stop moving, everything and everyone would stop too. The effect would be like a single car stalling on a highway during a busy travel day. There would be a chain reaction—the cars behind would have to slow down, and before long traffic would come to a halt.

The third purifying thought is that actions have consequences. This is also known as the law of cause and effect, or karma. The meaning of karma is understood by people all around the world. For example, in the West people say "what goes around comes around," and "you reap what you sow." The message is that whatever we do comes back to us. Our actions never simply dissolve into thin air but yield results, which we have to experience.

Karma does not play tricks. It is very direct. When we plant rice seeds, we get rice, and only rice. When a man and woman conceive, a human child results, and never one from another species. This is why the word 'inevitable' is frequently used in conjunction with karma.

Karma operates on all levels of experience. In social situations, when we approach others aggressively, they respond with wariness and suspicion. When we are gentle and kind, they are receptive and open. On a personal level, all that we are is the result of our past actions. Similarly, all that we think, say, and do right now will shape our futures. And there is also group karma, which binds individuals into families, religions, nations, and worlds. Personal karma and group karma can be extremely intricate and therefore difficult to comprehend, but both nevertheless remain rooted in the law of cause and effect.

Karma is not imposed on us from without. No outside entity, divine or otherwise, is responsible. Karma is self-generated. It is our responsibility. It begins with our minds, specifically with our thoughts and emotions. Positive thoughts and emotions lead to positive karma, and the opposite is also true. Therefore, if our lives are not going in directions that we like, we should heed the message of karma, look within, and make the necessary changes. We should release egocentric thoughts and negative emotions. We should cultivate openness and non-grasping, as well as love, compassion, and devotion. If we do this, we will become happier and more peaceful, and we will enhance the lives of others. If we persevere, the time will come when we totally liberate our minds; then we will transcend karma entirely.

The fourth purifying thought is that samsaric existence is very difficult. Samsaric existence refers to life as it is commonly understood and lived. As the teachings say, each of the four major chapters of life—being born, getting old, experiencing sickness, and dying—is very painful. The same can be said of being separated from loved ones, and of human emotions such as fear and loneliness. All of us want health, prosperity, success, and to live a long life. We want the same for family and friends, and we strive to make these desires manifest. But what we want and strive for and what we get are frequently not the same. This results in disappointment and frustration. In the cases when our attachment to a particular outcome is very strong, the result is often intense suffering.

Samsaric existence is generally unreliable. Sometimes we get the opposite of what we want. At other times we get what we want, but then it transforms, or we do. Sometimes we have to wait so long and endure so much to get what we want that we cannot enjoy it once it comes. At other times, it comes too soon, before we can handle it. The power of impermanence or change is at play at all times in samsara, and this makes the road from desire to its fulfillment very rocky.

The teachings say that even if we acquire the entire universe and enjoy it without interruption for decades, we will still have to give it up at the time of death. Nothing material accompanies us when we leave our bodies. Our homes, possessions, even the person we cherish most cannot come with us. The only thing we take with us at death is that which is immaterial and invisible—our minds. Therefore, while we are living we should reflect on the nature of samsara, understand that it offers no guarantees, and with that understanding moderate desire. Most importantly, we should look within. The great masters say that there is no greater joy than realizing the mind, and that this far surpasses even the greatest joys of samsara. They also say that unlike the joys of samsara, which are hard to obtain and impossible to keep, the joy of the realized mind, once attained, is everlasting.

If we deeply reflect on the meaning of these four thoughts, we will become better people. We will appreciate the beauty and potential of every single sentient being, including ourselves. We will treasure what we have and make the most of it. We will think, speak, and act in ways that bring benefit to ourselves and others, now and for the future. We will endure hardship, and use it to become wiser, stronger, and more compassionate. Ego-clinging will diminish, and the true mind, all-embracing and as vast as space, will dawn.

When should we contemplate the four thoughts? Many Nyingma masters have recommended that that we do so at the beginning of every practice session. They say that this will ground our practice right from the start and insure that it does not become scattered later on.

The Four Thoughts that Turn the Mind from Samsara are the ordinary method by which we purify our minds. The extraordinary method includes, as His Holiness says, "refuge, generation of bodhichitta, purification of obscurations, and the two accumulations." These, along with the practice of Guru Yoga, make up what is known as *Ngondro*.

The essence of refuge is trust and confidence in the Buddha, Dharma, Sangha, and in the Guru who is their embodiment. Refuge is the expression of our deep connection and commitment to Buddha Shakyamuni, Guru Padmasambhava, and the lineage masters, and to the paths they laid out which lead to spiritual awakening, as well as to all beings who take this journey. Bodhichitta is love and compassion for all beings. It is the heartfelt response to the fourth of the four thoughts just discussed, namely, that samsaric existence is very difficult. Bodhichitta has two aspects: aspirational and applied. Aspirational bodhichitta is the desire to be of the greatest possible service to others, to relieve their suffering and bring them happiness. Applied bodhichitta occurs when we put this desire into action through words and deeds. Bodhichitta is always united with the practice of wisdom, or nonduality, so that our love and compassion for all sentient beings becomes unconditional, that is, boundless, unwavering, and free from bias and attachment.

Sentient beings enter samsaric existence through four gateways, also known as the four kinds of birth: egg, womb, moisture, and miraculous. Moisture and miraculous births are spontaneous; they take place by themselves. Egg and womb births require parents.

Before taking birth, you were only consciousness, wrapped in a package of karma. Then your parents coupled and gave you a form. Your first home was your mother's womb, and your first food came directly from her body. When you emerged from the womb you could not speak; all you could do was cry. You had to rely on your parents completely and could not have survived otherwise. Your parents tirelessly cared for you, willingly sacrificing their own comforts and needs in order to provide for yours. At this time, what could you do for them? Nothing at all. Your parents' love for you was selfless. In that regard, they were your first spiritual teachers.

According to Buddhism, this is not the first time you have taken birth. It is simply the latest birth in an infinite series of incarnations. Your parents in this lifetime are therefore not the only ones you have known—every sentient being has been your parent at one time or another in the past. Therefore, your present existence is not only due to the kindness of your current mother and father, but to the kindness of the innumerable mothers and fathers you have had since beginningless time.

We should be grateful to all our kind parents who have raised us through the ages, and try to repay them to the best of our abilities. Even if we cannot say or do anything directly, we should always pray from our hearts for their well-being. For example, we can recite the *Four Boundless Contemplations:* "May all sentient beings have happiness and cause of happiness. May they be free from suffering and cause of suffering. May they never be separated from the supreme happiness which is without suffering. May they remain in boundless equanimity, free from both attachment to close ones and rejection of others." This prayer, although very familiar, is not common, but profound. It is a perfect expression of infinite, selfless love and compassion. Many great masters have chanted it throughout the centuries, and because of this it has become an integral part of the sound system of the universe. Truly, whenever we recite the *Four Boundless Contemplations*, we are lending our voices to an ongoing chorus. Our bodhichitta aspirations merge with those of the great masters who preceded us, and the results will be great. Mental and physical obscurations will be purified. Peace, love, and happiness will radiate throughout the universe. Hearts and minds will open, and realization will bloom. For this reason, we should recite this prayer, and others like it, for the sake of all our kind parents, and also for ourselves.

The teachings say that not only formal prayer, but even a single altruistic thought can change lives for the better. This is true not only for beings we want to help, but for ourselves. In a previous incarnation, Buddha Shakyamuni was born as a sentient being in the lowest of the hell realms. He was pulling a heavy iron chariot with another man. This other man, who was physically weak and hardly capable of such labor, was being whipped by the driver of the chariot. The Buddha felt great compassion for the man, and thought, "He is so weak—I wish I could pull this chariot by myself so he would not suffer so much." It is said that this single thought purified the Buddha's karma to the extent that he never again was born in the hell realms.

There are many stories that illustrate the enormous effect of compassionate thoughts and wishes. In Tibet, particularly during ancient times, there were very few bridges. If you wanted to cross a river, you had to do it on horseback. Poor people did not have horses; they had to cross by foot. Once a mother and daughter, who were very poor, were doing just that. The river was powerful, so they held each other's hands. But the currents were too strong, and they were swept away. The daughter thought, "May my mother survive, even if I do not." The mother thought, "May my daughter live, even if I die." Moments after these loving wishes were made, both the mother and daughter drowned. But owing to their great selfless compassion, they immediately took rebirth in Tushita Heaven. This story, just like the one above about the Buddha, shows the power of unconditional love and compassion. When our hearts and minds are focused on the well-being of others, good things will happen. For this reason, enlightened beings and great masters urge us to cultivate and expand bodhichitta continually.

The next practice is the "two accumulations," which is no other than the mandala offering. The two accumulations are merit and wisdom. We accumulate merit by cultivating the six paramitas: 1) generosity, 2) discipline, 3) patience, 4) joyful effort, 5) concentration, and 6) transcendent knowledge. We accumulate wisdom by becoming increasingly familiar with the sky-like nature of our minds and the natural freedom of all thoughts and sensory experiences. Merit and wisdom are actually two inseparable aspects of a single reality, but are divided in two for practical purposes, in order to suit our current dualistic mindset. Visualizing the objects of refuge and offering them the mandala encompasses all six paramitas; by doing so we accumulate merit. Then, when we dissolve the objects of refuge into ourselves and rest in the natural state of our minds without clinging to whatever arises, we accumulate wisdom.

Next comes the "purification of obscurations," or Vajrasattva practice. On the most profound level, we are already spiritually awake. However, due to the deeply ingrained habits of ignorance, anger, and attachment we cannot remember it. These three negative states are like dark clouds which totally block the sun and sky. The meditation on Vajrasattva clears away the dark clouds of our minds, so that we can once more be what we have always been—utterly spacious, bright and clear intelligent beings.

The next practice, Guru Yoga—"union with the spiritual teacher"—is proclaimed throughout the teachings to be of the utmost importance. His Holiness himself calls it "the vital essence of practice." Guru Yoga is based on devotion, which means appreciation for and confidence in the teacher and the lineage, and a sense of joy and gratitude that we have made such a profound connection. Devotion was first aroused when we took refuge. With Guru Yoga, it intensifies and expands. As this happens, all traces of doubt and hesitation disappear. We stop being spiritual gypsies—we have a home. This is necessary if we want to progress on our journey. By way of example, if we plant a seed, and keep moving it from one location to another, it will remain a seed, and eventually wither away. But if we plant that seed into good soil, leave it there and nurture it with water and light, it will sprout.

The scholar and siddha Ashvagosha composed a famous text known as the *Vajrayana Teaching on the Root Downfalls*, a translation of which is found in the second section of our *Stainless King* sadhana. In this text, Ashvagosha describes the fourteen principal samayas, or sacred vows, every tantric practitioner is obliged to uphold. Regarding the first and foremost of these samayas, Ashvagosha writes, "To achieve accomplishment and realization one must follow the teacher." Ashvagosha is saying that devotion to the teacher is the foundation of Vajrayana practice, the chief catalyst for progress on the path, and the ultimate cause of our future enlightenment. This same idea is expressed in teachings that pertain to the practice of the Three Roots. The Three Roots are lama, yidam, and khandro. Of these three, it is the lama (or teacher) that is the root of all blessings.

When devotion to the teacher is strong and stable, realization comes quickly, and it keeps deepening. Tepid or intermittent devotion might yield glimpses of realization, but they will not last. Also, slight devotion crumbles in the face of even minor obstacles, whereas great devotion can withstand anything. The devoted student sees hardships, however severe, as the teacher's blessings, and in so doing becomes even more devoted, and therefore even more accomplished. The ultimate result of this is complete realization of the true nature. At that time, the practice of Guru Yoga—union with the spiritual teacher—is realized, and the student and guru are one.

We begin the practice of Guru Yoga by visualizing Guru Padmasambhava in the sky in front of us, or above our heads. Guru Padmasambhava is the embodiment of all buddhas, bodhisattvas, and spiritual teachers throughout the universe. If we have one human teacher with whom we are particularly connected, we should imagine that he or she has taken the form of Guru Padmasambhava. If we have many teachers, we should imagine that all of them merge in a single state, in the form of Guru Padmasambhava.

Guru Padmasambhava is like a giant satellite dish, simultaneously receiving and transmitting infinite forms of spiritual communication. Time and space are no object to him. This means that if you want to receive instruction from a teacher in a faraway land or in another world-system, or if you would like to contact a teacher who passed away centuries ago or one such as Maitreya who is yet to come, you can do so through Guru Padmasmabhava. Tibetans say that it is impossible to taste the water of every river, but since every river flows into the ocean, if you go to the ocean you can taste them all in a single sip. The many rivers are all the teachers and teachings of the three times and ten directions. The ocean is Guru Padmasambhava.

Not only is Guru Padmasambhava the embodiment of all buddhas, bodhisattvas, spiritual teachers, and their teachings, he is also the embodiment of all enlightened qualities and abilities. His compassion, wisdom, and power are infinite. If you seek protection, he will protect you. If you want to be a better scholar, he will sharpen your intelligence. If you want to do a long retreat he will guide you to the place most conducive to the sadhana you are practicing, and provide for your material needs. Most importantly, Guru Padmasambhava will open up your heart and mind to the needs of others and grant you great ability to help them, and he will lead you to the pure land of great blissfulness beyond all concepts, the true nature of your own mind, which is no other than complete Dzogchen realization.

At this point His Holiness quotes the great master Lama

Shang Rinpoche, who said, "To nurture stillness, experiences, and deep concentration—these are common things. But very rare is the realization born from within through the Guru's blessings, which arises by the power of devotion." Lama Shang Rinpoche, also known as Shang Yudrakpa Tsondu Dakpa, was a student of Milarepa's heart-son, Gampopa. He lived during the twelfth century, and was the founder of the Shangpa Kagyu sub-school. His quote is very telling. We can learn and become adept at various meditation techniques, and in so doing achieve one-pointedness of mind, a sense of calm, and different degrees of spiritual insight. Over the centuries many people, even without teachers to guide them, have done precisely this. But when we lay open our hearts and minds to the teacher with absolute trust and utter surrender, the teacher will transfer his or her realization to us, and in that moment we will be enlightened. Blazing devotion is much less common than meditative skill, but infinitely more powerful. But even though it is uncommon, it is not beyond the reach and range of anyone.

His Holiness Dudjom Rinpoche, summarizing all he has taught in the first section of his *Mountain Retreat*, says, "Whether the meaning of the Great Perfection will be born in your mind depends on the preliminary practices." He then proceeds to quote Lord Drikung, also known as Kyobpa Jigten Sumgon, the great twelfth-century master and founder of the Drikung Kagyu sub-school. Lord Drikung said, "Other schools consider the main practice profound, but here it is the preliminary practices that we consider profound."

What do these quotations mean? From one perspective, they mean that Ngondro is the necessary prerequisite to, and foundation of, Dzogchen. Why? Right now our thoughts are busy and scattered, while our emotions are volatile. This renders us incapable of recognizing, much less abiding in, the nature of our minds. Even if we have gained a little meditative experience and have some familiarity with the natural state, we will find ourselves falling into the same conceptual and emotional traps again and again. Right now the pull of our past karma is very strong. A thorough and sustained mental purification is needed, which Ngondro provides.

From another perspective that is compatible with the first, Dzogchen is not higher than Ngondro, but an aspect of it. For example, every one of the Ngondro practices—this is true of Vajrayana practice in general—has two parts, ultimately inseparable, known as creation stage and completion stage. Creation stage practice enables us to identify and develop all of the mind's beautiful qualities—love, compassion, wisdom, devotion, generosity, and so forth. Completion stage practice enables us to tune into the absolute nature of the mind, which is infinite and inconceivable. From this perspective, practicing Dzogchen is no other than highlighting, or emphasizing the completion stage.

Many great masters continue to practice Ngondro long after they have achieved Dzogchen realization. Patrul Rinpoche completed the full Ngondro over twenty times. Vimalamitra attained the transcendental wisdom rainbow body, yet continued to practice the Dzogchen Ngondro throughout his life. His Holiness Dudjom Rinpoche himself told me that he completed three Ngondros. Following in the footsteps of these and other enlightened beings, you should do the Ngondro knowing that it is not just a beginning practice, but the complete practice. If you do so, when the time comes for you to focus more directly on Dzogchen itself, you will be like an accomplished artist putting the finishing touches on a masterpiece.

Nagarjuna

CHAPTER 13

TWO WAYS TO EMBODY THE TEACHINGS

"Second, the main practice consists in how, having cut through the misconceptions concerning view, meditation, and action, one accurately engages in the practice." With these words, His Holiness Dudjom Rinpoche introduces us to the second section of his *Mountain Retreat* teaching.

Before exploring His Holiness's teaching, we should reflect on the following. In modern times many Buddhist teachers are traveling all around the world to give teachings. Many texts are available, and many more are being translated. Through the Internet, a vast array of Dharma information can be instantly accessed for free. Establishing connections with teachers and teachings, studying and absorbing information—all this is important. But there is a saying in Tibet—"Even if you know the location of every fresh water spring in the world, if you do not go to one and drink, you will never quench your thirst." This means that if we want to achieve our spiritual goals, it is not enough to merely know the teachings. We must feel them—even be them. As the great master Khenchen Palden Sherab Rinpoche often said, there are two ways to accomplish this: the way of the scholar and the way of the yogi. Whichever way we take, it is best facilitated under the guidance of a qualified teacher.

If we are following the way of the scholar, we might begin by reading and contemplating the Buddha's Three Baskets teachings: *Vinaya*, *Sutra*, and *Abhidharma*. Then we might explore the writings of great Mahayana masters such as Nagarjuna, Asanga, and others that clarify and supplement all that is contained in the Three Baskets. Following this, we might examine the commentaries on all these teachings written by the great Tibetan masters. Traditionally, this would take place under the guidance of an academic institute or a monastic college.

When we follow the way of the scholar, we establish, step by step, a thorough intellectual comprehension of the teachings. But the way of the scholar does not stop there. The next step is to apply what is learned by study and contemplation directly to the world around us. The aim is direct realization of the true nature of phenomenal existence.

Let us apply the way of the scholar to the Madhyamaka, or *Middle Way* teaching. In Madhyamaka, it says that when we try to understand the true nature of any object of the phenomenal world, we tend to misconstrue it in one of the following ways, by assuming that:

1) It exists.
2) It does not exist.
3) It both exists and does not exist.
4) It neither exists nor does not exist.

These are known as the "four extreme views." They are extreme not only because they are partial, or one-sided, but ultimately because they are incorrect. According to the Madhyamaka teaching, no view—that is, no thought or system of thought, even the most rigorous and widely accepted—can adequately grasp and describe the true nature of any object. The true nature of any and all objects of the phenomenal world is beyond thought, or beyond the mind. And this is known as emptiness.

"Form is emptiness; emptiness is form." In his Madhyamaka teachings, such as this one from the *Heart Sutra*, the Buddha draws our attention to the emptiness of objects first. Why? Because our natural tendency is to look outside ourselves and to be captivated by the bodies or forms that we see. Since we are already looking outside, the Buddha urges us to continue to do so, only to look much more closely. When we examine an object closely, all our views about it dissolve, and in that moment we discover emptiness. The *Heart Sutra* continues, "In the same way feelings, perceptions, mental formations, and consciousness are also emptiness." Once we have looked at objects and ascertained their true nature we are no longer so captivated by them. Then looking within becomes much easier. Feelings, perceptions, mental formations, and consciousness are all aspects of the subject, which is also known as the self, or "I." When we look closely at the subject, what happens? All the views we hold regarding it dissolve and we discover that the subject, like its objects, is emptiness.

What about samsara, the state of confusion? What about the spiritual path that leads us out of samsara? What about nirvana, the goal? When we closely examine each of these we witness once more the dissolution of all of our views. All are emptiness. Indeed, the entire universe and all that it contains is emptiness. There is nothing that is not emptiness. In the words of the *Heart Sutra*, "Thus all dharmas are emptiness and have no characteristics." Emptiness means timeless, unchanging, and inconceivable. This is the true nature of all phenomena. No one created this truth, and it would be truth if no one proclaimed it. For this reason, the Buddha said, "Whether or not I have appeared on this earth, and whether or not I have given teachings, does not affect the true nature."

When we follow the way of the scholar according to Madhyamaka, we employ logic and reason in our analysis of objects, subjects, and their relations. The process is actually more complicated and time consuming than was indicated by the examples above. But the result is the same—the release of all views. Releasing our views is very important, and not only because they are one-sided and ultimately incorrect. The fact is that we do not hold our views lightly. We believe in and grasp them intensely. We believe that they are superior to the views of others. All this is animated and intensified by powerful, negative emotions. For many lifetimes we have promoted and defended our views. We have killed and died for them. This has been the cause of so much of the world's misery.

The teachings of the Buddha and the great masters are like spiritual bombs. They blow up our views, as well as the clinging and negative emotions which render them so toxic. But these bombs will not work unless we use them. The Buddha himself said that he can show us the way, but it is up to us to take it. We have to do the work ourselves. Following the way of the scholar, we study and contemplate the teachings, apply them to the phenomena of the world, and realize emptiness. And we also meditate. Meditation matures and ultimately completes the way of the scholar—it transforms knowledge into wisdom. Wisdom is the state of mind utterly free of views, clinging, and negative emotions. Once we have attained this state, our minds are as open as space and we see everyone with the eyes of compassion. This is the time when we truly benefit beings on a vast scale.

Throughout Buddhist history, many people have followed the way of the scholar and attained enlightenment. Some of these, in addition to studying and mastering the Buddha's teachings, also achieved expertise in mathematics, science, medicine, engineering, non-Buddhist philosophy, astrology, linguistics, poetics, and the fine arts. In great academic institutions such as Nalanda, these disciplines were taught as complements to Buddhist study and practice. Nagarjuna, Shantarakshita, and Naropa are among the Indian masters who were renowned for their spiritual realization, as well as for being experts on every one of these subjects. Tibetan masters of this caliber include Longchenpa, the First Khyentse, Jamgon Kongtrul, and Mipham Rinpoche.

The second approach to realizing the truth of the teachings is the way of the yogi. Here we do not go to an academic institute or monastic college, nor we do not engage in a systematic study of texts. Rather, we simply receive instruction from a qualified teacher and practice it with devotion and perseverance. By this alone, we can discover the true nature as it is, and spontaneously master all the branches of knowledge mentioned above. The way of the yogi was the way of Milarepa. It was also the way of Tsasum Lingpa, Jigme Lingpa, and many of the great tertons.

While yogis do not engage in any formal intellectual training before they begin to practice, they first must thoroughly comprehend the meditation instructions they receive from their teachers. While scholars begin with intense textual study and contemplation of the teachings, they must in the end practice meditation. Yogis first establish the meditation, and through that, realize the view. Scholars begin by establishing the view, then stabilize it through meditation. This means that although the yogi and scholar follow different ways, they arrive at the same destination. Each becomes a living embodiment of the teachings.

Mipham Rinpoche

CHAPTER 14

THE VIEW

The foundation of Dzogchen practice is establishing the view. This often begins with a verbal explanation, traditionally known as the "pointing out instructions." His Holiness Dudjom Rinpoche provides that here in the *Mountain Retreat* when he says, "First, as for the view that recognizes the true nature, our own mind itself is the nature of absolute reality. Divested of all conditional and artificial characteristics fabricated by the intellect, the true nature is established with certainty as awareness."

We usually use the word 'view' in reference to how much we can see of the external world. For example, we might say that a person who lives in the penthouse of a tall apartment building has an excellent view of the city, while one who lives in the basement of the same building has no view at all. We also speak of beautiful views, such as a range of mountains bathed in sunshine, or the nighttime sky lit up by stars. In Dzogchen, however, "view" does not refer to the quantity or quality of what we can see with our eyes. It refers to inner seeing—specifically, it refers to seeing your mind. To accomplish this, you must turn your attention away from externals. For this reason, as in a single voice, the great masters of Dzogchen proclaim, "Again and again, look within your own mind, and discover its true nature."

What happens when you look within your own mind? Thoughts and words vanish. You are completely awake, alert, and relaxed. There is nothing particularly to focus on. There is just total openness and freshness. Of course, these are words which describe this state. When the natural state is actually experienced, words are not needed. It is very important to remember this distinction. A decisive experience—not words—is what constitutes the true nature of your own mind, and this is the real Dzogchen view.

His Holiness says, "This awareness cannot be shown by example." The Dzogchen teachings often compare the true nature of the mind to the sky or to space. Sky and space are vast, open, and unchanging; so too is the mind. But mind is intelligent, and sky and space are merely gross phenomena. Ritual objects, such as a crystal or a mirror are also used as examples of the nature of the mind. These objects reflect everything external to them without being affected. Our minds do the same with regard to thoughts, emotions, and sensory experiences. But a crystal and a mirror, like sky and space, are inanimate—they are incapable of knowing. Examples like these are suggestive, but not entirely accurate. And examples are no substitute for the actual experience.

The great master Mipham Rinpoche, in his famous teaching known as *Dzogchen Manjushri*, says "As the moon is indicated by a pointed finger, in the beginning the true nature is indicated by mental analysis." The pointed finger includes study and contemplation, as well as all the descriptions, examples, and other skillful means our teachers use to give us a good idea of the true nature of our minds. These are all good, but not enough. This is why Mipham Rinpoche continues by saying,

"The original nature is beyond mental analysis. May we behold it, affirming its own nature." This means each individual must experience, conclusively and beyond doubt, the true nature of his or her own mind.

Right now many of us cannot recognize the Dzogchen view, much less maintain it, because our minds are wild and scattered. Thoughts and emotions continually distract us, and we habitually follow them. If we want to realize the Dzogchen view, we must harness the power of our wild minds, and Shamatha practice is the way to do it. There are many ways to do Shamatha meditation, but the essential practice always involves focusing the mind on a single object, such as the breath. In the beginning stages of practice we are easily distracted. But with repeated practice our ability to concentrate grows stronger, and we soon find ourselves becoming increasingly calm and comfortable. Eventually, our minds become peaceful, stable, and poised at all times. When this occurs, we have achieved the result of Shamatha meditation.

When you look directly at your mind and see it as it is, all that can be attained through Shamatha is spontaneously present. Stability and peace are right there, so there is no need to cultivate them by focusing on an object. In addition to this, your mind is wide-open, crystal clear, and brimming with compassion. This non-focus is the essence of Vipashyana. Thus, the moment you recognize the Dzogchen view you achieve the union of Shamatha and Vipashyana meditation.

Once you have recognized the view, the next step is to maintain it. Maintaining the view is the essence of Dzogchen meditation. At this time you are not trying to achieve anything more, for there is nothing left to achieve. However, you must watch out for distractions, which are none other than habitual thoughts and emotions. They will erupt and you will be very tempted to give in to them. If you do, you will lose the view.

The key point is to let thoughts and emotions come and go by themselves, without getting the least bit involved in their content. Let them pass through your mind the way the wind passes through the sky.

As your Dzogchen meditation gets stronger, distractions lose their power. You can maintain the view more easily, and for longer periods of time. This is a sign that your practice is progressing. When you can maintain the view at all times and in all circumstances, you will have attained enlightenment.

You have changed bodies and identities infinite times, gone through tremendous hardships in each of the six realms, but the open, brilliant nature of your mind has never changed. "It is neither corrupted in samsara, nor improved in nirvana," as His Holiness says here. The Buddha expressed the same idea in the *Avatamsaka Sutra*, saying that although worlds and beings come and go, the space in which all of this takes place remains the same. That space is your own mind.

Your own mind is the source, abiding place, and destination of all phenomena. We are talking about your simple, clear, ever-present intelligence. When you behold this state within yourself as it is, you know at last who you have always been. In the Dzogchen teachings this is called *self-awareness*, or *self-recognition*. It is also known as the realization of Buddha Samantabhadra.

Everything His Holiness Dudjom Rinpoche says in this section of the *Mountain Retreat* applies to the natural state of your mind, so it is important that you study and apply it with great care. For example, he says of your own awareness that it is "neither born, nor ceases to be; neither liberated, nor confused; neither existent, nor non-existent; neither delimited, nor falling to either side." You should look to your own mind and examine whether these assertions are true.

Ask yourself, "Has my mind been born?" When you do so you will be left silent. There is no answer. "Will it cease to be?" Again, there is no answer. If you keep looking in this way, you will come to realize that when it comes to the true nature of your mind, there are no answers, and no questions either. You cannot name, locate, measure, quantify, or qualify your mind in any way, nor is there any need to. Your mind is forever beyond the categories and assertions of the intellect. Thus, it is "free from complexities." When you look within and see your true mind, you achieve what the Dzogchen teachings call *kadag*, or the "all-pervasive, pure from the beginning state." This state is also known as "emptiness."

His Holiness says, "As the radiance of emptiness is unobstructed, the ocean of phenomena of samsara and nirvana appears spontaneously, like the sun and its rays." "The radiance of emptiness" means that your mind is not only pure, it is all-powerful and all-embracing. When you realize this, the universe is not separate from you. All the infinite phenomena and your own mind are in a single state—open, fluid, and sparking.

Emptiness and radiance have always been inseparable. The mind transcends the intellect and is inconceivable. Simultaneously, it manifests, knows, and accomplishes everything. Fully enlightened beings realize this completely, while ordinary beings like ourselves do not. We are taken in by sensory experiences, which we misinterpret as external phenomena, and by the thoughts and emotions our misinterpretation inspires.

In the language of Buddhism, fully enlightened beings are "originally perfect and temporarily perfect," while we are "originally perfect but temporarily obscured." Our original nature is the same as the buddhas,' but we do not yet recognize it—that is the only difference. The temporary nature of our non-recognition is like thick clouds obscuring the bright blue sky, or mud covering pure gold. Just as wind disperses clouds, and water cleans away mud, practices like Ngondro swiftly purify our non-recognition, so that the absolute perfection of our true nature shines forth in all its vastness and brilliance.

His Holiness says, "Thus awareness, in which appearances and emptiness are inseparably united, is the natural sovereign of the three kayas, and the nature of primordial reality." In this context, the term 'appearances' refers to the enlightened qualities of mind, such as unconditional compassion and nondual wisdom. Again, these qualities are one with emptiness, which also means that they are emptiness. In order to directly experience this, you should deliberately evoke one of these qualities—for example, unconditional compassion—and look at it closely. Ask yourself, "What is the nature of unconditional compassion?" The moment you ask this question, everything dissolves. All that is left is naked awareness itself.

The three kayas—dharmakaya, sambhogakaya, and nirmanakaya—are another way to describe the nature of your mind. They are not separate from one another; each kaya instantaneously embodies the other two. Dharmakaya refers to mind's openness, purity, and flexibility, and is a synonym for emptiness. Sambhogakaya refers to mind's arising energy, manifesting as unconditional love, compassion, and wisdom; it is a synonym for radiance, or buddha-nature. Nirmanakaya, which is the union of dharmakaya and sambhogakaya, means action—beneficial activity in response to the needs of others.

And what does Dzogchen mean? Dzogchen is the body of teaching and practice that comprises the ninth and highest yana of the Nyingma school of Tibetan Buddhism, as well as the state of mind this teaching and practice evokes. Dzogchen is actually short for *Dzogpa Chenpo*. *Dzogpa* means "perfection" or "completion," while *Chenpo* means "great" or "total." The message is that when you recognize this state of mind—when you unveil within yourself the Dzogchen view—you realize everything.

The universe is comprised of sights, sounds, smells, tastes, tactile sensations, and thoughts. All of these appear within your mind, and nowhere else. As your mind is perfect, so too is the universe. As the universe is perfect, so too is your mind. Inherent in this understanding is limitless compassion, and an extraordinary capacity to help others. Besides this, there is nothing else to realize. For this reason, His Holiness exclaims, "What a wonder it is thus to behold Samantabhadra's mind!"

That is the Dzogchen state of mind. With regard to Dzogchen as a body of teachings and practice, we have said that it is the ninth and highest yana. Why is it the highest? Because Dzogchen puts us in direct, experiential contact with the true nature of our minds far more quickly and directly than the other practices of the nine yanas. For example, the first three of the nine yanas are collectively known as the Sutrayana. Spiritual progress in the Sutrayana can be measured by what is known as the *Five Paths*:

1) Accumulation Path
2) Application Path
3) Seeing Path
4) Meditation Path
5) Path of No-more-learning

When we reach the Seeing Path we behold the true nature of our minds, beyond thoughts. However, it takes a long time to get to this point through Sutrayana practice alone. In Dzogchen, we reach this state instantaneously, the very moment we look into our minds. Of course, due to habitual patterns, this sudden realization does not last. We must stabilize it by meditating.

The Sutrayana is known as the Causal Yana. The six yanas

above it, collectively known as the Vajrayana, are the Result Yana. What is the difference between them? The Sutrayana is causal because it focuses primarily on virtuous behaviors of body, speech, and mind, which bring about an eventual realization of the true nature. The true nature is therefore seen as something that can only be attained in the future. The Vajrayana also focuses on virtuous behaviors, but it maintains that the result is ever-present, and therefore it is introduced from the outset. For practitioners of the Vajrayana, the result is not the goal, but the actual path. And of the six yanas that comprise the Vajrayana, it is Dzogchen that most swiftly and powerfully unveils the result.

All the schools of Buddhism agree that Buddha Shakyamuni gave 84,000 teachings. He gave 21,000 teachings to dispel attachment, 21,000 more to dispel anger, another 21,000 to dispel ignorance, and a final 21,000 to dispel all three together. These four groups of teachings correspond, respectively, to the Vinaya, Sutras, Abhidharma, and Vajrayana. Why did the Buddha give so many teachings on subduing negative emotions? Because it is precisely these negative emotions that prevent us from beholding the true nature of our minds. When they are dispelled, the true nature of the mind shines forth in its infinite glory. To recognize and abide in this state is the essence of the 6,400,000 Dzogchen Tantras, which are themselves the ultimate point of all of the Buddha's teachings. And this *Mountain Retreat* teaching of His Holiness Dudjom Rinpoche includes all of them.

Again, when we recognize the true nature of our minds we achieve everything. As His Holiness says, "There is not even an inch to go beyond this." But as we said earlier, knowing and even appreciating the words that describe this state are not enough. We must establish the meaning of these words firmly in our hearts and minds.

The first teacher of Dzogchen in the human world was

the great master Garab Dorje. He imparted his last testament, known as *Tsik Sum Nedek*, or "Three Statements which Strike the Essence," to his foremost disciple Manjushrimitra, just before entering mahaparinirvana. Many great masters have said that everything we need to know about Dzogchen theory and practice is contained in this teaching. The three statements are:

1) Decisively establish the view.
2) Decide on this, and nothing else.
3) Gain confidence that all phenomena are self-liberated within this state.

If we do not actualize the first of these three points—the view—we will never be able to actualize the other two.

By studying and contemplating the Madhyamaka teachings we can come to a thorough intellectual understanding of the view. This is important, but we must understand that the real view is beyond the intellect. For example, we can read all about what a certain food tastes like, but this will never be a substitute for actually tasting it. Once we taste it, we go beyond words. To know the view is to taste it, and that means to directly experience it. This is always possible. All that is necessary is to turn away from our usual projects and concerns, and look within.

Look within your mind. What do you see? There is nothing in particular to see, and nothing in particular to say. All the masters agree that when you arrive at the "nothing to see, nothing to say" stage—that is the view.

In one sense, the view is rather plain. It is simple, open awareness—no more, no less. For this reason, Guru Padmasambhava and other great masters have called it "ordinary mind." Ordinary mind does not appeal to us when we are seeking something otherworldly. This is why many people, having recognized the nature of their minds, are disappointed. They think, "This cannot be the Dzogchen view," and they set out in search of something they imagine must be greater. We can avoid this mistake by realizing from the outset that there is nothing rare, elaborate, or spectacular about the nature of the mind. It is simple, but at the same time, it is extremely powerful.

Once you have decisively established the view, you must maintain it. As we said, maintaining the view is the essence of Dzogchen meditation, and it corresponds exactly to the second point of Garab Dorje's legacy teaching. The task now is to not be distracted by the six sensory experiences. Do not block them from arising, and do not try to crush them when they do. Mind in its natural state is open and receptive—keep it that way. The six sensory experiences come and go, ceaselessly and spontaneously within your mind—let them. The important point is not to resist or cling to whatever arises, and above all, to relax.

When you go to a massage therapist for treatment, all you have to do is lie on the table. From that point, the therapist directs everything. The best thing you can do is not to interfere, to relinquish all control. Dzogchen meditation works in precisely the same way.

Of course, if we emphasize relaxation too much, our can minds can become dull and sloppy. For this reason, the Dzogchen teachings say that although relaxation is necessary, we should keep it fresh with clarity. This means that even as we relax, we should be alert and awake.

Up to now we have been referring to Dzogchen meditation in the form of silent sitting. But just as the Dzogchen view is utterly open and all-inclusive, so too is the meditation. This means we can and should employ any and all of the techniques of all nine yanas as supports—none of these are outside of Dzogchen. Cultivating bodhichitta and devotion always revitalizes our minds, as do the Vajrayana practices of chanting and visualization.

Within Dzogchen's own meditation tradition, a variety of techniques are taught and practiced in addition to silent sitting. For example, chanting syllables such as "AH" or "HUNG" is greatly emphasized, and not only for clarity's sake. Mind is infinite space. It is also energy, movement, and sound. When you abide in open awareness and chant, you are simultaneously tuning into all of these qualities of your mind. This is an excellent way to deepen and expand your understanding of nonduality. At the same time, you are fine-tuning the channels, winds, and essence elements of your subtle body.

QUESTION: *Could you elaborate on the relationship between thoughts and Dzogchen meditation, in particular, thoughts of compassion?*

ANSWER: *When we are practicing Dzogchen meditation itself, we do not invite any thoughts, or prevent them from arising. If and when they do arise, we neither engage them, nor push them away. We simply leave our minds open and free, and maintain awareness without analysis or judgment. Do not distinguish good thoughts from bad, accepting the one and rejecting the other. Let all thoughts, including thoughts of compassion, come and go as they please, and without any interference.*

If we are experiencing dullness or dryness in our meditation, it can be remedied by arousing devotion and compassion. Otherwise, when we are practicing Dzogchen, we should avoid indulging in thoughts of any kind—again, without rigidity or tension. Of course, in the beginning stages of Dzogchen practice, we are still relying on the thought of letting-go. This is needed because there is still the possibility of clinging to thoughts. But with determined practice, we do not have to remember to let go any longer. At that time letting-go is automatic, and whatever arises is the path of play.

Of course, before starting any session of Dzogchen meditation, we should think of all sentient beings, form a firm resolve to help them, and pray that they be free from suffering, enjoy temporal happiness, and ultimately attain enlightenment. Then, once our session is complete, we should evoke compassion once more, and dedicate the merit with the same good intention.

QUESTION: *In addition to praying for all beings, can we also pray for specific individuals? Will they feel the effects of our prayers?*

ANSWER: *It is excellent to pray for those with whom we are connected, such as relatives and friends, as well as for any individuals we have heard about who need help. And of course we should continually pray for all beings.*

Prayer is a spiritual superhighway that connects hearts and minds. It knows no barriers. Powerful messages that heal and inspire can be sent in an instant across the universe, as they're needed. All prayer is beneficial; one-pointed prayer is better; and prayer made while abiding in the state of naked awareness, suffused with unconditional love and compassion, is best.

External circumstances can determine whether or not our prayers are immediately effective. For example, if the people we are praying for are experiencing the consequences of heavy karma, it will take more time for positive results to manifest tangibly. We should not be discouraged, therefore, if at first our prayers do not seem to be having the desired effect. All this means is that the transformation must begin on the invisible plane. But if we are persevering, those we are praying for will eventually and directly experience positive changes. Wind and water re-shape mountains over time. Prayer is even more powerful than these.

QUESTION: *I can understand feeling compassion for people we know and love, and for beings who are helpless. But it is a difficult thing to imagine being compassionate to people who deliberately do harm. Unconditional compassion like that seems unfathomable.*

ANSWER: *Unconditional compassion is within your reach because it is your nature. You need only transform the thoughts and emotions which obstruct it. One of the most accessible and most powerful methods for accomplishing this is dedicating the merit, which means to share the positive energy you generate with all beings. As you practice the dedication of merit, you will gradually experience an unfolding of compassion within yourself. You will develop a deep and everlasting bond with all beings. You will directly and indirectly help them. You will give without expecting anything in return. Your identity will expand beyond the limiting confines of I, me, and mine and become truly universal. When this happens, unconditional compassion will not only be fathomable to you—it will be who you are.*

Longchenpa

CHAPTER 15

MANIFESTATIONS OF MIND

At the start of every formal practice session, re-kindle your connection to the lineage. Then consider the suffering that beings undergo in samsara, reactivate your commitment to help them, and sincerely pray for their welfare. Devotion and bodhichitta are not just how to start your meditation, or merely a beginner's practice; they are the foundation and heart-essence of the spiritual path.

Once you have given rise to devotion and bodhichitta, re-establish the Dzogchen view—open, clear, and relaxed. Experience this vividly. As His Holiness says, meditation means to maintain the view continuously. Therefore, for your meditation to work, it is of the utmost importance that you recognize the true nature of your mind, beyond doubt or hesitation..

When we unite the practice of devotion and bodhichitta with Dzogchen meditation, we become gentle and kind, humble and natural. Great masters of the Dzogchen view possess all these beautiful qualities in abundance. Of course, as we read in their life stories, they also have inconceivable spiritual power. They see the flexible nature of the laws of cause and effect, and are attended by buddhas, bodhisattvas, dakinis, and dharmapalas, as well as by invisible beings of all classes. There is nothing they do not know or cannot do, yet they do nothing to distinguish themselves from others. The great masters are almost always silent about their powers, and keep them hidden. If they do speak of or display them, it is only to help and inspire others, and never for egotistical purposes.

We should follow the example of these great masters. In particular, we should not boast about our spiritual accomplishments. Boasting does not help others, but rather provokes their annoyance and resentment. It certainly does not help us—the teachings are quite clear that we weaken and possibly ruin what we have attained when we boast about it. Boasting about accomplishments that we do not have is particularly bad.

Whether we boast overtly or under the cloak of humility, whether we do so directly or manipulate others into doing it for us, boasting is nothing but the ego. We want others to admire us; we want to increase our reputation. Whenever these urges arise, we should never indulge them, but always let them go. Rather than trying to promote our ego, we should keep realizing the view.

With that understanding, let us examine the view once more. Your own mind and the infinite universe share the same nature—infinite, open, and free from all concepts. There is no boundary or difference between what is commonly referred to as the subjective and objective spheres. This is why the great masters repeatedly teach that all the phenomena of samsara and nirvana are equal.

The view is all encompassing, all-inclusive, and does not distinguish between inside and outside. However, if you want to experience it, it is necessary to look within. For this reason, many Dzogchen masters instruct their students, "Go away, search for your mind, and when you have found it, come back to me with a report."

Your mind is the source from which everything arises, abides, and dissolves. The universe and all that is contained within it—space and time, worlds and beings, all phenomena and every transformation—are the display of your mind. In a word, mind contains everything. This teaching appears repeatedly throughout the sutras and tantras, as well as in the commentaries written by Longchenpa and other great masters. In the *Tenth Bhumi Sutra*, Buddha Shakyamuni said, "Oh, Noble Sons, the three realms are nothing but mind." The term "three realms" has a variety of meanings. For one, it refers to three immense world systems: the realms of desire, form, and formlessness. The human realm, the world we know and inhabit, is a part of the desire realm—but only a small part. Virtually all the other realms are imperceptible to us. The three realms can also be understood as body, speech, and mind, or the tangible, subtle, and intangible dimensions of human experience. And there are other meanings besides these. The Buddha is saying that whether conceived as immense world systems, as modes of human experience, or in any other way, the three realms are not outside, but within.

Not even the Buddha exists outside. The *Guhyagarbha Tantra* says that if you search throughout the ten directions and three times for the Buddha, thinking that he is an externally-existing being, you will never find him; he is nowhere else but here and now within your mind. Longchenpa offered this example, which also appears in several tantras. A man owns an elephant that is peacefully living in the man's backyard. But the man, believing his elephant is lost, leaves his home and wanders the earth in search of it. His actions are futile. He will not find what he seeks until he returns to his own home.

The great master Nagarjuna said that no matter how often

charcoal is washed, it will never become white; that no matter how hard a common stone is polished, it will never turn to gold. Similarly, he says, if our minds were not already enlightened by nature, all efforts we might make to discover this would be futile. But this is not the case—we have buddha-nature. Therefore, if we take the teachings to heart and practice them with joyful effort and devotion, we will traverse the five paths, ascend the ten bhumis, and reveal the treasure that we not only possess, but that we actually are.

One sun does not shine on the rich and another on the poor. There is only a single sun and it shines equally on all beings. In the same way, buddhas do not have one type of mind, and sentient beings another. The nature of the mind is the same whether you are the Buddha, an experienced yogi on retreat in a cave, a novice meditator, or an insect.

The nature of the mind is known by many names and can be expressed in many ways—for example, as the "union of wisdom and compassion." Wisdom refers to openness or space, which means freedom from thoughts and negative emotions, as well as the absence of hope and fear. Compassion refers to abiding love and affection for all beings, along with the spontaneous ability to help them. The great masters say that as your ability to abide in the Dzogchen view increases, your compassion increases with it. Once your Dzogchen view is absolutely stable, your compassion will be boundless. For this reason, the teachings say whoever actualizes the view spontaneously actualizes the union of wisdom and compassion.

Wisdom is also known as emptiness, while compassion is also known as clarity. Just as wisdom and compassion are united, so too are emptiness and clarity—they are two aspects of enlightened mind. With regard to emptiness, as I have said before, an intellectual understanding is not enough; you must make it a matter of personal experience. The unfailing way to experience emptiness is to look within your mind. You can do this directly by simply looking, or by employing a question, such as "Where is my mind?" or "Who am I?" The moment you look within, or ask yourself one of these questions, all ideas and emotions dissolve. What remains is inexpressible. If we try to express it we can call it openness, space, or purity. We can call it emptiness. We can call it dharmakaya, which means "truth body," or "reality body."

You look within, and at that moment experience emptiness. A moment later, your mind stirs, and a thought suddenly arises. Then another thought arises, and on and on it goes. You do not have to intentionally do any of this—it happens naturally. This is because your mind is brimming with power, and this power spontaneously expresses itself in the form of thoughts. Your mind is like a child who never gets tired, who plays continuously. This unceasing play of your mind is inseparable from emptiness and is known as "clarity."

The teachings speak of two kinds of clarity: internal and external. Internal clarity refers to what I just spoke of, that is, the mind's great playful energy. External clarity refers to all phenomena, everything we see, hear, smell, taste, and touch. Phenomena seem to exist outside, independently of ourselves. But in fact internal clarity gives rise to external clarity. This means our minds manifest the universe, and not the other way around.

Just as emptiness is known as dharmakaya, clarity is known as sambhogakaya. Sambhogakaya refers to richness, or fullness. Your own mind is the source of the unceasing creativity of the universe manifesting in the dance of forms. Your mind embodies everything—what can be more full or rich than that? Sambhogakaya is often translated into English as "enjoyment body," and is synonymous with the term "great blissfulness." This bliss is your actual experience when you abide in the view at all times and places. It is ceaseless joy that is independent of circumstances. Effortlessly, automatically you radiate this joy to others.

The clarity or sambhogakaya state manifests as the Five Dhyani Buddhas: Akshobhya-Vajrasattva, Ratnasambhava, Amitabha, Amoghasiddhi, and Vairochana. Again, these buddhas do not exist externally, but are aspects of your mind. Vairochana is the vividness of self-awareness—you totally know what you are. Ratnasambhava is richness and abundance—all the beautiful qualities of all the buddhas are naturally inherent within your mind, and you can access them at will. Akshobhya-Vajrasattva is the indestructible nature of this state. Amitabha is uncontrived intelligence, the "limitless light" that radiates ceaselessly, without limits. Amoghasiddhi is action—doing whatever is necessary effortlessly, perfectly, and always for everyone's benefit.

The clarity or sambhogakaya state also manifests as the five wisdoms: mirror-like wisdom, equanimity wisdom, discriminating wisdom, all-accomplishing wisdom, and dharmadhatu wisdom. Regarding the first of these—mirror-like wisdom—a mirror reflects whatever appears before it. In the moment of reflection, mirror and image are united. Your mind functions like that. Sights, sounds, smells, tastes, tactile sensations, and thoughts are what make up the universe. When any of these appear, they do so within your mind, without any boundary or partition. This is nonduality, or the merging of subject and object—clear, intelligent, and perfect.

The wisdom of equanimity refers to the complete absence of bias and judgment. You are not forcing anything. You are not trying to restrict or control anything. Everyone and everything are welcome within your mind. There is ample space for all to come, stay, and go, and there is never any crowding or congestion.

The discriminating wisdom is your unlimited capacity to

see and comprehend the details of any phenomenon that arises within your mind. For example, if a person appears to you, you will instantly notice all of his or her physical characteristics. At the same time, you will know with perfect clarity every nuance of his or her psychological state.

The all-accomplishing wisdom means the moment you see that something needs doing, you do it, spontaneously and without error.

The wisdom of dharmadhatu refers to the infinite space and freedom of your mind, which gives rise to the five buddhas and five wisdoms. For this reason, the dharmadhatu wisdom is no other than the view itself.

Emptiness and clarity, or the dharmakaya and sambhogakaya of your mind, emanate ceaseless forms, which are known as nirmanakaya. Nirmanakaya, which literally means "emanation body," has a variety of meanings. In this case, it means thoughts. At this time, you do not categorize or rank thoughts or choose among them. Labels such as high and low, good and bad, and even spiritual and mundane are not applicable when you are abiding in the true nature. Nirmanakaya emanations possess all of the qualities of sambhogakaya and dharmakaya. They are magical displays of your mind's great energy, perfect in their coming, perfect in their abiding, and perfect in their going. You experience all of this directly, and are free from hope and fear, accepting and rejecting.

The five buddhas, five wisdoms, and three kayas are spontaneously present within your mind. Practitioners of the Sutrayana will realize this in three, seven, or thirty-two countless aeons. Diligent practitioners of the Vajrayana will realize it within their lifetimes. The Vajrayana is powerful and swift acting—this is why it is so highly praised. In particular, devoted practitioners of Dzogchen, the highest Vajrayana teaching, can attain the transcendental wisdom rainbow body while still alive. The great master Chetsun Senge Wangchuk, to cite one example, accomplished this in only seven years.

What makes the Vajrayana so much more effective than the Sutrayana? The great master Karma Chagme explains that the difference lies in the fact that Vajrayana practice emphasizes the visualization of deities, while Sutrayana does not even speak of it. The deities symbolize the transcendental wisdom rainbow body, suffused with great blissfulness. Thus, the moment you visualize the Buddha, Guru Padmasambhava, Tara, or any other enlightened being, you are immediately tuning into the sambhogakaya nature of your mind. This means you are taking your own innate enlightenment as the actual path, and not deferring it for the future. This practice is so powerful. Why is it absent in the Sutrayana, and taught only in the Vajrayana? The teachings say that the buddhas do not deliberately withhold information, but rather instruct beings according to their readiness and capability. In this regard, the Vajrayana in general, and Dzogchen in particular, should be understood as the teaching for those who are spiritually very developed.

CHAPTER 16

THE VIEW REVISITED AND HOW TO KEEP IT

Although the true nature of the mind embodies all three kayas, at this time we will focus solely on its dharmakaya aspect. This is in keeping with the first statement of Garab Dorje's legacy teaching, as well as with the great commentary on that teaching written by Patrul Rinpoche entitled, *Khepa Shri Gyalpo*, or *The Wise and Glorious King*. These two teachings, as well as the teachings of all the great Dzogchen masters, state that once fresh, naked dharmakaya awareness is perfectly understood, the sambhogakaya and nirmanakaya are understood also. In other words, at the very moment we realize dharmakaya we realize the other two kayas. Otherwise, if dharmakaya remains unknown to us, or if it is only hazily known, we will continue to misinterpret and mishandle sambhogakaya and nirmanakaya. We will be startled by mind's great energy and cling to and chase the thoughts and emotions which are its natural display. For these reasons, if we want our Dzogchen practice to be successful, it is necessary to recognize and abide in the open, luminous quality of mind.

Dharmakaya is always present. You do not have to go somewhere special or do anything spectacular to reveal it. Wherever you are, your mind is with you—why not look at it? As we have said, you can do so directly, or you can ask yourself a question such as "Where is my mind?" The moment you do this all of your thoughts vanish. Everything is open and pure. And just like that, the dharmakaya is revealed. The simple, direct process whereby you instantaneously behold your dharmakaya mind is known in the Dzogchen teachings as *Trekcho*, which can be translated into English as "cutting thoroughly."

Recognizing dharmakaya is the Dzogchen view. Once the view is recognized, it needs to be maintained. How do you do this? First of all, continue to cultivate devotion and perform meritorious activities. Also, practice non-distraction and non-grasping. Let your mind rest in the open, vast dharmakaya state, and try not to stray from it. When sights, sounds, smells, tastes, tactile sensations, and above all thoughts and emotions arise, do nothing—let them come, be, and go.

In the beginning, some conceptual support in the form of oral and written instructions is necessary for us to do Dzogchen practice. Words are given because words are what we're used to. If, as beginners, we fail to keep these words in mind, we will have no choice but to give in to habitual patterns. However, if we do keep these words in mind and practice accordingly, we will become increasingly familiar with and capable of abiding in the dharmakaya state, and there will be less and less need to refer to the instructions in their conceptual form. With further practice, we will totally merge with the view and meditation. At that time we will abide in the dharmakaya state naturally and spontaneously, without the slightest need to refer to anything, conceptual or otherwise.

The dharmakaya state is vast and luminous, like a

clear autumn sky. The teachings say that three atmospheric conditions—clouds, dust, and mist—can arrive singly, in pairs, or all together to totally obscure the sky-like mind. The teachings were compiled a long time ago. If they were being written today pollution would probably be added to that list. Clouds, dust, mist, and pollution are of course metaphors for the thoughts and emotions we believe in and act on. When we get involved with these thoughts and emotions, we forget the dharmakaya state.

Our task as Dzogchen practitioners is to abide in the view. We do not have to do anything about thoughts and emotions except to let them come, be, and go. But this is easier said than done. Thoughts and emotions are clever like foxes, and resilient like weeds. They can change their colors like chameleons and their sounds like mockingbirds. And they are as convincing as great actors. If we are not alert, if we believe in, cling to, and use thoughts and emotions as a basis for our speech and action, any progress that we have made will be compromised. If we persist in this, it is possible that everything we have accomplished spiritually can fall apart.

Be strong when thoughts and emotions arise. Stay mindful, alert, and conscientious. Recall and apply the instructions that you have received. This will anchor you. The view is open and free—keep the view. Do not identify with your thoughts and emotions, no matter how powerful and true they seem. And be patient. Whatever arises will pass.

Strive to maintain the view at all times, whether you are sitting, standing, walking, or lying down. Whenever you do a formal meditation session, assume the *Seven Postures of Buddha Vairochana*. This is the classic meditation position taught by the Buddha, Guru Padmasambhava, and all the great masters. It provides an exceptional physical support for the view, and also stimulates the health of the body in general. *The Seven Postures* are as follows. First, sit down on a cushion and arrange your legs either in the double vajra (full-lotus), single vajra (half-lotus or "bodhisattva posture"), or simply crossed legged. Second, place your hands in the equanimity mudra. To do this, put the outer edge of your left hand on your lower abdomen, about two inches below the navel center, with the palm facing up. Place the back of your right hand in the left palm, and allow the tips of your thumbs to touch. Some masters prefer to keep a small space between the two thumbs. Both ways are correct. Third, keep your back straight. Fourth, let your head incline forward slightly, so that the entire spinal cord is perfectly aligned—like a column of golden coins, as the teachings say. Fifth, keep your shoulders relaxed and your elbows off your ribs. Sixth, bring the tip of your tongue to the roof of your mouth, and gently keep it there. But if this is uncomfortable you do not have to do it. Seventh, relax your eyes in a half-open position and gaze downward towards the tip of your nose. When you are practicing Dzogchen, keep your eyes in the relaxed and half-open position, but look straight ahead instead of down. In either case, it is important to keep your eyes still. And with regard to the breathing, keep it natural.

The great master Kamalashila was the foremost disciple of Shantarakshita, who, along with Guru Padmasambhava and King Trisong Deutsen, founded Tibetan Buddhism in the eighth century. Kamalashila came to Tibet at the King's invitation, shortly after Shantarakshita's mahaparanirvana. King Trisong Deutsen asked Kamalashila to write a book on Mahayana theory and practice; Kamalashila complied by writing three. In his books, Kamalashila gave many teachings on the benefits of the *Seven Postures*.

What are the benefits of this position? One important benefit is that it balances the wind energy that courses through our channels in five principal ways. These five are known as:

1) Descending Wind
2) Digestion Wind, or the Fire-like Wind
3) All-Pervading Wind
4) Life-Sustaining Wind
5) Ascending Wind

By crossing our legs in any of the three positions, we are balancing the Descending Wind, which enables us to properly eliminate feces and urine. By placing our hands in the equanimity mudra, we are balancing the Digestion or Fire-like Wind, which keeps our stomachs, intestines, and our entire metabolic system in good working order. By keeping our backs straight we are balancing the All-Pervading Wind, which keeps our muscles supple and strong. By relaxing our shoulders and keeping our elbows off our ribs, we are balancing the Life-Sustaining Wind, which facilitates healthy respiration. When we incline our heads slightly forward so that our spinal cords are perfectly aligned, we are balancing the Ascending Wind, which stimulates our speech and mental centers. When we keep our eyes relaxed, half-open, and still, our concentration becomes sharp. When we breathe naturally, our minds slow down, and we feel peaceful.

Just as good posture is important, so too is prayer. When we pray to the buddhas, bodhisattvas, and realized masters, we are tapping into the wellsprings of a living lineage. This is the lineage of unconditional love and compassion, indestructible nondual wisdom, and miraculous power, and it flows unceasingly like the great rivers of the world flow into the ocean. Prayer is the expression of deep respect and appreciation for the lineage. It is also the expression of the humility and grace necessary to receive everything that it has to offer. And what we receive we gladly share with others, in the spirit of bodhichitta.

The spiritual journey is not a path of sorrow, but of joy. The entire universe is a divine mandala, and all living beings are buddhas. Enlightenment is everywhere, in everyone. The more we practice the teachings, the more we see this. The more we see this, the happier we become. This happiness, we discover, is not dependent on external forces at all, but is intrinsic to our being. The utmost and final happiness, also known as great blissfulness, is indestructible.

Happiness in all its manifestations, including the final one, arises from the sambhogakaya and dharmakaya nature of mind. This means that happiness is simultaneously both pleasurable and devoid of substantial existence. To test this, deliberately invoke happiness within yourself, then look directly at it. What happens? Happiness dissolves, and there is nothing to hold. All thoughts and emotions, whether we consider them pleasant or unpleasant, are like that. They are transient mental events, and nothing in themselves. As I mentioned earlier, thoughts and their relationship to dharmakaya mind is like the wind moving through the sky. The wind can change speeds and directions furiously and unpredictably. Still, the sky remains unmoved. Likewise, the absence of wind, or utter stillness, does not change the sky. To apply this metaphor to meditation, disengage from the habits of labeling, judging, and analyzing your thoughts and emotions. Also, give up the belief that having no thoughts and emotions is better than having them. It bears repeating—recognize your dharmakaya mind, and let thoughts and emotions come, be, and go, without resisting and without clinging. Rest, wide-awake, in simply that.

Great masters say that in order to progress, we need to incorporate three things into our practice: stability, gentleness, and clarity. Stability refers to maintaining the dharmakaya state. This is not easy, particularly when we are beginners, because thoughts and emotions are loud and insistent. The great master Patrul Rinpoche has compared them to roaring waves. We no longer want to be swept away by those waves. This has happened far too often in the past. The solution is mindfulness. Remember the instructions and apply them. Be open and aware, and when thoughts and emotions arise, do not chase them. Should you find yourself pursuing your thoughts and emotions, stop at once, and return to the dharmakaya state. If you keep practicing like this, your ability to remain in the natural state will increase. Eventually you will find yourself abiding in it at all times, without any effort.

The second thing we need is gentleness. We should not place excessive demands on ourselves or try too hard. Truly, when it comes to Dzogchen practice, anxiety or force of any kind is unnecessary and unproductive. The mind is open and energetic. It generates, supports, and dissolves thoughts and emotions—this is its nature. As we said earlier, it is not necessary to do anything or go anywhere special to realize this. All that is necessary is to tune into what is already happening. If we are simple, peaceful, and relaxed—if we are gentle—we will realize that the goal has already been attained.

Clarity, the third thing that we need, refers to mental alertness, or brightness. Stability and gentleness by themselves can lead to dullness, drowsiness, and lethargy. If these states are allowed to fester, our capacity to operate effectively in the relative world will be compromised, and we will make no further progress in meditation. Therefore, whenever our energy is sinking, we should re-invigorate it at once by straightening our posture and applying one of the skillful techniques of the Vajrayana. Praying to the lineage masters and arousing bodhichitta are particularly effective.

Tsasum Lingpa

CHAPTER 17

MEDITATION

His Holiness Dudjom Rinpoche says, "Having thus cut from within all doubt and misconception about the view, maintaining the view continually is called 'meditation.'" Once you have a good feel for the Dzogchen view the next step is to sustain it. Let your mind rest in the natural state. Do not investigate, analyze, or label anything. "Now I am meditating, now I am holding the view"—even seemingly harmless thoughts such as these should be released. Invite nothing, hold nothing, and don't chase the objects of the six senses.

Although you are not chasing the sense objects, it is important to keep the six senses open and alert. Do not guard against experience; at the same time do not deliberately provoke it. If nothing arises, fine; if something arises, that is equally fine. Suddenly something arises—a sight, a sound, a thought. What do you do now? You simply continue as before. Remain open and alert; other than that, do nothing. What happens if you do this? The sight, sound, or thought fades away. In the teachings, this is known as "self-liberation," which means that whatever arises, dissolves by itself, automatically. This coming and going, this self-liberation, is the natural flow of all the phenomena of the universe. Through the Dzogchen practice of remaining wide awake while not interfering with whatever arises, you come to see it very clearly.

As His Holiness says, "Whatever manifestations of the phenomenal world may arise, remain in a state of natural freshness without grasping them, like a small child looking inside a temple." When small children enter a temple, they see all the statues, mural paintings, and ritual objects just as we do, but they do not name, analyze, or judge them—they simply look. And when they leave the temple they do not dwell on what they saw. We should be like these small children. When phenomena arise we should not subject them to any kind of intellectual scrutiny, but simply see them without grasping.

Of course, great masters who are free from discrimination, and the ego-clinging and pride that accompany it, can employ their intellects whenever and however they like. They can name, analyze, and judge without losing the flavor of dharmakaya awareness. Regarding this, Omniscient Longchenpa said that strong practitioners don't need to impose any structures or discipline on their minds. Mind is empty when it is in the no-thought state, and empty when it is thinking. Why prefer one to the other? But until we reach this level, we need to follow some structure and discipline on our minds, chiefly letting go of thoughts.

In other Buddhist teachings, the process of training the mind to abide in the natural state is called "taming the wild elephant." There are many ways to do this. For instance, the *Guhyagarbha Tantra* teaches that when we practice visualization, mantra recitation, and completion stage meditation with good concentration, devotion, and perseverance we will certainly subdue all duality and realize the dharmakaya. Then, once our dharmakaya realization is stable, sambhogakaya and nirmanakaya spontaneously arise in all their glory. Realizing that the mind is the natural embodiment of the three kayas is the enlightenment of the primordial Buddha Samantabhadra. At that time the meditation and post-meditation states merge and become one, no-thought and thinking are a single taste, there is no difference between buddhas and sentient beings—everything and everyone is whole, complete, and perfect.

As we read the *Mountain Retreat* text, we see that after spending some time describing meditation, His Holiness suddenly switches gears, and once more teaches us how to realize the view. He does this because at the beginning stages of practice we cannot maintain the view for very long. We need to know how to retrieve it when we lose it, and there are many ways to do so. His Holiness says: "When past thoughts have ceased, and future thoughts have not arisen, in the interval is there not a perception of nowness, a virgin, pristine, clear, awake, and bare freshness which has never changed by even a hair? Ho!" This is a classic and powerful Dzogchen pointing out instruction which has been given, in one form or another, by many great masters over the centuries. It provides an easy and direct path for introducing the nature of the mind. To paraphrase His Holiness, everything that has happened is gone—do not review it. Everything that might happen is mere speculation—do not invite it. The moment you release your preoccupation with the past and future you find yourself in the present moment, or the single-instant state, with your awareness stripped of concepts. This is the view.

What is the duration of the single-instant state? The teachings explain it as follows. If you stack sixty-four lotus or rose petals tightly in a vertical column, a single-instant is the time it takes you to pierce through all of them at once with a needle. Look at your mind this very instant. Be the view. Now strive to maintain it at all times. That is meditation.

Another technique is to think that your mind is sent out into space, then have your awareness look back to where it came from. What do you see? Nothing that you can say. That is the dharmakaya state.

QUESTION: *How do the great masters who meditate in secluded areas deal with wild animals?*

ANSWER: *Some of the great masters in my area of Tibet used to say that animals are more frightened of humans than humans are of animals. They also said that whenever we practice in areas where wild animals roam, it is good to chant strongly and use the bell and damaru, particularly at night—this scares the animals away.*

I will tell a story about Khenpo Karpo. He was an excellent Nyingma and Kagyu master, and one of his main practices was chanting the Seven Chapter Prayer *of Guru Padmasambhava. He taught Shedra at Rumtek Monastery in Sikkim during the time when His Holiness the Sixteenth Karmapa was still alive. Khen Rinpoche and he were good friends, and I knew him also.*

Khenpo Karpo did many retreats at Tso Pema, or Lotus Lake, which is located in Himal Pradesh, India. In ancient times, people tried to burn Guru Padmasambhava and Princess Mandarava at this site, but they did not die. They transformed the fire into a lake, and sat together, totally radiant, in the center of a lotus. From that moment, Tso Pema has been a renowned pilgrimage spot. During the 1970's, my father went there quite often for retreat. He stayed at the one simple hermitage that then existed. Since then the area has been developed considerably—several temples and monasteries have been built, and a giant statue of Guru Padmasambhava has been erected.

Khenpo Karpo did his retreats at Tso Pema in a cave-like cell made of boulders and hand-built walls. It was well-known that wild tigers roamed the area, but he was certain that this enclosure was strong enough to keep him safe. One night, while he was meditating, he heard a tiger's roar. Khenpo felt that the tiger was very close, and became frightened. He did not have a damaru or bell, so he picked up his few cooking utensils and started banging them on the walls. This did not scare the tiger at all. In fact, the tiger roared even more powerfully and started making loud snorting and grunting noises. Khenpo Karpo could not actually see the tiger, but sensed that it was right above the open entrance to his cell. By now he was very afraid. He thought, "What can I do?" Suddenly he remembered that he had matches. He started lighting them and throwing them up into the air, one after another, all the while yelling, "Ki! Ki! Ki! Ki! Ki!"—the battle cry of the warriors from eastern Tibet. And it worked—the tiger disappeared.

QUESTION: *I am unclear about the relationship between individual effort and the realization of the three kayas.*

ANSWER: *At this very moment and for all time your own awareness is the embodiment of the inseparable three kayas. As I have said, dharmakaya is great openness, sambhogakaya is creative energy, and nirmanakaya is whatever arises. The three kayas of your own awareness are naturally, spontaneously, and continuously present and active. Individual effort on your part will neither hinder nor help this process. This does not mean that other kinds of effort are unnecessary. For example, effort is needed to visualize deities, chant mantras, and do prostrations—it is impossible to make progress on the spiritual path otherwise. It is the path of effort that frees your mind sufficiently so that you can abide in non-effort. But right now we are talking about the natural, unchanging state of your own mind and its nondual relationship to phenomena. Observe yourself closely. When your eyes, ears, and mind are open and alert, forms and colors, sounds and thoughts appear without any provocation—coming and going, just like that. If you are wholly without grasping, then seeing, hearing, and thinking, as well as the other three sensory experiences, are perfect and complete just as they are, and effort is quite beside the point. At that moment the three kayas are unveiled—you are the Primordial Buddha.*

QUESTION: *Do all minds ultimately merge and become one, or will there always be many minds? And can you explain once more how everything is mind?*

ANSWER: *There is not and will never be a single mind that is shared by everyone—there will always be limitless individual minds. Everyone, whether enlightened or not, has his or her own mind. Each individual mind can and does reflect everything and everybody. At the same time, sentient beings may interpret the reflections differently. For these reasons, the teachings say that everyone is the sovereign ruler of his or her universe.*

Your world is comprised of sights, sounds, smells, tastes, tactile sensations, and mental events. All these are your experiences and occur within your mind. How will you respond to them? It is entirely up to you. Of course, until you are completely enlightened, karma plays a part. The teachings speak of three major karmas, created many lifetimes ago, to which all living beings are bound. These three are: sentient being karma, collective or group karma, and individual karma. Sentient being karma refers, in this case, to your being a human, and not some other species. Human bodies and minds are constituted to perceive and interact with phenomena in very specific ways, that, for example, birds and fish are not. Collective or group karma means that you have been born into a certain family, within a certain culture and time, and have been socialized accordingly. Individual karma includes the particularities—your unique patterns of thought—that make you the one-of-a-kind person that you are. The three karmas seem quite powerful. But again, look closely. Where do they exist? Nowhere else but in your mind.

When you are dreaming, you experience the world quite vividly, just as you do when you are in the waking state. When you awaken, you realize that you were dreaming, and that all those experiences were entirely internal—the play of your mind. You review the past and anticipate the future—where does this take place if not within the mind? And what about the present moment? It too is mind. Everything is mind. But it is not enough to agree with this statement. Explore these issues thoroughly. Go beyond agreement. Come to know for yourself.

Garab Dorje

CHAPTER 18

MEDITATION CONTINUED

We have learned techniques that enable us to experience the true nature of our minds, the open and blissful state free from thoughts. But as His Holiness says, "One doesn't remain forever in that state; doesn't a thought suddenly arise?" No sooner do we achieve absolute stillness of mind, when suddenly, without warning, the mind moves, and a thought appears. It is like the calm surface of mountain lake's rippling. How and why this happens is quite mysterious. At the same time, there is nothing to worry about, as it is entirely natural. What should we do at this time? We should be like surfers, and ride the wave of thought by keeping our minds on the single-instant state and our feet securely on the surfboard of awareness.

When experienced surfers go out on the ocean to ride the waves, they do not concern themselves with yesterday or tomorrow. They root themselves in the here-and-now, so that they can ride each wave as it comes, with poise and concentration—otherwise they will fall, and possibly drown. Similarly, as Dzogchen meditators, we should not allow ourselves to be distracted by past and future thoughts. We should remain wide-awake and relaxed in the present, and when a thought arises keep our footing by not being fixated and by not interfering. We let the thought come and go. And we do this one thought at a time.

As we have said, mind is space, and thoughts are the wind that moves naturally, spontaneously, and inseparably through space. There is no way to catch the wind. From the dualistic perspective, mind is a vault, and thoughts are the messages it contains. Some thoughts are believed, some are denied, and still others are ignored, or saved for a later date. We think about our thoughts, and create identities based on them. We speak and act on behalf of our thoughts, and thus involve other beings. Conversation and interaction spark new thoughts, which inspire more speech and action, which in turn develops even more thoughts. On and on the cycle goes. There seems to be no other way to live. This is what His Holiness calls the "chain of delusion."

The chain of delusion—also known as samsara—is an addiction to the seeming reality of thought. The Dzogchen view is to be free from this entirely. As beginners, most of us can maintain the view for a short time only, since our propensity for believing in and following thoughts is quite strong. This is because we have been addicted to our thoughts for many lifetimes. But no addiction, however great, can withstand the power of a mind that is determined to break it. Therefore, let us abide in the Dzogchen view as long as we can, and make a firm decision not to chase thoughts. We should remind ourselves, again and again, to let thoughts come and go. If we forget and find ourselves chasing thoughts, let's stop at once and bring our minds back to the view. This takes considerable effort in the beginning, less effort as our practice grows, and ultimately, one day, it is entirely effortless. To summarize, rest naturally in the open, radiant space of mind, and keep releasing. As His

Holiness says, "This itself is the main practice uniting the view and meditation of Trekcho."

At this point His Holiness quotes the great Dzogchen master Garab Dorje: "When awareness arises abruptly from the natural state of the primordially pure expanse, this instant recollection is like finding a gem in the depths of the ocean. This is the dharmakaya which has not been contrived or made by anyone." We have been bound by the chain of delusion for so long, but the true nature of our minds, even though unrecognized, remains spacious, whole, and ever perfect. Now, owing to the kindness, inspiration, and practical instruction of His Holiness Dudjom Rinpoche and other realized beings, we have the means to experience it. The moment we apply a Dzogchen instruction—for example, when we ask "Where is my mind?"—lifetimes worth of obscurations dissolve on the spot, and the open, radiant, thought-free mind blazes forth in all its glory, just like that. It is shocking how fast this happens. This mind is peaceful, blissful, and bright; beyond beginnings and endings. The more deeply we experience it, the more valuable we know it to be. This is dharmakaya, the ultimate nature, enlightenment itself.

His Holiness continues, "Just as when stone meets bone, you should experience this with great energy day and night without distraction. Not allowing emptiness to remain in the domain of theory, bring everything back to awareness itself." To reiterate—now that we have discovered the nature of our minds, we must maintain it at all times. We should not drop this gem, and let it fall back into the ocean. In Tibet, after great practitioners were introduced to the nature of their minds, they would meditate in solitary places like hermitages or caves. They stayed there for weeks, months, and even years in order to stabilize their realization. Many practiced so diligently that they wore holes in their meditation cushions—their rear ends would actually touch the rocky floors. This is the meaning of the phrase, "When stone meets bone." For this reason, my father often said, "It is better to wear out one meditation cushion than to wear out a hundred pairs of shoes."

Gampopa was the great master Milarepa's foremost disciple, and over the span of many years he received all of his teachings. One day, on a big boulder near Mount Kailash in western Tibet, master and disciple met for the last time. Gampopa was returning to his home in central Tibet. Milarepa gave him his final instructions. They made their farewells, and finally it was time for Gampopa to leave. With every step, Gampopa felt a deep, almost unbearable yearning. For his part, Milarepa did not move. He sat on the same boulder, watching his spiritual son. Suddenly Gampopa stopped walking and turned around. At that moment, Milarepa stood up and started waving his arms, signaling Gampopa to return. Gampopa thought, "The master is calling me, I must go to him." As soon as Gampopa returned, Milarepa said, "I forgot to give you my last teaching," As Gampopa wondered what it might be, Milarepa turned around, pulled up his robe and pointed to his bottom. Gampopa saw that it was very bony, and that the skin was rough and hard, like leather. Milarepa said, "Son, now you can go."

The ultimate meaning of Milarepa's last teaching to Gampopa is that if we want to achieve our spiritual goals, we need to practice continually, with courage and commitment. We may not wear out our bottoms or our cushions, but we will wear out our addiction to thinking, and that is enough. Therefore, with devotion and bodhichitta as our foundation, let us look within, re-connect to the view, and rest wide-awake in the face of whatever happens. With open minds and hearts, we should let the six sensory experiences move as they will, without interfering and without being distracted.

It is important to remember that this is spiritual practice, and not intellectual exercise. Once we understand the meaning of the words that describe how to meditate on the Dzogchen view, we should apply them without hesitation. We should merge at once with the true nature, and remain there, relaxed and carefree. As His Holiness says, "Experience this great energy, day and night, without distraction. Not allowing emptiness to remain in the domain of theory, bring everything back to awareness itself." If we practice in this way, stone will surely meet bone, in the deepest, most meaningful way.

Milarepa

CHAPTER 19

ACTION

The word 'action' means movement or activity of any kind; more specifically, it means behavior or conduct. In the context of this *Mountain Retreat* teaching, action refers to the thoughts, words, and deeds that enable us to maintain the Dzogchen view and meditation at all times.

The supreme support for maintaining the Dzogchen view and meditation is devotion. For this reason, at the very beginning of the "Action" section, His Holiness Dudjom Rinpoche emphasizes once more the practice of Guru Yoga. His words are very important: "Now, about how to improve meditation by putting it into action to accurately engage in the practice, as was said before, the most important thing is fervent devotion, to pray with ardor from the heart, without ceasing for even a moment to regard the Guru as the real Buddha. This is the one remedy that cures all diseases, and is superior to all other ways of dispelling obstacles and making progress. With it, levels and paths will be traversed with great momentum."

Because the true nature of the mind is so utterly simple, it would seem that maintaining it should be simple too. But this is not the case. As the teachings say, once we have recognized and are working to stabilize our dharmakaya realization, challenges will definitely arise on the external, internal, and secret levels. By practicing Guru Yoga, we will meet and overcome these challenges, as well as deepen and expand our dharmakaya realization until it becomes unshakeable.

Devotion to the teacher is the supreme catalyst for those who seek complete spiritual awakening. This has been the experience not only of yogis who received little or no academic training, but also of well-trained scholars like Longchenpa and Naropa. Longchenpa was already a master of all nine yanas of the Buddhist path, as well as of the ten arts and sciences, when he met his root teacher, the great Dzogchen master Kumaradza. Longchenpa studied with Kumaradza and practiced his teachings for a number of years. One day, Longchenpa said to his teacher, "As an expression of my devotion, I will go into retreat to actualize all that you have shown me." Longchenpa went to the Chimpu caves at Samye Mountain and remained there for approximately three years. He was very poor at this time. All he had to eat was several pounds of flour and twenty-one *ngulchu* pills. A single old sack served as his meditation cushion, blanket, and coat. The conditions were very difficult, particularly during the winter, but Longchenpa's devotion never wavered; he took Kumaradza's teachings to heart and perfected his Dzogchen realization. He became the greatest writer on Dzogchen in Tibetan Buddhist history, and is renowned as the "Second Garab Dorje," and the "Garab Dorje of Tibet." All of this happened because of his devotion.

Naropa was a great scholar and debater at Nalanda Monastic University in India during the latter part of the tenth century. If this was the limit of his accomplishment we might not even know his name today. But Naropa was and still remains one of the most compelling and inspiring figures in Buddhist history. How did this happen? Long after he became a successful scholar and debater, Naropa had a dream that compelled him to seek his master, Tilopa. Naropa had to give up his homeland as well as a very comfortable lifestyle in order to do this. Many years passed and many obstacles had to be overcome before Naropa actually met Tilopa. And this was just the beginning. The histories say that Tilopa put Naropa through twenty-four harrowing trials. Because of his unshakeable devotion to Tilopa, Naropa was able to endure them all. This burned away all of his obscurations, and he became enlightened. Naropa became a great teacher and siddha, and is honored as one of the forefathers of the Kagyu lineage.

The Longchen Nyingthig lineage, which comes from Guru Padmasambhava, is renowned as a lineage of devotion. All the practitioners who became major holders of this lineage, whether scholars, yogis, or a combination of both, did so owing to their undying trust in and commitment to their masters. Here is one story. The great master Jigme Lingpa had many superb students—one of these was Jigme Gyalwai Nyugyu. One time, when Jigme Gyalwai Nyugyu was on retreat in Tsari in eastern Tibet, Jigme Lingpa was staying far away to the northwest. Upon rising each morning, Jigme Gyalwai Nyugyu faced the northwest, and chanted devotional prayers to his master. One morning, his yearning and longing was so great that he actually fainted. When he awoke, he recognized that there was no view or meditation to cultivate, and no one to do the cultivating. Later, when Jigme Gyalwai Nyugyu reported this to Jigme Lingpa, the latter exclaimed, "My son, that is it! You realized the fourth and final Togal experience, the 'exhaustion of phenomena.'" Jigme Lingpa instructed him to meditate on that state until it became stable. Jigme Gyalwai Nyugyu followed his master's instruction, and fully accomplished it. Later, he became the root teacher of Patrul Rinpoche, as well as of many other great masters.

This great emphasis placed on devotion might lead us to believe that it is some kind of dogma. The truth is quite the opposite. Devotion does not come from outside, nor can it be coerced. It is an already existing inner force. For most of us much of the time, this force goes unrecognized, because we are so preoccupied with our thoughts and emotions. But should we meet a master, someone we strongly sense is not an ordinary being but rather a living example of spiritual excellence, our devotion begins to stir. Then as we relate to that master, accept his or her instructions, and put them into practice, our hearts and minds begin to open. We become more comfortable with ourselves, our relationships improve, and we notice similar effects occurring in the master's other students. At the same time, whenever we observe the master, we see that his or her words and deeds are never mundane or self-serving, but always inspiring and helpful—full of love, compassion, and wisdom. With this evidence, our trust and appreciation of the master deepens, and our practice intensifies.

Mature devotion is synonymous with indestructible commitment and confidence. At this stage you can say with full assurance, "I have an excellent teacher and I am on an excellent path. All my spiritual goals are well within reach." You know precisely where you are and where you are going, and there is no turning back. This measure of conviction is of the utmost importance—nothing substantial can be accomplished by a shaky mind. As it is said, if you dig one hole deeply, it will catch the rain and you will have all the water you will ever need. But if you dig one shallow hole after another, you will only get puddles.

Ultimately, devotion is the constant call of your own enlightened mind. In the beginning it is almost impossible to understand or even hear this call. This is why the master appears. He or she hears your call perfectly, takes it for you, and nurtures you until you can answer it for yourself. Does devotion still manifest at that time? Yes, in the form of undying gratitude. We can see this in the songs of Milarepa. Before his enlightenment, Milarepa prayed constantly to his root teacher Marpa for inspiration, guidance, and to remove obstacles. After his enlightenment, whenever Milarepa gave a teaching, he always prefaced it by praising Marpa.

The path to enlightenment is filled with obstacles. While some of these are external, most are internal, and they are the most challenging. Buddha Shakyamuni taught that there are five major internal obstacles: 1) laziness; 2) forgetting the instructions; 3) dull, sinking energy or wild scattered mind; 4) too much effort; and 5) too little effort.

We can overcome the first two obstacles by re-invigorating our motivation. Spiritual practice enables us to increase and expand our positive qualities, as well as decrease and ultimately remove all that is negative. Spiritual practice enhances our relationships with others, gives us the strength to withstand fluctuating circumstances, and prepares us perfectly for the moment of death. It is the direct, unfailing path to happiness. What do we possibly gain by giving it up?

Dullness of mind and sinking energy—the third obstacle—are problems that arise when you are actually practicing. The solution, as His Holiness says here, is to "revive alert awareness." There are many ways to do this. For example, you can re-awaken your devotion, as was just stated. Arousing love and compassion for all sentient beings and contemplating the *Four Thoughts that Turn the Mind from Samsara* will also help. Check and adjust your posture. In particular, straighten your spine. You can also bring your awareness to your eyes—take a good look at whatever is in front of you and concentrate on it for a while. It is also good to gaze upwards, to gaze at the sky, or to go outside and be in the natural light. If conditions are such that you must stay indoors, try to increase the light in your room by opening curtains, lighting candles, and so forth. Dullness of mind and sinking energy can be caused by simply being too warm, so if it is convenient and appropriate, remove some clothing or open a window. Over-eating, or eating too many heavy foods might also be a cause. In this case, eat less or eat lighter. It is also beneficial to do practice while walking or even exercising—this is very invigorating.

If the opposite occurs and your meditation "scatters and becomes wild," as His Holiness says here, it is important to re-focus and relax. There are many excellent techniques for doing this. For example, lower your gaze and focus gently on your breathing. You can re-arrange your body posture so that it is more casual. If necessary, lie down. It is also highly effective to place your awareness on your navel chakra, or to the point four inches below it. You can also concentrate on a sacred image, one that is particularly meaningful to you. In short, the antidote for the scattered and wild mind is Shamatha.

The fourth and fifth obstacles to spiritual progress are related to effort—either we are trying too hard in our practice, or not enough. The antidote to the first of these is gentleness and patience. The antidote to the second is a greater sense of urgency and more discipline.

Whenever and however we work with our practice energy, we should do so simply and effortlessly. We should retain and apply the Dzogchen view and meditation, and refrain from conceptualizing as much as possible. This means we should not label, analyze, or judge what we are doing. There is no need to look to the past or to the future. Rather, we should stay in the present, and make the necessary adjustments as seamlessly and tracelessly as the wind changes direction.

It is important to reiterate that practice should not be intermittent, but a continuous state. There should never be a time when we are not practicing. For this reason, His Holiness says that we should abide in the view, practice meditation, and apply the teachings on action "while eating, sleeping, walking, sitting," as well as "in or out of meditation periods."

As we continue on this path, thoughts and emotions keep coming, and some will be intense, even shocking. Our minds are very open now, so anything at all can arise. Our practice, however, remains the same. We remain relaxed and wide-awake, free from "all sorts of cogitation," as His Holiness says here. This means that we should not add more thoughts and emotions to this process; we need only witness. This is why the teachings remind us, again and again, "Do not affirm or negate, nor accept or reject, any thought or emotion. Let it come, let it be, let it go."

His Holiness says, "There is no need to meditate on emptiness as an antidote distinct from the nature of these undesirable thoughts and obscurations. If you recognize the nature of these undesirable thoughts with awareness, at that very moment they will be liberated by themselves, like a snake untying its own knot." Rather than focus on emptiness, we should carefully observe how thought functions. To do this we must release ourselves from our usual biases and assumptions, and observe our minds as if we are exploring a brand new world.

Look within. At first, there is nothing to see but the open space of mind. Suddenly a thought appears. It seems to bear a message and has some degree of intensity. But the thought does not remain that way for long—suddenly it disappears. All that remains is the open space of mind.

In the past, we fixated on the brief moment when a thought

seemed to carry a message. But when we observe our minds closely, we discover that the message being brought by thought dissolves even as it is being conveyed, very much like writing in the sky.

The metaphor given by His Holiness regarding this process—"like a snake untying itself"—is very fitting. A snake coils, then uncoils itself automatically. In the same way, your mind creates a thought, then quickly re-absorbs it. It really is that simple.

It is easy to understand this teaching intellectually. It is quite another matter to apply it when we are in the middle of feeling hatred, lust, arrogance, or envy. But this is precisely what we need to do. We should bring our practice to the point where thoughts and emotions, no matter how intense they seem, cannot move us. This will not occur if we deny, reason, or fight with them. It will happen only by letting go in a state of total awareness.

CHAPTER 20

MORE ACTION

His Holiness says, "The two deadly enemies which have bound us to samsara since beginningless time until now are the grasper and the grasped. Now that by the grace of the Guru we have been introduced to the dharmakaya nature residing in ourselves, these two are burnt up like feathers, leaving no trace or residue. Isn't that delectable?"

"The grasper and grasped"—also known as "ego-clinging"—dominate the minds of sentient beings. Ego-clinging has created innumerable problems throughout time, and continues to do so. The Buddha spoke of this throughout his teachings, as did all the great masters who followed him. Dharmakirti, one of the *Six Ornaments of India*, said that the process unfolds in the following way. First, you conceive of yourself as an individual, and then you conceive of everyone else as being other. Once this occurs, you want to preserve your individuality. This is the basis of attachment. Simultaneously, you are wary of and guard against others, whom you suspect will hinder or harm you. This is the basis of aversion, or anger. When circumstances are quiet, attachment and aversion lie dormant. But when you want to assert your individuality, or when you feel you are being threatened, attachment and aversion burst into flames.

Ego-clinging is synonymous with "I." "I" is not just the thought of being an individual, but includes anything and everything we can identify with. Almost every individual privileges his or her identifications. In the worst situations, we argue, fight, and will even kill or be killed for them. For this reason, the great master Shantideva, in his masterpiece, the *Guide to the Bodhisattva's Way of Life*, compared "I" to a demon, and he told us again and again to give it up. For the same reason, Guru Padmasambhava created many unique and powerful tantric sadhanas, which through practice enable us to transform this "I" into something wholly positive.

Every time we look within and recognize the true nature of our minds, "I" disappears. In the early stages of practice we are not able to sustain this recognition for very long, so "I" always returns. But if we continue to practice, the time will come when occasional recognition becomes continuous and never-ending. On that day, the great troublemaker "I"—roots, trunk, limbs, and branches—is gone forever.

His Holiness says, "Having received the profound instructions of such a swift path, if you do not put them into practice, they will be just like a wish-fulfilling gem put in the mouth of a corpse—what a loss!" We are very fortunate to have received these sublime teachings. We know the simple and sure method by which suffering is uprooted and dharmakaya awareness, the quintessence of enlightenment, is revealed. We now have complete control over our spiritual destiny—it would be a shame if we did not practice. The wish-fulfilling jewel grants all requests, but it is very hard to obtain. Once obtained, it does not work automatically—it has to be invoked. A corpse is oblivious not only to the power of this jewel, but to its very existence. Let us not be like corpses. Let us appreciate and use this precious jewel that we have received.

At this point His Holiness addresses a common meditative experience. We connect with the natural state, then our awareness suddenly drops. Thoughts arise, one after another, and we vaguely follow after them. His Holiness calls these "black thoughts," not because of their content, but because of their effect. These thoughts are like a fog. They obscure and reduce our vision, and make us listless. Should this experience occur, we must not disparage ourselves. Feeling bad is a thought too, and we are striving to release thoughts, not create them. All that is necessary is to revitalize our awareness and return to the natural state.

His Holiness teaches that the nature of thought is dharmakaya. Each thought is open, flexible, utterly free, and inconceivable. Each thought is inseparable from mind itself. As we said several times, the relationship of thought to mind is like wind to space. To realize this fully, we need to become stable in Trekcho. If we cannot remain relaxed and aware and let every thought release itself, we will not be able to see thought for what it is. Instead, we will do what we have always done—believe in and react to that thought with more thoughts, and also with words and deeds. The teaching that the nature of thoughts is dharmakaya should not be misinterpreted as a license to chase them. Rather, it is the realization that there is no reason or way to chase thoughts, since there is nothing to chase. Can we chase the wind?

Many practitioners mistake dharmakaya for a state of mental stillness, or the no-thought state. The no-thought state is one of the fruits of Shamatha practice. It is good, but temporary, and more importantly, it is not dharmakaya. Dharmakaya transcends no-thought, as well as thought. At the same time, it gives rise to both and is their actual essence. As Dzogchen practitioners, we should not strive to eliminate thought and achieve the no-thought state. Rather, we should remain aware and at ease. We should leave our six senses open, and let phenomena, including thoughts, come and go. We witness the stream of events in a carefree way, just as an old man watches children playing.

QUESTION: *Is it useful to analyze strong thoughts and emotions that stem from unpleasant childhood experiences?*

ANSWER: *It is best to abide in the true nature of the mind, and let all mental events come and go. No matter how strong a thought or emotion may be, whether it concerns the past, present, or future, do not analyze it. Say to yourself, "I will not accept or reject any thought or emotion." Be aware, be brave, and do not waver in your commitment. Truly, the swiftest, most powerful way to resolve thoughts and feelings is to let them self-liberate.*

If we need more conceptual support, we can understand this practice through the framework of the six paramitas. For example, when we allow a mental event to arise, express itself, and go, we actualize the paramita of generosity. When we neither think about, speak, or act on a thought or emotion, we complete the paramita of morality. The ability to let all of this take place in its own time and in a relaxed way is the perfection of the paramita of patience. Being faithful to your commitment to neither accept nor reject a thought or emotion fulfills the paramita of joyful effort. To clearly behold a mental event releasing itself by itself is the essence of the paramita of concentration. Finally, when we realize that no thought or emotion can help or hinder us in any way, we attain the paramita of wisdom.

If we were mistreated as children, or at other times during our lives, we should practice forgiveness. Even if we were entirely innocent, we injure ourselves by harboring resentment and anger. In general, we should not spend too much time thinking about the past. We should learn all that we can from it, then let it go forever and move forward with confidence.

QUESTION: *How does compassion relate to dharmakaya and the continual process of letting go?*

ANSWER: *Belief in thoughts and emotions covers up dharmakaya mind, while letting go of thoughts and emotions unveils it. Dharmakaya mind has many beautiful qualities; one of these is compassion. The more you let go, the more compassion you discover. When you have at last let go of everything, your compassion is boundless.*

QUESTION: *In Dzogchen practice the goal is to release all conceptions as gently and naturally as possible. In this context, the word 'Trekcho'—cutting through—seems aggressive, almost inappropriate. Is there another way to define or understand this word?*

ANSWER: *Absolutely. You can replace "cutting through" with "transcend," or "release."*

Venerable Khenchen Palden Sherab Rinpoche
Meditating

CHAPTER 21

TASTING MOLASSES AND OTHER EXPERIENCES

There is a well-known Tibetan saying: "hearing that molasses is sweet is one thing, but experiencing its sweetness directly on your own tongue is quite another." We have heard and read about the Dzogchen view. We know what it is intellectually and can articulate it to others. All of this is fine. But the time has come for us to directly experience the Dzogchen view—not only know it, but to feel and live it; not just once in a while, but all the time.

Although the term "Dzogchen view" can sound supernatural, what it actually means is quite ordinary. The Dzogchen view means to be who and what you are.

"Who am I?" When you ask yourself this question there is no answer, at least not in words. There is just awareness—open, free, and clear. Awareness is the answer; awareness is who you are.

Awareness does not look forward to the future or back to the past. Awareness is content and relaxed here and now. It does not hope for and fear anything. It needs nothing, and is therefore beyond seeking. All of this is who you are.

Because Dzogchen is the highest teaching, people often believe that they are not ready for it, or that they cannot handle it. But why should this be, when your own awareness is ever-present and ever-available?

Ask yourself, "Who am I?" or "Where is my mind?" Identify awareness and abide in it. This is the task that we all are ready to accomplish.

Awareness is open, free, and clear. It sizzles with vitality, creativity, and power, and gives birth to infinite experiences. Every experience is the expression of awareness. But until you are totally free from ego, you must not cling to what arises. Continue to abide in awareness itself, and do not believe in, be proud of, manipulate, and catalogue anything. It does not matter whether these experiences are pleasant or unpleasant, spiritual or worldly. Let everything that appears within your mind and to your other five senses, whether good, bad, or neutral, be released back to its source.

Some experiences are unique to individual practitioners, others are quite common. Most practitioners will go through what is known as the "five stages of meditative experience." These five stages are generally associated with Shamatha, but since Dzogchen is the union of Shamatha and Vipashyana, Dzogchen practitioners will experience them as well. The five stages are: 1) movement; 2) gaining experience; 3) familiarity; 4) stabilization; and 5) fulfillment.

The first stage of meditative experience is well-known to all practitioners. As soon as you sit down to practice your mind erupts. Your thoughts are wild, loud, and relentless—it feels as if they might sweep you away. This is the movement experience. Great masters compare this stage to many streams simultaneously gushing down a mountain during a rainy season. So much mental turbulence is disconcerting, but the fact that you are noticing it is positive. How is this? Previously you were always getting lost in the content of specific thoughts. Now, for the first time, you are understanding the richness of your mind as a whole and seeing it more panoramically. Your awareness is getting sharper. Although it may not feel like it, you are actually meditating. So this is an excellent start.

Stay inspired, keep practicing, and soon you will reach the second stage: gaining experience. Great masters say this stage is like the rushing waters of the mountain streams converging into a single river down in the valley. At this time your mind is still turbulent, but less disturbing. Individual thoughts are still strong, but not so compelling. Meditation is making sense, and there may be glimpses of the Dzogchen view. You are progressing.

Keep persevering in your practice, and you will definitely reach the third stage: familiarity. At this time you have attained a measure of inner peace. You can abide in the Dzogchen state for a while, and when you stray, your mindfulness always brings you back. This is like a bird which always returns to its feeder. Great masters compare this stage to a mighty river, like the Ganges or Mississippi. Such a river, when viewed from a distance, seems perfectly calm. But as one approaches it, one sees and hears some turbulence. In this way, the third stage of meditative experience is a mixture of stability and restlessness. But stability is increasing. You are definitely more in charge.

Keep going, and the fourth stage of meditative experience—stabilization—will be reached. Great masters compare the stabilization stage to a lake or an ocean that is deep, wide, and still. This means that your Dzogchen view is very strong. Turbulent thoughts and emotions are rare, and when they arise, you can easily handle them. However, it is important to be mindful of the subtle, almost undetectable thoughts and emotions that continue to course through your mind, and which are like tiny ripples appearing on the surface of a lake or an ocean. If these thoughts and emotions go undetected, they will eventually gain momentum and become very disturbing. Clearly observe them and allow them to self-release, just as you did during earlier stages. Always stay relaxed.

If you keep up your practice, the fifth and final stage—fulfillment—will be attained. Great masters say that at this stage your view is like a mountain—majestic and unshakeable. You realize that every one of the six sensory experiences is a display of the true nature. Everything you see, hear, smell, taste, feel, and think is perfect, just as it is. You are utterly open and free, and your compassion flows spontaneously and without obstruction, whenever and wherever it is needed.

These five stages of meditative experience are positive. But while you are on this journey some other experiences, such as negative thoughts and emotions, will also manifest. Some of these may be provoked by external circumstances, while others seem to arise from nowhere and for no reason. Some will be familiar to you, and others will be utterly foreign, as if they were implanted into your mind from outside. There can be deep fluctuations in the intensity of these thoughts and emotions. You might have unusual dreams. Furthermore, you can see visions and hear voices that seem to emanate from beings who are spiritual, demonic, or both. Do not regard any of these experiences as true. Do not believe in or analyze them. Let them come and go. There is nothing else you need to do.

Among the experiences common to all practitioners are bliss, clarity, and no-thought. These three states arise naturally from good practice. At the same time, they need not and should not be sought after. Nor should you let them make you proud.

Bliss means that you feel happy, and that you know your happiness is not conditioned by external events, but rather is an integral part of yourself. This is a sure sign of progress. But as the great masters say, although bliss is positive, it is only an experience. Never become attached to it.

Clarity is synonymous with vitality, or energy. It is a feeling of radiance and inner strength. Your mind is bright, clear, and alert. Your intelligence is sparking. Furthermore, you sense that these experiences are intrinsic to your being, and independent of anything outside. All this is very good, but it is just as important that you do not fixate on it. Clarity is a manifestation of good meditation practice, but not the final result. Keep going.

The no-thought state means that you can remain in meditation for two, three, or five minutes—perhaps even longer—without a single thought or emotion arising. More importantly, it means that your mind is open and spacious, and that you are comfortable and relaxed. You sense that these qualities do not depend on specific environments or actions, but rather that they are aspects of your nature. All this means that you are moving in the right direction. But it does not mean that you should cling to or yearn for the no-thought state. The coming and going of thoughts and emotions is natural. It is one of the expressions of your mind's clarity. Do not privilege no-thought over clarity, or you might end up being reborn in the animal realm—a dull, lethargic state of mind. Be aware, be alert, and keep letting go.

Bliss, clarity, and no-thought may arise in that sequence. They can also occur simultaneously, or in any order. However they manifest, the essential point is to abide continuously in the state of dharmakaya awareness. Once again, we must not attach too much significance to these or any other experiences. As His Holiness and other great masters say, it is important that we do not use these states as fuel for arrogance. Self-importance, whether its object is worldly success or meditative experience, is always an impediment to our spiritual progress.

His Holiness now quotes a well-known Dzogchen saying,

"Theory is like a patch; it will fall away. Experiences are like mist; they will vanish." "Theory" refers to formulas, phrases, strings of words, quotations from scripture and the great masters—every conceptual and verbal description of the teachings, including the very ones you're reading now. Theory has an important place, particularly when we are beginners, but when difficult circumstances arise in real life, only genuine realization will help. Furthermore, once genuine realization is born within, there is no longer any need for theory. When you taste molasses for the first time and have its flavor on your tongue, do you need to consult the words you read that attempted to describe it?

"Experiences are like mist; they will vanish." Mist is insubstantial and ephemeral. It comes mysteriously, is constantly shifting, and quickly dissolves. Every experience is like this, and so are the meanings we give to it. Sights, sounds, smells, tastes, tactile sensations, thoughts, and emotions, as well as sublime meditative states—let none of these control you.

Experiences keep coming, good as well as bad. What you thought was resolved will return with greater vigor than before, and new experiences will also arise. There will always be ample opportunity to grasp onto and be controlled by these experiences, until the time when both practitioner and path completely release. In the past many people, having made considerable progress, reverted to believing in and acting upon the creations of their minds, and they lost their way.

With sustained practice we attain some stability. We deal competently with external events, as well as with our thoughts and emotions. Meditation and post-meditation merge to some degree, and life becomes relatively smooth. At the same time, the teachings feel very familiar, and formal meditation seems less necessary than before. Many people in the past, having come to this point, decided they had reached an advanced stage, and that they no longer needed to practice. The subjective, judgmental aspect of their minds was still operational, and they gave in to it. They lived out the rest of their lives and died having progressed only part-way. His Holiness says, "You old meditators, still novices in practice, watch out—there is a danger you may die with your head encrusted with salt." The head of a corpse encrusted with salt may be unfamiliar to Western people, but is well known to Tibetans. It is unpleasant to see, and it smells even worse. His Holiness' message could not be more clear. We must keep practicing, and not give in to thoughts and emotions that suggest we are already enlightened. We must complete what we started.

Vimalamitra

CHAPTER 22

AN OLD FRIEND, A SNAKE, AND A THIEF IN AN EMPTY HOUSE

Thoughts and phenomena come and go by themselves. By remaining aware, patient, and relaxed, by not interfering with the natural processes of our minds and phenomena, we will certainly realize this. According to the Dzogchen teachings, realization of the coming and going of thoughts and phenomena—known as self-liberation—occurs in three interconnected and increasingly subtle stages.

The first stage is likened to meeting an old friend, or someone you know. When you meet an old friend there is no need for pretense or guardedness. The two of you already know and trust one another; you just slip into conversation, everything flows quite nicely, and there is the same sense of comfort when the time comes for parting. Being with an old friend is in all respects easy. In the same way, as your practice matures, the natural flow of thoughts and phenomena—their appearing, lingering, and departing—becomes increasingly familiar to you. You do not have to wrestle with what arises. You can relax and let go, knowing that the true nature takes care of everything. In this way life becomes increasingly uncomplicated and enjoyable.

The second stage of self-liberation is like the undoing of a snake's knot. When a snake becomes knotted, it immediately uncoils itself. The process is extremely simple and direct. With regard to Dzogchen practice, this means that your mind is open, clear, and without any focus. A thought occurs to you and you observe as it dissolves, just like that.

This level of simplicity and directness is attained when you are no longer very interested in judgment and analysis. In other words, your own subjectivity—your habitual reactions to the flow of experience—is losing force. It is becoming easier not to interfere with what arises. You are increasingly able to let the true nature work for you.

This process reaches its culmination during the third stage, that of self-liberation, which is like a thief in an empty house. By this time you have transcended ego. You do not need to name, sort, and rank phenomena, or assert or flaunt your will in any way. You have mastered the art of simply being. At the same time, this empty house of yours—your body—still has doors and windows. This means that your mind and five sense organs are still open and receptive to phenomena. Your interaction with the world continues. The difference now is that nothing can distract or deceive you. You know phenomena do not exist independently of your own awareness. They are images that appear in the mirror of your mind.

As you cultivate this state in a relaxed way over time, beautiful qualities, inseparable from the openness and power of your mind, manifest abundantly. Your love and wisdom surge like a mighty river. You become simple and humble, deeply respectful and appreciative of others. You work tirelessly on their behalf, according to their needs, your talents, and the complexities and subtleties of the interdependent coordination system. Interdependence is comprehended swiftly and clearly, as your inborn intelligence has fully bloomed.

All this means you have accomplished the unity of emptiness and compassion. It also means that you have mastered the Dzogchen teachings in terms of view, meditation, conduct, and result. Your mastery can occur in the sequence just described, in any order, or all at once.

What does it mean, to have mastered the view? It means that for you there is no longer any difference between absolute and relative truth, or between buddhas and sentient beings. All your concepts about high and low, good and bad, have completely worn away. Mastering meditation—what is that? It is the merging of day and night. Waking experience and sleeping experience have fused into a single, seamless, translucent state. The whole of life is like a dream. What does it mean to master conduct? It means that you are beyond acceptance and rejection. Every single experience is blissful. You have achieved the one-taste awareness of wisdom mind. Finally, what is mastery of the result? It is knowing that your own mind is the embodiment of the inseparable three kayas.

Profound, unshakeable inner strength now marks your realization, and it manifests in what is known as the "four confidences." For example, if a thousand buddhas appeared you would have nothing to ask them. You know that you know, and you know that your knowledge is complete. Nothing is needed. There is nothing to gain. This the first confidence.

Similarly, if a thousand enemies surrounded you, or if all the circumstances of your life unravel, you would be unmoved. You have nothing to lose. That is the second confidence.

Hope is extinguished. You no longer yearn and strive for enlightenment, or anything else for that matter. This is the third confidence.

Fear is extinguished. You do not worry about not attaining enlightenment, and you do not try to get out of samsara. This is the fourth confidence.

When you possess the four confidences you are equal to Garab Dorje, Manjushrimitra, Shri Singha, Jnanasutra, Vimalamitra, as well as Guru Padmasambhava and his twenty-five disciples. Your mind is pure, unchanging, and infinite—you are a sky-yogi, identical to Longchenpa and Jigme Lingpa. And although others may perceive you as an ordinary human being, secretly you are the Buddha—not in name, but in reality.

There is a story in the Dzogchen texts which illustrates how simple and direct the path to this realization can be. There was a prince, happy and content upon his throne. Then he went outside and started mingling with the crowd. All of a sudden he forgot who he was. He wandered off, and became enmeshed in mischief and trouble. Then one day he remembered, "I am the prince." He returned to the palace and sat down upon his throne. All that mischief and trouble vanished.

Right now we are like the wandering prince. But the palace and throne are always present—only a moment of recollection away.

CHAPTER 23

CLARIFYING RELAXATION: A REMINDER

When a lion or tiger is walking and gets close to its destination it will stop, look back, and one last time survey all the territory it has covered. In the same way, many great masters who give teachings will, as they near completion, stop and briefly review the material they have already taught. At this time we will follow in their footsteps. Up to now we have been following the path laid out by the great master His Holiness Dudjom Rinpoche in his *Mountain Retreat*. We have discussed, with some thoroughness, the first two sections of his text, namely the "preparation" and the "main practice." "Preparation" deals with the foundation of the journey—refuge and bodhichitta, purification and devotion, as well as contemplating the four thoughts that turn the mind from samsara. The essence of "preparation" is to arouse a heartfelt desire to benefit beings, a deep connection to the lineage, and an understanding of the innate purity of the universe. The "main practice" deals with Dzogchen meditation.

Dzogchen meditation means to relax your mind in its natural state. The word 'relax' is sometimes misinterpreted as an excuse to "let loose;" that is, to abandon all rules and structures and chase whatever impulses seem most compelling or convenient. Obviously, this is not what His Holiness and the other great Dzogchen masters have in mind.

The actual meaning of this instruction is as follows. Open the doors of your six sense faculties. Be receptive to sights, sounds, smells, tastes, tactile sensations, thoughts, and emotions. This does not mean that you hunger for or invoke these experiences, but rather that you allow your eyes, ears, and so forth to function naturally, and to receive whatever comes.

When a sensory experience arises, do not name, question, or judge it at all. Do not encourage it to stay, and do not force it to hurry up and go. Remain open and aware; besides that, do nothing.

The sensory experience that has come does not stay long. It will go, and when it does, let it.

When you relax your mind in its natural state, do not be like a cat waiting for a mouse, hyper-alert and ready to pounce. Be at ease. Observe whatever arises like an old man watching children play. Does an old man worry about or analyze children's games? Does he jump into the sandbox with them? No, he just watches, unconcerned and perhaps even a bit amused.

Gompai is a Tibetan word. It is often translated as "meditation," but what it actually means is "getting used to," or "becoming familiar with." In the context of Dzogchen practice this means to acclimate yourself to the practice of remaining open to and aware of the natural flow of whatever arises. This is an alien experience in the beginning, because you are used to making subjective demands upon and meddling with phenomena for so long. But with practice it gets easier.

Relax your mind in its natural state. Whatever arises—let it come, let it be, and let it go. Keep doing this, and you will become increasingly gentle and strong, content and compassionate. Keep doing this, and life becomes more and more enjoyable. Keep doing this, and the Great Perfection of all that is will be revealed in all its glory.

His Holiness Dudjom Rinpoche

CHAPTER 24

POST-MEDITATION: DREAMS, VOWS, AND SAMAYAS

As we have discussed, there are two dimensions to a practitioner's life: meditation and post-meditation. Meditation in this context refers specifically to formal practice, performed in distinct sessions that have a beginning, middle, and end. Post-meditation refers to everything else. In the modern age, most of us spend most of our time in post-meditation. If we want our spiritual growth to develop swiftly and efficiently, the relatively short time that we spend in formal practice will probably not be sufficient. We will need to find ways to apply what we learn during meditation to all our other activities.

When we practice Vajrayana in formal sessions, we visualize deities and chant mantras; then we dissolve the visualization into ourselves and meditate in the Dzogchen state. This is a profound training on realizing that forms and sounds are inherently pure while being inseparable from our minds. There is no reason that we should limit ourselves to this training only in formal sessions. After all, during post-meditation, forms and sounds keep appearing. We can continue to practice by realizing their inherent purity and simply not judging them. And even though we are not deliberately cultivating forms and sounds by visualizing and chanting, they still appear nondually within our minds—all we have to do is tune in. If we practice in these ways, we are integrating meditation and post-meditation beautifully, and our realization will continuously expand.

In the *Diamond Sutra*, Buddha Shakyamuni taught "All conditioned phenomena are like dreams, illusions, bubbles, or shadows; like drops of dew, or flashes of lightning. They should be contemplated accordingly." Sentient beings and buddhas, samsara and nirvana, "I" and others, space and time, every single interpretation of the meaning of life—nothing is real. And as the Buddha also said, even if there is a state of mind higher than enlightenment, it too is unreal. It is not difficult to apply this teaching during post-meditation, and the rewards of doing so are great. If we look upon everything as a dream or an illusion, our grasping and clinging to phenomena will diminish. Our hearts and minds will open, and our appreciation for sentient beings and all that we experience will grow. And all this will deepen our realization of nonduality.

It is also important that we maintain vows and samayas during post-meditation. Vows and samayas are tips and guidelines for travelers on the spiritual path. They are the fruit of the experience of great beings who completed their training, and they are given to us so that our journey will be as safe and smooth as possible.

Maintaining vows and samayas can be difficult, because what the experts say is good for us often contradicts what we want. For example, even though nutritionists recommend that we eat more vegetables and fruit, how many of us listen? Most of us would rather eat ice cream and pie. Even when we are informed of the possible negative consequences of our behavior, we persist. The ego is stubborn, and old habits are hard to break. The word 'vow' is the English translation of what in Tibetan is known as *dompa*. *Dompa* actually means restraining ourselves from doing that which is negative. "Samaya" is a Sanskrit word, translated into English as "sacred bond," or "covenant." In Tibetan it is known as *damtsig*, which is the imperative to see the innate purity and perfection of the universe. Most of us require a considerable amount of time to accomplish this. Here, too the ego manifests its stubbornness. It wants to see the universe the way it always has.

Vajrayana practitioners uphold what is collectively known as the *"three vows:"* 1) pratimoksha vow, 2) bodhisattva vow, and 3) tantric samaya. These three embody all the vows and samayas of Buddhism. The pratimoksha vow is to avoid all harmful thoughts, words, and deeds. The bodhisattva vow is thinking, saying, and doing only that which is beneficial to ourselves and others. The tantric samaya is seeing the universe and all beings and phenomena as perfect and pure. It also includes fulfilling all our practice commitments, such as completing the Ngondro.

As Vajrayana practitioners, we should uphold the three vows not only during formal meditation sessions, but at all times. By doing so, we gradually wean ourselves from belief in the independence and superiority of the ego, as well as from the thoughts, words, and deeds that support it. We recognize and appreciate the dignity of others, and our ability to benefit them increases. We behold the true nature of the whole of reality, indestructibly beautiful and inseparable from our minds. In these ways, the spiritual progress we make in meditation never fades, but actually intensifies during post-meditation.

On the other hand, if we do not uphold these vows and samayas during post-meditation, whatever we have learned from formal practice will not be strong enough when challenging internal and external circumstances arise. We will likely revert to the same old patterns and attain the same unsatisfactory results. Then we might blame the practice and leave the spiritual path entirely. But when we leave the path we are actually leaving ourselves.

The great masters teach that there are four ways vows and samayas can be broken or lost. That is, through:

1) Ignorance: we simply not do know what they are.
2) Disrespect: we know what they are, but disdain them.
3) Carelessness: we know what they are, have respect, but lose mindfulness.
4) Emotional weakness: we know what they are, have respect and are mindful, but are overwhelmed by our attachment or anger.

Some great masters, such as Asanga, add the following:

5) Mental dullness, or lack of clarity.
6) Fatigue.

The Buddha, Guru Padmasambhava, and other great masters created this checklist, as well as the entire network of vows and samayas in general, not to burden us with extra homework, but rather so that we can monitor ourselves, avoid or at least minimize mistakes, and correct ourselves when necessary. When we can do this consistently, we will be our own masters.

If and when we break a vow or samaya, it is necessary to mend it as quickly as possible. To delay only compounds the problem. By way of example, when drips of water fall from your ceiling, you should stop the leak right away. If you do not act promptly, the ceiling will disintegrate and eventually collapse, and your house will be ruined.

The teachings say that broken vows and samayas, as well as mistakes in general, have one virtue: they can be restored. One of the most renowned ways to accomplish this is through Vajrasattva practice, either by itself or in conjunction with a liturgy of confession such as *The Stainless King*. Praying for the well-being of others and performing good deeds are also excellent, as is cultivating devotion to the spiritual teacher through Guru Yoga. Particularly supreme is Dzogchen Trekcho. Letting whatever arises release itself without a trace fulfills every vow and samaya.

Vajrasattva

CHAPTER 25

VOWS AND SAMAYAS OF THE FIVE BUDDHA FAMILIES

Everything we need to know to keep progressing on the path is expressed in the vows and samayas of the Buddha, Vajra, Ratna, Padma, and Karma families.

The Buddha family's vows and samayas include taking refuge, bodhichitta, and morality. These three are the foundation of the Buddhist path. For this reason, the Buddha family is considered to be the source of the other four families. This is also why, in murals and thangkas that depict the Five Dhyani Buddhas, Vairochana, the presiding deity of the Buddha Family, is always placed in the center.

Refuge means that you trust wholeheartedly in the Buddha, Dharma, and Sangha. Bodhichitta means that you are dedicated to actualizing and manifesting limitless love, compassion, and wisdom. Morality means avoiding negative actions, doing only what is positive, and adapting your conduct to the laws and customs of the culture in which you live.

The great master Nagarjuna said that when we practice good conduct, our world becomes a heaven. Even the tiniest good deed reverberates much farther than we know. When we take this advice to heart and practice it in conjunction with refuge, we are upholding the vows and samayas of the Buddha Family.

The essence of the many vows and samayas of the Vajra family is to keep the bell and dorje united. Vajrasattva, the lord of this family as well as the lord of the other four, is always depicted holding these implements. The bell symbolizes wisdom, or emptiness; the dorje symbolizes compassion, or skillful means. Keeping them united means to cultivate wisdom and compassion as a unity, which is the very heart of Vajrayana Buddhism.

The vows and samayas of the Ratna family can be summed up in a single word: generosity. We should give whatever we can to others in order to enhance their lives. There are four principal gifts that we can offer. The first includes gifts of a material nature, such as food, clothing, and shelter. The second is protection, and includes actions such as rescuing beings from dangerous situations, keeping them out of harm's way, and comforting them when they are anxious or afraid. The third gift, known as "words of wisdom," is practical advice that inspires and encourages beings to develop spiritually. The fourth gift is the motivating force which generates and perfects all acts of genuine generosity—the unity of compassion, wisdom, and humility. Compassion means that you want to free beings from suffering, and to help them every way you can. Wisdom means that you know precisely what to give, and when to give it. Humility means that you do not feel important or superior to others, and that you do not expect or need acknowledgement or reward. Ratnasambhava is the lord of the Ratna family. His name can be translated as "Jewel-Born." This signifies that in rediscovering your own infinite richness, your ability to give will be boundless.

The vows and samayas of the Padma family are embodied in Buddha Amitabha, the "Lord of Speech." Amitabha represents the infinite array of teachings that lead beings to enlightenment. Within Buddhism, there are many schools, sub-schools, and lineages, and many great masters. Amitabha is present in all of them. In fact, he is present whenever and wherever the message of non-violence, love, compassion, and wisdom is being taught. Knowing this, we should avoid sectarianism. We should be broad-minded and respect all good paths. We should also strive to make our own speech—which both includes words and transcends them—increasingly inspiring to others. This is how we uphold the vows of the Padma family.

The Karma family is next. Karma means "action"—specifically, any and all actions that fulfill the temporal and spiritual wishes of all beings. We uphold the vows and samayas of the Karma family when we dedicate our lives to this task. During formal practice sessions, we employ the various skillful techniques of the Vajrayana and make prayers for universal peace, prosperity, and enlightenment. Between sessions, we use our talents to benefit others, ever mindful of their needs. With continuous and dedicated practice, our power to help others grows increasingly selfless, effortless, and effective. In time, it becomes universal, truly "all-accomplishing," which is the meaning of the name of the lord of this family, Buddha Amoghasiddhi.

Guru Padmasambhava

CHAPTER 26

VIEW AND CONDUCT

At this point His Holiness quotes Guru Padmasambhava, who said, "Though my view is higher than the sky, my conduct regarding cause and effect is finer than barley flour."

The view that is higher than the sky is the totally liberated mind—freedom from all concepts. The conduct that is finer than barley flour refers to words and deeds based solely on what benefits others and inspires them toward spiritual awakening. View and conduct are not independent of one another. They must be practiced as a unity. For this reason, Guru Padmasambhava also said, "Do not lose conduct in the view; do not lose the view in conduct." We lose our conduct in the view when we use our view as an excuse to speak and act randomly and carelessly. We lose our view in conduct when we forsake spaciousness and follow and enforce rules rigidly and proudly.

There is a famous Dzogchen saying: "The view should be brave, and the conduct timid." You need a brave view because the ego is cunning and likes to be in charge. It knows how to win and will not give up without a fight. Train yourself to remain still and relaxed in the face of its infinite demands. Keep letting go until your ego merges with infinite space. This is the brave view of the Dzogchen warrior. With regard to conduct—be patient and kind, attune yourself to the needs of others, and say and do only what gives them peace and inspiration. Remember, you do not always have to speak or act in order to be of benefit to others—silence and stillness can be very powerful too. When you unite the brave view and gentle conduct like this, you are following the path of the great Dzogchen masters.

Guru Padmasambhava also said, "Descend with the view; ascend with conduct." This instruction is particularly appropriate when your view has become stable. Your ego and its expressions are no longer dominant, and you are very much at home in the infinite space beyond words and deeds. Guru Padmasambhava is saying that although you can soar in the sky all by yourself in perfect freedom, you must not remain separate there. You should come down to earth, be with others, and help them grow.

CHAPTER 27

THE MAJESTY OF GURU YOGA

His Holiness Dudjom Rinpoche says, "All the samayas of the Secret Mantra vehicle, as many as can be enumerated, are gathered into the samaya of the Guru's body, speech, and mind." The way to realize this swiftly and powerfully is by practicing on Guru Padmasambhava.

Guru Padmasambhava is the essence and embodiment of all buddhas and bodhisattvas, all gurus, devas, and dakinis, and all dharmapalas. He is the Lord of the Vajrayana teachings, as well as the buddha for this time. Although his enlightened activities in India and Tibet during the eighth and ninth centuries are well-chronicled, he is not only a historical being, however profound, but also a living buddha who is and who will always be available to help sentient beings. The ways and forms in which he manifests are limitless and always in accord with the needs of specific individuals. Ultimately, Guru Padmasambhava is the nature of your own mind, your own spiritual perfection, which you have yet to realize.

To practice on Guru Padmasambhava, visualize him in

the sky in front of you, or above your head, in the form that he is commonly depicted on thangkas and statues. With faith and confidence, feel his presence, pray to him and receive his blessings. Finally, let your mind mingle with his. This is one way to do Guru Yoga.

What are the samayas of Guru Yoga? The body samaya is seeing every single sentient being as a perfect emanation of Guru Padmasambhava, or of your root teacher, if you are practicing that way. The speech samaya is hearing all sounds as the sound of his mantra, or as his sacred speech. The mind samaya is to experience all of your thoughts as the play of his enlightened awareness.

Diligent practice of Guru Yoga ripens your being, and prepares you to receive the mind-to-mind transmission of authentic Dzogchen realization. The specifics of how and when this will occur is utterly dependent on the intensity of your devotion, the strength of your samaya, as well as the unique qualities of your relationship to your root teacher.

Nyoshul Lungthok was one of the great masters in Tibetan Buddhist history. Like all great masters, he was a student first, spending about twenty years apprenticing with and attending to his root teacher, Patrul Rinpoche. One time the two of them were staying in a hermitage near Dzogchen Monastery in eastern Tibet. Every evening Patrul Rinpoche would go outside, lie down, and gaze at the sky. He was doing the Dzogchen practice known as "uniting the three spaces." One evening, while he was lying down as usual, Patrul Rinpoche called Nyoshul Lungthok, and asked, "My son, did you tell me that you have not yet recognized the nature of your mind?" And Nyoshul Lungthok replied, "That is true sir, I have not." Patrul Rinpoche said, "There is nothing you cannot know. Come, lie down next to me, and look at the sky." Nyoshul Lungthok did as he was asked, and the conversation continued in the following way.

"Do you see the stars in the sky?"
"Yes."
"Do you hear the dogs barking in Dzogchen Monastery?"
"Yes."
"Do you understand the words we are saying?"
"Yes."
"Well, that is the meditation."

At that moment, Nyoshul Lungthok attained complete Dzogchen realization.

All Patrul Rinpoche said was that seeing, hearing, and knowing in a natural, uncontrived way is Dzogchen practice. He gave a teaching that his student undoubtedly had heard, in one form or another, many times before. It could not have been the content of the instruction alone that created this realization in Nyoshul Lungthok. What happened then? What happened was a teacher's wisdom and compassion, and a student's devotion were coalescing for years, and a profound spiritual love was born. Everything was in place so that, in a single moment, the sight of stars, the sound of barking dogs, and the exchange of simple words between a spiritual father and his son were enough to set the son's mind free—forever.

Shantideva

CHAPTER 28

MORE TIPS

When we meditate in a secluded environment, the distractions we face are those generated internally by our minds. With diligent practice we become more capable of dealing with these distractions and in so doing we attain a good measure of stability. But when we rise from the cushion and go into the world, the environment is more chaotic. Sights, sounds, and other sensory experiences arise unpredictably, in varying forms and intensities. Interactions with other people are particularly challenging and trigger powerful thoughts and emotions. Applying what we have learned in meditation might seem difficult, if not impossible at these times. But it does not have to be, as long as we employ mindfulness, alertness, and conscientiousness.

Mindfulness means to remember the instructions. Be open and relaxed and do not believe in and follow transient phenomena. What comes will go, by itself. Alertness means to apply the instructions at all times, not only during formal sessions. The goal is to transcend the mind-made duality of meditation and post-meditation, and to abide in the Dzogchen state continuously. Conscientiousness means to be consistent and persevering. The path can suddenly twist—be ready. Keep your eye on the goal, even if it seems far off. Stay balanced and if you happen to fall, get up, dust yourself off, and keep going.

In the *Guide to the Bodhisattva's Way of Life*, the great master Shantideva said when we are mindful, alert, and conscientious we draw all the virtues towards us, and simultaneously cast all non-virtues away. We become so strong that when negative emotions arise—Shantideva compares them to wild beasts with gaping mouths—they cannot harm us.

If you continue to cultivate these qualities, you will be able to use every experience, good or bad, as the path to enlightenment. If you do not, you will be easily thrown off course. For this reason, in his *Letter to a Friend*, the great master Nagarjuna compared mindfulness, alertness, and conscientiousness to nectar, and their absence to poison. He recommended that you drink this nectar continuously—it will sustain you until you reach your goal.

Enlightenment is your nature. To reveal it, you need deep-rooted faith in your teacher, in the teaching, and in yourself. And you must practice until you reach your goal. With such determination, even murderers can transcend their evil pasts and attain the highest realization. Ajatasatru, Angulimala, and Nanda are three men who did precisely that, according to Indian Buddhist history. Ajatasatru murdered his own father, King Bimbisara, and while under the influence of Devadata, even attempted to kill the Buddha several times. Angulimala, after having received negative instructions from his teacher, murdered almost one thousand people. Nanda killed his own mother. But they met masters and became inspired. They received instruction, and practiced devotedly. Each one believed in, purified, and utterly transformed himself, becoming an arhat.

In Tibet the best example of this is of course Milarepa. To avenge his mother he learned black magic and destroyed an entire house along with most of its inhabitants. Afterwards he felt tremendous remorse and desperately sought a way to purify his horrible mistakes. Finally he met the great master Marpa, who put him through excruciating trials. Yet Milarepa's devotion to Marpa was unfailing and he endured every trial, purified his negative karma, and became one of the greatest yogis in Buddhist history.

Indestructible faith in the guru is very powerful. Such faith begins when you recognize your guru's extraordinary abilities. The guru is free from ego, knows the teachings perfectly, and has complete insight into the hearts and minds of beings. The guru sees that your nature is enlightened, and wants you to know it—right now, if possible. He or she also knows the reasons you do not see it, knows the remedies, and patiently offers them to you. What the guru says and does in your presence is profound and multi-layered, created especially for you, and is meant not only for today, but for the future too—and sometimes even for the past. When you watch your guru interact with others, you see that he or she always makes them happy, and leaves them in a better place. Should a situation or environment darken or become volatile, it cannot disturb the guru's inner peace, and he or she transforms it without effort, in an instant, into something bright and positive. And this is only the beginning.

As His Holiness Dudjom Rinpoche says in his teaching, the relationship between guru and disciple is of the utmost intimacy and power—it is the first Vajrayana samaya, and the embodiment of all the others. We uphold it by always respecting the guru, by putting his or her instructions into action, and by never letting ourselves be deterred from the path. Whoever practices like this will eventually become just like the guru.

First Buddhist Council

CHAPTER 29

THE SANGHA

His Holiness says, "In general, the samaya with your Dharma brothers and sisters comprises holding all those who have entered the door of Lord Buddha's teachings in high esteem."

At the beginning of every practice session we proclaim, "I take refuge in the Buddha, I take refuge in the Dharma, I take refuge in the Sangha." Many of us are quite sure of the importance of the Buddha and Dharma, but less certain about the Sangha. Some of us would like to ignore it altogether. But Sangha is vital for our spiritual growth.

Sangha means "spiritual community." It is comprised of everyone who is practicing the Dharma, who is striving to grow spiritually in order to be an agent of good in this world. This is a beautiful and noble quest, one that requires enormous dedication and courage. It is no small feat to transform self-importance into unconditional wisdom and compassion. For this reason, every practitioner deserves our respect.

Every Dharma practitioner shares a common lineage to the Buddha and is working for the same goal. At the same time, every practitioner is unique. No two start from the same place and no two process and manifest the teachings in the same way. When practitioners meet, there are bound to occasionally be intense exchanges, which make for good learning opportunities.

Practitioners stimulate each other's growth. This is why the teachings say the Sangha is the source of inspiration. One practitioner overcomes powerful obstacles, becomes spiritually stronger, and moves you to greater diligence and resiliency. Another practitioner's unique interpretation of the teachings ignites your understanding. Stimulation and inspiration can take many forms—sometimes even as a sudden test. For example, a Dharma brother or sister says or does something that you perceive as insulting. Do you retaliate? Or do you let go and respond positively?

Seasoned practitioners are called "spiritual warriors." They do not earn this title by practicing all by themselves, sitting on the porch eating Häagen-Dazs ice cream. They interact with Sangha members, and with other sentient beings, too. They invite the spontaneous and chaotic into their lives. And they love challenges. They meet them by remaining aware, by letting go, and by speaking and acting in ways that are always appropriate and beneficial.

Having reminded us of the importance of Sangha in a general sense, His Holiness now says, "More particularly, all those who have the same guru and the same mandala are vajra brothers and sisters." The bonds shared among those who study and practice under the guidance of a single guru are extremely powerful. The guru is both the father and the mother, and the guru's students are his or her spiritual sons and daughters.

On the most general level, the Sangha includes all beings, in all forms, throughout the universe. Everybody who has lived, is living, and will live is Sangha. We should share our love and wisdom with every one of them. At the same time, let us acknowledge and celebrate our special connection to our vajra brothers and sisters. As the teachings say, these connections were not formed by accident. They are the result of good karma and past aspirations. Our vajra brothers and sisters have been our close spiritual companions over the course of many lives. And they will continue to be so, until each of us attains enlightenment.

Four Friends

CHAPTER 30

THE TEN NON-VIRTUES AND THE TEN VIRTUES

We want everlasting happiness, and believe we will attain it by pursuing and achieving our desires. But because of the fundamental truth of impermanence, any happiness attained on the path of desire is transitory at best. For this reason, the teachings say that the pursuit of desire inevitably leads to frustration, or worse.

Everlasting happiness is our nature. It is whole and complete right now. It is not to be found by pursuing the objects of desire, but by looking within. Our hearts and minds are vast and all embracing. When we realize this our happiness is achieved, and we can help others to find their own happiness. This is the purpose of practicing Dharma.

His Holiness says, "Whatever you might be able to accomplish with your three doors, do only that which is truly beneficial to others." The expression "three doors" is a famous Buddhist metaphor for body, speech, and mind. Why are these likened to doors? Because they are the portals or gateways through which happiness and suffering manifest. Since we wish to be happy and to be free from suffering, it is very important that we use our three doors wisely. One of the most simple, direct, and powerful ways to do this is to avoid the ten non-virtuous actions and cultivate their opposites.

The ten non-virtuous actions include three by body, four by speech, and three by mind. The three by body are 1) taking the lives of others, or killing; 2) taking that which has not been given, or stealing; 3) and sexual misconduct. The four by speech are 4) lying, 5) slander, 6) harsh speech, and 7) gossip. The three by mind are 8) covetousness, 9) violent thoughts, and 10) extreme views. If you perform these ten non-virtuous actions, you create suffering for yourself and others, and not only during the moments immediately following the deed—the suffering will extend far into the future. If you avoid these actions, suffering is reduced and ultimately eliminated.

You will create happiness for yourself and others by doing the opposite of the ten non-virtuous actions, that is, by cultivating the ten virtuous actions. Instead of taking life, save life. Save an animal that will be slaughtered, or find a good home for a shelter dog or cat that is scheduled for euthanization. Rather than stealing, be generous. Material things, protection, and words of wisdom—give these to others, according to your abilities and their needs, as selflessly as possible. Instead of engaging in sexual misconduct, respect your own and others' vows and commitments, and do only that which honors the wishes and dignity of living beings.

Slander is malicious speech which harms and even destroys reputations and relationships. It can even lead to murder. To illustrate this, the Buddha told the following story. Once upon a time there was a lioness and a female buffalo who were the best of friends. Both had babies. The two mothers wanted their children to be close, and said to them, "We want you to be best friends, as we have been. But beware of slander. Do not listen to negative remarks other creatures might make." Shortly after saying this, both the lioness and the female buffalo died peacefully.

The young lion and the young buffalo grew to be strong and beautiful, and just as their mothers had hoped, they became the best of friends. Now, every time the lion went out to hunt, a certain fox followed him. The lion always left a little food behind for the fox, but otherwise never acknowledged him. "He is so arrogant," thought the fox. "He should suffer. I cannot harm him physically. But I can destroy his relationship with the buffalo."

One day, after finishing his meal, the fox, with his tail dragging on the ground, meekly approached the lion and laid down on the ground. "What do you want, fox?" asked the lion. And the fox said, "I have something to tell you." The lion asked, "What is it?" And the fox replied, "Great uncle, I don't think you will listen." And he scampered off.

The next day, the same thing happened. This time the lion said, "If you don't tell me I'm going to knock you out."

"Okay, okay. It's just that I am really worried about you."

"Why?"

"Your best friend, the buffalo, says that he is going to challenge you to a fight."

"I don't believe it."

"Whether you believe it or not, he said it. In fact, he is training for the fight right now."

The next day the fox and lion continued the conversation. The lion asked the fox, "How is he training to fight me?" The fox said, "He thrusts his horns in and out of the earth, he makes loud snorting noises. Why don't you spy on him, and see for yourself." The lion went and saw the buffalo doing precisely what the fox reported. At this point the lion decided that he must prepare to fight.

During this time the fox was also planting seeds of suspicion into the buffalo's mind. Finally the buffalo asked, "How is he training to fight me?" The fox said, "He rolls onto his back, stretches out, then springs back up. He paws the earth and shakes his head; he opens his mouth and roars." The buffalo spied on the lion, and saw him doing exactly what the fox had described. At that moment the buffalo realized that he must train for a fight.

The behaviors the fox claimed were special preparations for battle were natural to each animal. The lion and buffalo observed each other doing these things many times before, never thinking anything of it. But the cunning fox convinced them to interpret these behaviors as marks of evil intent. Thus, the next time the lion and buffalo saw each other they immediately sprung into action. The lion leapt onto the buffalo, and tore into his neck; at the same time the buffalo thrust his horns into the lion's stomach. Both died on the spot. At that moment the gods cried out, "How awful! Two good friends destroyed each other because of a fox's slander!"

This is of course just a story. And slander does not necessarily lead to killing. It does, however, hurt beings and drive them apart. We should avoid it and instead speak words that are kind, uplifting, and which foster harmony.

In the same way, we should avoid lying and tell only the truth. We should also refrain from speaking harshly. Instead, our tone should be gentle and soothing. Gossip, which includes spreading rumors about people as well as all forms of meaningless chitchat, serves no good purpose. We should give it up entirely, and say only that which is meaningful and life enhancing.

Speech is powerful. From ancient times and until now, speech has been a supreme catalyst, influencing sentient beings in myriad ways, both good and bad. Among the Buddha's twelve enlightened activities, it is his teaching—his speech—that has had and continues to have the greatest impact. The speech of great beings inspires others to seek and find beauty and light. The speech of neurotic beings sows confusion and discord. Positive speech can open minds. Negative speech can cut the heart into pieces. The teachings say that the wounds caused by negative speech are more painful and long lasting than those caused by arrows and spears. Therefore, we should always be thoughtful before we speak, making sure our words are governed by wisdom and kindness.

With regard to the mind—covetousness, which is incessant desire, should be dropped. Instead we should cultivate its opposite, which is contentment. Those who are content have true peace of mind, and that is the greatest wealth. Those who are not content, even if they are rich, are agitated. They never have enough and are always looking for more. As it is said, without contentment, even a billionaire is a pauper. Once upon a time, a man was transporting a sack of grain to his home. He stopped at an alehouse, put the sack down just outside the door, and entered. A monkey walked by, reached into the sack, and grabbed a handful of grain. He scampered up the nearest tree, and began eating. Suddenly a single kernel dropped to the ground. The monkey forgot all about the grain in his hand, swiftly descended the tree, and began searching frantically for the fallen kernel. At that moment the man came out of the alehouse. He saw what had happened, picked up a big stick and whacked the monkey. The monkey cried and ran off. He not only lost the handful of grain, but was wounded too. There are many stories like this one. The point is that we do not need so much for a good life, and once we obtain it, we should be content. We should also not be so foolish to gamble what we have. As the saying goes, why risk a mountain for a mustard seed?

It is also important to forsake anger in all its forms, and cultivate its opposite, which is loving-kindness. This is one of the principal messages of the Dharma. There are many benefits to cultivating loving-kindness. First of all, it heals bodies and minds. It removes obstacles. It draws new sentient beings towards us and strengthens already existing bonds. It makes us do good things in the world. It attracts the admiration of invisible beings, who respond by becoming our guardians and Dharma protectors. It insures that after death, we will be reborn in the upper realms. In short, when we cultivate loving-kindness we create happiness for ourselves and others, not only in the present, but far into the future.

Finally, we should abandon extreme views. There are many kinds of extreme views. The worst of these are beliefs that sanction and celebrate the harming and killing of beings. The following is a story which illustrates the results of such beliefs. In ancient times there lived a wealthy man who instituted and practiced animal sacrifice for the sake of his religion. When he was near death, he said to his son, "Promise me that you will continue this splendid tradition." And his son agreed. The years passed. One day, as the son was sharpening his blades, preparing for a sacrifice, an arhat who was gifted with clairvoyance sat down nearby to meditate. A few moments later, an animal being led to the sacrificial altar started making the most pathetic noises. The arhat looked at the animal and said, "What are you complaining about? It was you who set this in motion." The animal was the seventh incarnation of the father. In each of his previous six incarnations he had also taken birth as an animal, and was sacrificed by his son every time.

Extreme views manifest even among Dharma practitioners. For example, some of us who uphold all the vows feel this makes us more noble than others. Some of us who can maintain our minds in the natural state look down on those on a gradual path. This goes to show that beautiful spiritual qualities can become compromised, even corrupted, when taken over by the ego. The solution is to remember that realization and ego-inflation are two completely different things. What you can do well does not make you better than others. Remember humility, and respect all beings. Look directly at the "I" whenever it asserts itself, and let it go.

QUESTION: *Avoiding the ten non-virtuous actions and performing their opposites—how does this relate to vows and samayas of the Guru's body, speech, and mind?*

ANSWER: *When you avoid killing, stealing, and sexual misconduct, and cultivate their opposites, you fulfill the samaya of the Guru's body. When you avoid slander, lying, harsh speech, and gossip, as well as covetousness, violent thoughts, and wrong views, and cultivate their opposites, you fulfill the samayas of the Guru's speech and mind.*

QUESTION: *The Dzogchen view is freedom from hope and fear. But we need faith on the path to realize this view, and that implies at least some hope and fear. How does all this actually function when we are on the path?*

ANSWER: *If you want to drive from New York City to California, you need faith in yourself. You need a good vehicle and an efficient route. You also need ample provisions, as well as contingency plans should something go wrong. Once you have acquired all of this, you start your journey. You keep your eyes on the road and go with the flow of traffic. Should road conditions change, you make adjustments. You take time to rest and eat, you might stop from time to time to gaze at pleasant sites, but you do not linger in any place for too long. Hours and days pass. You cross one state line, then another. You notice the landscape is changing. These are undeniable signs of progress.*

Of course, until you finally arrive in California, hope and fear will manifest from time to time. Will I really make it? What if something goes wrong? It is important not to indulge these feelings—let them go. If something goes wrong, correct it; otherwise, just keep driving. Do this, and you will surely reach your destination. This is a metaphor for how to proceed on the spiritual path.

The teachings say that when you have traveled sufficiently—how long and how far depends on the individual—you will realize that there has never been a starting point, a path, or a destination. There has never even been a traveler. Simultaneous with this understanding is the end of hope and fear.

QUESTION: *When I encounter others during post-meditation, I do not see them nondually. They appear separate and different. What adjustments can I make?*

ANSWER: *First, keep your sense organs open and relaxed, and let sights, sounds, smells, tastes, tactile sensations, and thoughts come and go as they please. At the same time, continually recall that everything is the display of a divine mandala, or if your prefer, simply a dream, or a display of magic. Also, try not to prejudge or dictate to the people you encounter. Embrace them with love, be receptive to their uniqueness, and help them in any ways you can. If you cultivate these attitudes continuously, the walls that create separation and difference between yourself and others will crumble, and nondual vision—your own true nature—will reveal itself.*

QUESTION: *Is there a connection between ignorance, negative karma, and a natural disaster such as the tsunami of 2011?*

ANSWER: *Ignorance is non-recognition of the true nature, which manifests in the belief in "self" and "other." When you harbor this belief, it is inevitable that you will privilege yourself over others. This becomes the basis for ignorance, attachment, anger, arrogance, and jealousy. When you are motivated by these mental states and speak and enact them, you create negative karma. Similarly, when your words and deeds are motivated by love, compassion, and wisdom, you create positive karma.*

There are many types of karma, all of which can be categorized under two headings: individual and group. Individual karma is generated by a single person, who alone bears its consequences. Group karma is generated and experienced by a closely-knit collective of people whose connections extend over the course of one or more lifetimes. Karma is profound and complex. It works mysteriously within the life of a single individual. The mystery deepens considerably when two or more individuals are involved. Therefore, even though we may not know all the details, beings who share a common fate—including those affected by the tsunami—are karmically linked.

His Holiness Dudjom Rinpoche

CHAPTER 31

THE ONLY THREE THINGS TO CONSIDER

His Holiness says, "At all times, there are only three things to be considered: the Dharma, the Guru, and sentient beings." "At all times" means that you should always be in practice mode. Strive to release all distinctions between meditation and post-meditation.

The Dharma, the first of the three things to be considered, is the message of the Buddha. It is the path of spiritual awakening, grounded in unconditional love, compassion, and wisdom. Apply the essence of practice in life. If someone is struggling, respond with kind, supportive words. If you are wronged, forgive. If you are in a noisy environment, listen to the sounds without judging or analyzing them. All of this is Dharma. And of course whenever you do a formal practice session that begins with refuge and ends with the dedication of merit, that is Dharma too.

Dedicating the merit is very powerful. The same is true of making prayers of aspiration. What is the difference between the two? The great master Longchenpa explained it in the following way. When you dedicate the merit, you are sharing positive energy that has already been generated. It is like a gift. When you make prayers of aspiration, you are generating additional positive energy and directing it to the future. It is like a pledge. Both of these practices are sublime expressions of bodhichitta, which literally means the courage to attain enlightenment.

Bodhichitta is one of the extraordinary teachings of Buddha Shakyamuni. It is often called his "Lion's Roar." When a lion roars, the sound is so impressive and authoritative that all the other animals immediately become quiet and attentive. This "Lion's Roar" is the proclamation that all beings can grow spiritually, that each one can contribute greatly to the improvement of the world, and that there are no limits. This is a stirring message, wholly positive. Who could find fault with it?

We should arouse bodhichitta at the beginning and ending of every practice session. This is the teaching of Longchenpa and many other great masters. When you begin your session, open your heart and mind to embrace all beings, wishing them every manner of temporal and spiritual happiness. Vow to attain enlightenment in order to help them. Then, just before you end your session, dedicate the merit to them.

How does the dedication of merit work? The Buddha used the following example. When a drop of water falls on a beach, it quickly dries up, but when a drop of water falls in the ocean, it merges with the ocean and lasts forever. The drop of water symbolizes any positive action and the spiritual energy it contains. If you keep it for yourself, it will not last very long. But if you share it with all beings, it becomes part of the universe.

The great master Shantideva said that even an enormous amount of positive energy accumulated over aeons is fragile if you hoard it for yourself. A single act of anger on your part can destroy it all, as swiftly and easily as a gust of wind extinguishes the flame of a single candle. But when you share all your positive energy with all beings, it not only becomes indestructible, but actually increases.

There are three types of positive energy, or merit: 1) that which you generate yourself, 2) that which you witness others generating, and 3) that which has been, is being, and will be generated by all beings throughout space and time.

When it comes time to actually dedicate the merit, draw upon all three types of positive energy. Share this infinite treasury of spiritual wealth with your friends, family, and all beings. Pray that everyone enjoys long life, health, prosperity, and the swift fulfillment of all their good wishes, and that they ultimately realize enlightenment. When you do this, you are expanding and deepening your vision, and you are helping to reshape this world into the pure land that it has always been.

The second of the three things to consider is the Guru. The Guru is the spiritually awakened being with whom you have a profound karmic link. He or she knows your mind thoroughly and tailors the teachings for you in such a way as to speed up your spiritual progress. If you follow the Guru's instruction diligently and precisely you cannot fail.

The third of the three things to consider are sentient beings. Everything we think, say, and do for them should be governed by bodhichitta. Once again, there are two types of bodhichitta: aspirational and applied. Aspirational bodhichitta is related to mind and is therefore boundless. Applied or engaged bodhichitta, which pertains to words and deeds, is limited by our abilities and the receptivity of others, among other factors. Regarding aspirational bodhichitta, we should always include everyone in our prayers and practices. In terms of applied bodhichitta, we should do what we can to help others and strive to increase our current abilities, as well as develop new ones.

Enlightenment Stupa

CHAPTER 32

THE FOUR MODES OF LIBERATION AND SIGNS OF PROGRESS

The stronger your practice gets, the more spacious and attentive your mind becomes. Thoughts and emotions will still arise, however, and often seem more intense and real than ever. The situation is similar to what happens when you remove clutter from your house—the individual objects that remain stand out much more vividly. At this time it is important to reactivate mindfulness, alertness, and conscientiousness. Remember the instructions, apply them, and move forward. Do not believe in and follow thoughts and emotions. Keep letting go.

Your ability to let go will be perfected as you tune into what the Dzogchen teachings call the *Four Modes of Liberation*.

The first of the four modes is *yedrol*, which means "originally liberated." The term "originally" does not refer to that which occurred once, a long time ago; it refers to that which is eternal and fundamental. "Liberated" of course means "free." The message of *yedrol* is that your mind freely creates thoughts and emotions, and since this is entirely natural, nothing about it has to be changed.

The second mode of liberation is known as *rangdrol*. *Rangdrol* means "self-liberated." The message here is that just as thoughts and emotions arise naturally, they depart naturally. Once again, you do not need to add or subtract anything to this process.

The third mode is *cherdrol*, which means "liberated through bare attention." This means that simply by being relaxed and alert you will behold the truth of the first two modes. This requires some effort, because for a long time we have been fascinated by the meanings of thoughts and emotions. Be aware, and observe the workings of your mind with equanimity. You will see quite vividly that thoughts and emotions arise from the pure space of your mind, convey their message, and then dissolve back into that same space. All this takes place swiftly and seamlessly, like letters drawn on water.

The fourth and final mode, called *shardrol*, means "liberated upon arising." This is an expression of the deepening of your awareness and is the full flowering of the previous three modes. At this time thoughts and emotions arise less frequently, and when they do, they dissolve immediately.

The condensed message of the four modes of liberation is that your mind naturally and spontaneously generates thoughts and emotions, that these come and go freely in the open space of your mind, and that if you are alert, relaxed, and persevering, you will see this very clearly.

As the great Dzogchen masters always say, thoughts and emotions arise for practitioners and non-practitioners alike; the crucial difference lies in the way they are handled. Non-practitioners are impatient. They fixate on the meaning. They do not let thoughts and emotions complete their journey to emptiness. Dzogchen practitioners know that the meaning of a thought or emotion is just a temporary phase in what is essentially a journey of space within space.

What are the signs of progress on this path of letting go? First of all, you are less attached to everything. You are confident as well as humble. Difficult circumstances do not bother you so much, and you know you can handle them. Your ability to discern and manifest what others need for their worldly and spiritual well-being becomes quite strong; indeed, your mere presence is soothing to them. Boundaries of every kind dissolve. The universe becomes your home.

Machik Labdron

CHAPTER 33

THE FOUR DEMONS

The path to enlightenment is essentially a purification process. It can be likened to cleaning a long-neglected chimney or toilet. You must encounter and remove a great deal of encrusted intellectual and emotional filth, born from many lifetimes of bad habits.

When you practice Dzogchen, you become aware of your mind's innate openness and purity. At the same time, you experience the volatility of your negative karma. You see that your nature is enlightened. You also see the reasons you cannot sustain this recognition. All this happens swiftly, and can be extremely daunting. His Holiness says, "The great profundity of this Dharma carries obstacles with it in the same way that great profit goes together with great risk." For this reason, you must be on guard.

Wisdom Dakini Machik Labdron advises us to be aware of four demons: 1) intangible demons, 2) tangible demons, 3) exciting demons, and 4) the demon of grasping. These are manifestations of the karmic purification that occurs on this path. They are called "demons" because they are tricky, hard to resist, and potentially destructive.

Intangible beings belong to the invisible world. Generally only practitioners with a karmic connection to such beings will encounter them directly; the rest of us will not. His Holiness describes how such a meeting might occur: "At the place where you practice, spirits will show their forms and call you by name. Taking the guise of the Guru, they will make predictions."

Tangible demons, by contrast, are of this world, and will be experienced in one form or another by every practitioner. There are two types of tangible demons: physical and mental. The first includes disease, abuse from others, reversals of fortune, and natural disasters such as earthquakes and floods. The second includes hallucinations, nightmares, and wild, unprovoked mood swings. One common manifestation of this is a sudden disgust with spiritual practice.

Exciting demons are pleasant experiences; these can appear in worldly or spiritual ways. The former manifests as enticing sensory objects—whatever you are most attracted to. The latter can include visions and dreams of buddhas and bodhisattvas, recollecting past lives, reading the thoughts of others—there are many possibilities.

The fourth demon of grasping manifests the moment you believe in and hold on to any of the first three. If you submit to any of them you derail your spiritual progress and quickly get lost in the world of hope and fear. If you do not submit, there are no demons anywhere, just an ongoing flow of transient experience. For this reason, grasping is ultimately the only demon.

As you progress on this path, everything intensifies. Your most enduring thoughts and emotions erupt with greater force and in more extraordinary forms than ever. New thoughts and emotions burst forth as well. External circumstances will turn against you. You will feel as if you are under siege.

Do not be afraid—root yourself and apply all that you have learned. Pray to your root teacher and to the lineage masters. Arouse bodhichitta. Identify and experience the power of your awareness, and rest in it. Above all, keep releasing—the raging storms will pass, and your realization will be all the stronger for having weathered them. As His Holiness says, "Appearances will become insubstantial like mist. Confidence in the Guru and in his instructions will grow as never before."

Beware—every time you have attained a new level realization, your "I" will seek to appropriate it. "What a great yogi I have become!" Advanced practitioners, seduced by such thoughts, recreate the obstacles they have just overcome. It is therefore very important that you remain ever cognizant of the grasping demon. If a cat has nine lives, your "I" has nine million—and possibly more.

His Holiness says, "If bad circumstances that arise on the path are relatively easy to deal with, good circumstances present much greater difficulties." Bad circumstances are like getting a thorn in your foot—it hurts and you remove it at once. But good circumstances are quite another matter—you want to keep them.

Good circumstances manifest both temporally and spiritually. In the temporal domain, your income and reputation might increase and you will have much greater access to objects of desire. In the spiritual domain, your love, compassion, and wisdom will deepen and expand, and others will notice it. They will praise you, seek your company and counsel—they may even begin to call you "Guru." If you take any of this too seriously and for any length of time, your self-importance will grow. You will put more energy into preserving and augmenting your status, and less into your practice. For this reason good circumstances are known as "demons of distraction."

Do not yearn for good circumstances, and do not worry if they fade away. Remain attentive and continuously read your own mind. Again, be on he lookout for the grasping demon, and for thoughts like "I am great" and "I am better than others." If you believe in thoughts like these and highlight them you are moving in the wrong direction. As the great master Mipham Rinpoche taught, the clearest sign of realization is when genuine humility takes root in your being. Therefore, it is pointless to feed and indulge your ego.

His Holiness says, "Until the expression of your inner understanding has reached perfection, it is wrong to recount your experiences to everyone; so keep your mouth shut." One of the important tantric samayas is keeping secrets. Great masters are very hesitant about speaking of their realization or displaying their powers. In fact, they do so only when they know for certain that it will inspire and help others. The Buddha, Guru Padmasambhava, and all the great masters attained the unchanging state of egolessness suffused with unconditional compassion. We are not at that stage yet. Our egos are still very tricky and our compassion ebbs and flows, so we need to be very clear about our intentions. We may have completed long retreats, had visions and dreams of deities, and our experience of nonduality may be blazing, but before we share this information with others, we must first ask ourselves, "For what purpose?" Is it that we want to be seen by others as advanced practitioners? Do we secretly hope they will spread tales of our realization, so that our reputation increases far and wide? Or do we truly believe that by sharing this information with them, they will benefit? We should examine ourselves like this, and if we discover that our motivation is the least bit tainted by ego-clinging, it is better that we remain silent.

His Holiness says, "Do not belittle the gaining of merit through the cause and effect relationships of relative truth, deceiving yourself with mere words about emptiness." It is easy to proclaim the Dzogchen view, but to fully establish it as a way of life takes time and effort. Many practitioners, prematurely believing that they have attained this view, disregard the laws of cause and effect and completely lose their way, injuring themselves and others. Until we attain complete realization, we should continuously reflect on and practice the teachings on relative truth and absolute truth, while always uniting view and conduct.

His Holiness says, "Village ceremonies for the taming of demons and so on are performed in order to get food, so don't stay too long in populated places." This is far less of a problem in the West than in the East. In Tibet, for example, it is customary for families to invite monks, nuns, or ngakpas to their homes in order to perform ceremonies. For as long as the ceremony lasts—one, two, or three days and sometimes even longer—the family is expected to serve them the best food they can afford. Then, once the ceremony is complete, they are expected to give them a sizable donation. As it is said in *The Words of My Perfect Teacher* and elsewhere, many people get caught up in this way of life, and their motivation and discipline decay. They perform the ceremonies mechanically, becoming alert only when it is time to eat and collect their fees. Between practice sessions they lounge about and gossip about the family that is sponsoring them.

The purpose of these ceremonies is to remove obstacles to long life, health, and prosperity on both the worldly and spiritual levels, as well as to create auspicious circumstances for the future. The monks, nuns, and ngakpas who preside over these ceremonies should be focused solely on the welfare of their patrons and other beings and on correctly performing the rituals. Material concerns must be de-emphasized. And gossip is to be avoided at all times.

In general, all interactions with others should be free from hipocrasy. If you are seeking your own advancement, it should never be at someone else's expense. Whether you are at your job or at home, you should be kind, honest, and trustworthy, while mindfully keeping your words and deeds in accord with Dharma.

His Holiness also says, "Don't associate with negative people or with those whose views and actions are not in harmony with yours." If your ability to abide in the true nature is strong, you can associate with anyone. But until that time comes, you should exercise caution. Human beings influence each other for better and for worse. You should avoid, or at least seriously restrict your contact with people who are consistently under the sway of negative emotions and who lead unhealthy lives. And it is important to completely abstain from all destructive habits, such as smoking.

During the time of Buddha Shakyamuni, smoking did not exist, and so there was no prohibition against it. But the Buddha said that his Vinaya teachings should always be adapted to changing times and circumstances. Guru Padmasambhava predicted many times that people in future generations would become addicted to smoking, as well as to other toxic substances. His Holiness Dudjom Rinpoche himself published a small book on the dangers of smoking, which has been translated into English. Scientists have proven beyond doubt that smoking destroys health and shortens lifespans. And many of us have seen this for ourselves—we have witnessed friends and relatives get sick and die, in some instances long before their time, from lung cancer and other smoking-related diseases.

Alcohol should be consumed in moderation and as a samaya substance only. When taken in excess it distorts the mind, which can lead to very destructive behavior.

What happens when you drink too much? The teachings describe the process as follows. First, you become relaxed, and then your inhibitions peel away. You become talkative.

Your complexion reddens and you feel bold. By the time you are drunk, all sense of decorum is gone and your language and behavior become crude. You might get belligerent, challenge others, and start a brawl. A Tibetan folk saying describes this alcohol-induced bravado quite well—"During the day, a coward; at night, a great warrior."

The next day you wake up in a stupor. Your friends tell you what you did the night before and you can hardly believe it. You would like to hide for shame, but how can you hide from yourself?

If you continue down this path you can become addicted to alcohol. At this point your entire world revolves around drinking. You drain your finances, squander your talents, and ruin your health. You stop caring about others. Ultimately, you end up throwing your precious life away. And it is not only alcohol addiction that accomplishes this; drug abuse will do the same.

Alcohol and drugs are powerful substances. Even a highly advanced practitioner can lose mindfulness and be rendered helpless if he or she overindulges. The following story, which occurred during the time of Buddha, illustrates this quite well. Once upon a time, between the cities of Shravasti and Shambu, near the mountain called Chimvat Chawdy, there lived a husband and wife. They were very wealthy, but had no children. The husband desperately wanted a son. Towards this end he continually supplicated the sun, moon, and stars, and gave charitably to the poor. Finally, his prayers were answered, and a child was conceived. From that moment circumstances seemed to conspire against husband and wife. Many things went wrong; in particular, their wealth started to dwindle. But the husband was happy nonetheless. He said, "Whether the child is a boy or a girl I will name it Leong." Leong means "welcome."

A boy was born, but by this time his parents were in poverty, and many members of their extended family had become sick or had passed away. Then, before too long, the husband and wife themselves died.

None of the surviving relatives wanted to take care of the baby. They said, "Since the moment of his conception he has brought nothing but hardship and tragedy to our family. His father named him 'Welcome,' but he should really be called 'Unwelcome.'" And so Leong was left all alone in the world.

The years passed. By now Leong was in his early teens, and was living in Shravasti as a beggar. One day, as he was picking through garbage and crying, the Buddha gathered his students and deliberately walked in that direction. When Leong saw them approaching he was certain that they would mock him. But the Buddha welcomed him and said, "Come with us."

Leong went to Jetavan Grove and was ordained. He received teachings, practiced diligently, and because his karma was so ripe, he became an arhat very quickly. An arhat is someone who has defeated the ego and all the negative emotions. But despite Leong's having attained such a high realization, he remained an object of scorn, both within the spiritual community, as well as without. People still called him "Unwelcome," and gossiped about how he brought his family to ruin. The Buddha decided the time had come to glorify Leong, and to make his spiritual power known to the world.

Around this time a nearby village was being terrorized by a naga named Soname. Some villagers approached the Buddha, and pleaded with him to subdue Soname, but the Buddha did not immediately answer. A day or two later, the Buddha was sitting with Shariputra, Maudgalyaputra, and other great arhats. When the topic of subduing the naga came up, the Buddha gently looked at Leong. Leong immediately understood, "This is my time."

Not long after this, the Buddha gathered all of his students. He asked them, "Who among you will subdue the naga Soname?"

Leong was sitting far away, but clearly saw the Buddha looking at him. He quickly raised his arm, like an elephant king thrusting his trunk to the sky. Everybody was shocked, and started murmuring, "What is this? He must not know what he is doing." But the Buddha gave Leong his silent approval.

The next day Leong went on his mission. He went into Shravasti, obtained his food, and put it in his begging bowl. He did not eat right away, but instead walked to the spring where the naga resided. People had been avoiding that spot out of fear. When Soname saw Leong approaching, he thought, "Ah, here comes one of the new monks. He must not know my strength. I will have my way with him!" Leong sat down majestically by the spring, and ate his lunch. When he was finished he got up and slowly washed his begging bowl in the spring water.

Soname was enraged. This person had made the water dirty! Soname created a storm—the clouds darkened and there was a great rain, with thunder and lightning. Leong, in the meantime, was meditating on loving-kindness. Then, through his spiritual power, he summoned the naga, who was in the form of a snake, into his begging bowl. Leong quickly turned the bowl over and Soname was trapped. At that moment the sun burst from the clouds and was shining brightly. Leong said, "Let's go see my teacher." He took the snake in his begging bowl to the Buddha at Jetavan Grove. Word spread that he had subdued the naga. From that moment Leong was renowned as a great arhat.

One day Leong was invited to lunch by one of his father's old friends. This man was quite rich—he had over 500 horses on his farm—and was very honored to host such a great arhat. Beer was served with lunch, and Leong and his host drank it with great gusto. At the time the Buddha had not yet issued any prohibitions against alcohol. By the time Leong left his father's old friend, he was completely drunk. On his way back to Jetavan

Grove he collapsed by the side of the road, and there he lay, totally unconscious.

The Buddha and his students were just finishing lunch, and he deliberately led them along a different route to Jetavan Grove. Eventually they saw a monk sprawled by the roadside, his robes flapping in the breeze. "Who is this?" asked the Buddha. And everyone said, "It is Leong the arhat." The Buddha asked, "The same Leong who subdued the naga?" And everyone said, "Yes, the same one." Then the Buddha asked, "Do you think he can subdue a naga now?" All his students shook their heads no. "Such is the fault of alcohol," the Buddha continued. And from that moment on he prohibited it.

CHAPTER 34

INTEGRATING PREPARATION, THE MAIN PRACTICE, AND POST-MEDITATION

We have been following in the footsteps of His Holiness Dudjom Rinpoche, studying his precious words and receiving his blessings. Now, as our exploration of his *Mountain Retreat* draws to a close, let us review the three statements he made early on which outlined the three main topics of the text.

His Holiness started with: "The preparation—having cut the ties of grasping and clinging, how to purify one's own mind stream by keeping the mind turned toward the Dharma." Although by force of habit we see phenomena as relatively stable and independently existing, they are in fact ever changing and inseparable from perception. It is impossible to grasp and cling to that which is always moving, and just as importantly, there is also no need to do this—the entire universe and all that comes and goes within it is has never appeared anywhere else but within our minds.

We should not attach ourselves to any system of interpretation. Names, categorizations, and judgments are fabrications. All phenomena have been, currently are, and will always be perfect and pure, forever beyond the intellect. The Great Perfection is already the nature of everything. In this way, we should continually restrengthen our natural connection to the Dharma.

The second topic is: "The Main Practice—having cut misconceptions about the view, meditation, and action, how to accurately engage in the practice." His Holiness' *Mountain Retreat*, although small in size, is filled with pith instructions, or golden nuggets of essential advice. Truly, everything a diligent practitioner could ever need for his or her spiritual journey is contained within this text. Devotion and bodhichitta, awareness and continuous letting go—if we cultivate these as His Holiness teaches, our intellectual and emotional veils will be lifted and we will swiftly reawaken to the state of Buddha Samantabhadra.

Finally, we reach: "Post-Meditation—how to keep up the samayas and vows, and complete all the subsequent actions of this life with Dharma." Samayas and vows are not commands issued from some authority outside ourselves. They are not designed to invade our privacy or restrain our freedom. The entire purpose of samayas and vows is to keep our spiritual practice vibrant and on course. Remember, we are opening our minds and hearts to the full beauty of the universe, to all beings and to ourselves. To open is also to expose oneself to the unexpected, uncomfortable, and undesired. Samayas and vows enable us to anticipate and competently deal with all of this, and ultimately to transform it into fuel for our journey.

The great master Karma Chagme, writing in the beautiful, colloquial prose style for which he is renowned, uses the following example. "You are poor and starving, then someone shows you the gold that had been hidden beneath your kitchen floor. You now have the gold. But gold by itself will not fill your stomach." His Holiness Dudjom Rinpoche and other great masters have taught us that the universe and all beings are already enlightened. To know this is good, but if you leave it as such, all you have is a really excellent idea. Karma Chagme continues, "You must take that gold to market, and use it to buy barley. Then, in order to make tsampa, you have to clean, roast, and grind that barley." The great master is talking about transforming the excellent idea of universal enlightenment into a living reality through diligent practice.

To accomplish this swiftly, maintain your mind in its natural state. This is the essential teaching of the *Mountain Retreat*. The natural state is not in the past or in the future, but always here and now. It is not outside, but totally within. To experience it, ask yourself, "Where is the source of my mind?," "Who am I?," or if you prefer, simply gaze within your mind. As soon as you apply one of these techniques, you will behold an open, serene, wakefulness that is totally free from thoughts and emotions—that is the natural state. Once you have discovered it, the next step is to maintain it with gentle mindfulness.

The natural state is open and serene; at the same time it is like a vast cauldron bubbling with inexhaustible energy. The natural, spontaneous expression of this energy is the continuous coming and going of thoughts. Witness this, but do not interfere with or attach any importance whatsoever to what you are witnessing. Simply be aware, without hope, fear, or fixation. Precisely this is what is called "liberating," and "letting go."

At times you will be distracted by strong thoughts. When this occurs, direct your awareness to your heart center. For a short time rekindle your devotion to the buddhas and lineage masters, then once again ease your mind into its natural state. At other times your mind will become dull and tired. The solution here is the same—devotion. As His Holiness says, "Devotion is the single medicine which cures every disease."

When you are alone you can shout the PHET syllable, as taught by the great master Patrul Rinpoche in his famous Dzogchen teaching, *The Wise and Glorious King*. Shouting PHET instantly puts you in the natural state. It also wonderfully clarifies a dull and tired mind.

Another excellent practice for evoking and clarifying the natural state is this one: focus your eyes, gaze strongly into a bright blue sky, and send your next exhalation into space.

Make use of these practices. Keep your view strong, and be modest and humble. For inspiration, read the life stories of the great masters. Do not sell yourself short or make excuses—you are always stronger than your karma. Honor your worldly obligations, serve others, and make time for formal practice. Unite meditation and post-meditation, and keep releasing. Do this, and you will realize that enlightenment has always been your nature.

CHAPTER 35

SKILLFUL MEANS AND WISDOM

Just as a human being needs two legs to walk and a bird needs two wings to fly, a Dharma practitioner needs to cultivate skillful means and wisdom in order to grow spiritually. If we cultivate one without the other we will not get very far. If we cultivate both with enthusiasm and perseverance we will continually progress on the path and ultimately attain enlightenment. The essence of skillful means is compassion, devotion, and everything else that is positive. The essence of wisdom is the Dzogchen state; that is, the mind ungoverned by thoughts and emotions.

The great master and future Buddha Maitreya said that if we perform the following ten virtuous Dharma activities, our skillful means practices will become very powerful. 1) The first of these is reproducing Dharma texts. In ancient times, this was very labor intensive. Materials were hard to acquire, everything had to be written by hand, and as a result Dharma texts were rare. Today, with the advent of modern publishing technologies, Dharma texts are far easier to come by. But regardless of the circumstances of production, the teachings of the Buddha and the great masters are highly beneficial to beings; thus, making them available in textual form is a virtuous activity in any era. 2) The second virtuous activity, as taught by Maitreya, is making offerings to temples, statues, texts, and any other representation of the Three Jewels. 3) The third one is being generous to sentient beings. What is the difference between making offerings and being generous? Both making offerings and being generous involve giving. The difference lies in what is given—the Three Jewels receive our devotion, and sentient beings receive our compassion. 4) The fourth virtuous activity is chanting the teachings. As mentioned earlier, in Tibet, as well as in other Buddhist countries, monks and other qualified individuals are sponsored by families to read Dharma texts in their entirety, in order to promote temporal and spiritual happiness. 5) The fifth virtuous activity is memorizing the teachings. The sixth, seventh, and eighth are 6) explaining, 7) listening to, and 8) contemplating the teachings. 9) The ninth is putting the teachings into practice. 10) And the tenth is meditation. These are the ten virtuous Dharma activities as taught by Maitreya.

The buddha and bodhisattva Avalokiteshvara gave a similar teaching. He too advocates the performance of ten virtuous Dharma activities. As Avalokiteshvara is much beloved in Tibet, this teaching is widely practiced by the Tibetan people. The first three activities are sponsoring and creating representations of 1) enlightened body, 2) speech, and 3) mind in the form of statues, texts and teachings, and stupas. 4) The fourth one is protecting the lives of others. 5) The fifth is financing, building, and maintaining roads, bridges, and hospitals, as well as other public works. The sixth and seventh are 6) making offerings and 7) being generous. 8) The eighth is keeping temples, shrines, and articles of religious faith clean, as well as our own homes. 9) The ninth is circumambulating temples, stupas, and other objects of veneration—this is a very popular practice in Tibet.

10) And the tenth virtuous activity is good conduct. Whenever we perform any of these activities, we should do so with the wish that all beings attain enlightenment. Avalokiteshvara said, "Those who practice like this are my beloved children, and they will meet me in Dewachen the moment they leave their bodies."

When we perform virtuous activities, our positive energy and ability to help others increases. When we abide in the nonconceptual Dzogchen state, our minds become totally open and pure. This is how to practice the unity of skillful means and wisdom. As our practice matures, we will roam freely on the journey of life and death, happy and without regret. We will be like the great masters who gazed like lions, leapt like tigers, and flew away like garudas.

It is important to recollect and appreciate our good fortune—this is also a skillful means practice. We are connected to these profound teachings, as well as to the great masters who have actualized and selflessly shared them throughout time. We live in a beautiful country where access to the teachings and teachers and the freedom to practice are unrestricted, and where the necessities and even the comforts of life are relatively easy to obtain. As individuals, each one of us is intelligent, capable, and to a large degree free. We have time to listen to, contemplate, and practice the Dharma; we can thrive and grow. By contrast, many people around the world are denied basic human rights, including freedom of religion. Many have to work at difficult, tedious jobs for long hours simply to survive. This is not to say that this country or any other is perfect, or that those of us who live here do not experience hardship. There is room for improvement on every level. We should not ignore this, but at the same time we should not fixate on what is wrong when so much is right. Our lives are mostly good. We are filled with and surrounded by light. Let us make use of it, deepen and expand it, and share it with others.

Padampa Sangye

CHAPTER 36

THE EVER-PRESENT GROUND

The path to enlightenment is grounded in devotion and bodhichitta. Devotion is faith in and loyalty to your spiritual potential and to the guides and inspiration that are leading you to its actualization—including the Buddha, Dharma, and Sangha, Guru Padmasambhava and the lineage masters, as well as the teachings in both their theoretical and practical aspects. Bodhichitta is the process of opening your own heart and mind to the hearts and minds of others, as well as fully developing your abilities, so that you will be an ever-active force of good in this life and in lives to come.

Along with devotion and bodhichitta, it is important to acknowledge and embrace impermanence. Impermanence means phenomena are constantly changing, and that life passes quickly and ends in death. Death is powerful. It is the complete dislocation of everything you know. And death is coming—for many beings, it will come today.

Although reflecting on impermanence may at first seem morbid, if you persist in it you will discover that it is truly helpful. A good understanding of impermanence frees you from attachment. What is yours is yours for only a very short time—this is the way of nature. When you embrace this you will appreciate whatever comes your way, and you will be able accept its transformation and ultimate departure with grace.

A complementary practice to reflecting on impermanence is to see everything as a dream. When you dream, you are a subject interacting with a seemingly objective world. When you awaken you realize that whatever took place in that dream actually happened solely within your mind. The world of waking experience is similar to a dream in that it seems to exist objectively. But when you examine it closely, you realize it is an uninterrupted flow of sights, sounds, tastes, smells, tactile sensations, and thoughts. Like a dream, it is completely your own experience, and entirely within your mind.

A dream is also not tied to or dependent on what in waking hours are believed to be truths and facts. You can be a different being in your dreams—you can even be a tree or a mountain. You can journey forward and back in time, visit different world-systems, dance in the sky. Waking experience can be like that too, except that when we are awake we strongly believe in boundaries and limitations.

Whatever you are doing and experiencing, say to yourself as often as you can, "This is a dream, and I too am a dream." This simple practice will help you realize the unity of the world and your mind, and will open you to the infinite potential of each and every moment. If you keep practicing like this, your commitment to conventional truths and facts will change. The duality dream will end, and the enlightenment dream will begin.

We have already discussed meditation posture, but here we will explore it from another angle. Many great masters say you should arrange your body so that it is "crossed like woven fabric, straight as an arrow, bent like a hook, and tight like a bronze sword." 1) The first of these, "crossed like woven fabric" refers to sitting with your legs in the full vajra, half vajra, or basic crossed-legged position; The half vajra is also known as the "bodhisattva posture" in Tibet. 2) "Straight as an arrow" means keeping the spinal cord straight up. 3) "Bent like a hook" means your chin should tilt slightly in and down, so that your neck is aligned with the rest of your spine. 4) "Tight like a bronze sword" refers to contracting your abdomen slightly up and in.

When you sit with your back in a vertical position, it opens the central channel. When you tilt your chin slightly forward and down, it slightly closes the two side channels. When you contract your abdomen slightly up and in, it brings the two side channels closer to the central channel. This is a very auspicious arrangement, which pacifies mental turbulence and enables you to experience the deep peace of your mind, as well as its great energy and blissfulness.

As the teachings say, when the body is balanced, the channels are balanced; when the channels are balanced, the winds are balanced; and when the winds are balanced, the mind is balanced. Therefore, once you have arranged your body in this meditation posture, keep it—be still and stable like a mountain. Also, keep your eyes relaxed and perfectly still. This will keep discursive thought to a minimum, and will allow the beautiful qualities of your mind to blaze forth with even greater range and intensity.

These four aspects of proper meditation posture are of course included in the *Seven Postures of Buddha Vairochana*. If you can sit comfortably in this position, that is excellent; but if your physical condition does not permit it, make adjustments as needed.

The next foundation of good practice is to continually cultivate the two Vajrayana stages: 1) creation stage and 2) completion stage. Cultivating these two stages will help you reawaken swiftly to the true nature of reality, as it is. By practicing the creation stage you realize the purity and perfection of the entire universe and all the phenomena it contains. By practicing the completion stage you realize that the universe and all the phenomena it contains are transient experiences, which occur nowhere else but within your mind, and that your mind is inconceivable. During formal meditation sessions the creation and completion stages are kept distinct and performed in sequence. But as your practice matures you come to realize that they are one and the same.

At the end of every meditation session, as well as whenever you perform or witness a virtuous deed, dedicate the merit. Share the positive energy with all beings, wishing them every manner of happiness and prosperity. It is best to perform the dedication free from all notions of yourself as the doer, and others as the recipients.

When difficult circumstances arise, let them go, Dzogchen style. Do not name, judge, or wrestle with what arises—simply witness. When this is difficult, you can use other methods. Pray to Guru Padmasambhava and the lineage masters for assistance. Follow the example of the great master Shantideva, who said, "I accept all obstacles and hardships as opportunities to practice bodhichitta." Be patient, and remember that no situation, good or bad, is forever—change is coming. The main thing is to apply the teachings at once, and to persevere. If you do so you will purify negative karma and become spiritually stronger.

We should take and apply our good practice energy with us no matter where we go or what we do. The is the essence of post-meditation. We should be mindful of spoken and unspoken codes of good behavior, and try our best to read the nuances of each situation. There is a time for action, and a time to rest. When it is appropriate, we should not hesitate to apologize and forgive. Life is far too precious and fleeting to create and harbor ill feelings. The great master Padampa Sangye said, "Oh, Tingri villagers! Our gathering is like a dream—it will soon disperse."

Mindful of the words of this great master, with loving-kindness and non-attachment in our hearts and minds, let us make the most of this life and our time together.

QUESTION: *Can you give us a condensed explanation of how to practice Dzogchen meditation?*

ANSWER: *Be natural, relaxed, and carefree. Open your mind and your other five senses. Do not search for anything, and do not prevent or block anything either. Whatever arises is a pure movement and already free. You do not have to add or subtract anything. Rest wide-awake in the face of whatever arises—this alone is sufficient.*

Whenever a powerful thought or emotion arises, do not suppress or analyze it. Let it come, let it be, and let it go—this is the essence of the four modes of liberating that we discussed earlier. Also, be aware of what in Tibet is called namtog ongyur, *or "crawling thoughts." These are gentle, subtle, at times almost imperceptible thoughts and emotions, which move like shadows through your mind and which function like lullabies. What happens when a small child listens to a lullaby? She falls asleep.*

Do not get carried away by thoughts and emotions, whether powerful or gentle. At the same time, do not consider them wrong; they are natural manifestations of your mind's boundless power. There has never been a time when your mind was not manifesting thoughts and emotions. Your mind is like the ocean, and thoughts and emotions are like the ocean's waves. Both the ocean and its waves are of a single substance, and they cannot be separated. The same is true of your mind, and thoughts and emotions. If you relax and witness and do not interfere, you will see this very clearly. In seeing this, you will be free.

QUESTION: *How does Prajnaparamita compare to Dzogchen?*

ANSWER: *The great masters say that Prajnaparamita and Dzogchen share the identical view and result—great emptiness—but use different methods to realize it. The Prajnaparamita way is to first carefully scrutinize external phenomena and establish their intrinsic emptiness. Only at that point does one proceed internally, to the mind. The Dzogchen way is internal right away—mind itself is the path. Prajnaparamita is primarily an analytical path, whereas Dzogchen is primarily yogic. Of course, analysis is not wholly absent in Dzogchen. Questions such as "Where is my mind?" and "Who am I?" are utilized, but only briefly, and only to cut through the maze of thoughts and emotions which cover the nature of mind. In the final analysis, Dzogchen is a swifter and more direct path than Prajnaparamita, although either one will lead you to enlightenment.*

During this discussion we have been speaking exclusively of Dzogchen Trekcho. We have not mentioned Dzogchen Togal. While Trekcho leads you to the state beyond conceptions, Togal unveils the infinite power and creativity of that state. Many great masters have said other systems or traditions of meditation cannot do this, not even Mahamudra. Togal is supremely unique.

CHAPTER 37

PREPARING FOR DEATH AND TOGAL

Good Dzogchen practitioners do not have to prepare for death. They know that whatever happens is the display of their own infinite minds. Therefore, when death arrives they simply restrengthen their awareness; then, with great confidence, they release their illusory bodies and active mental states into the sphere of dharmakaya, and effortlessly move on to the next stage.

Those of us who have not attained such realization must prepare for death. We should reflect on the fact that our lives have never been static, not even for a moment, but rather have been the expression of constant change. We took birth, grew older, went through many different experiences, and now the time has come for body and mind to separate. There is nothing unnatural or unusual about it—in dying we simply complete one cycle of impermanence, so that another one can dawn. As we contemplate these matters, we should abide in the natural state, and not allow ourselves to be distracted by fear and other emotions.

As His Holiness says, as death approaches we should free ourselves from any remaining attachments. We came into this world with nothing, and we should depart the same way. If there is time, we should distribute all of our belongings to others. Otherwise, we should give everything to Amitabha, Guru Padmasambhava, and Avalokiteshvara in the form of a mandala offering. Then we should pray, "May this act of generosity bring great benefit to all beings." After praying, we should release all connections to what we have given away. What was ours belongs to others now, and is no longer our concern.

At that point you should form the following thought. "Soon I will be entering the dharmakaya state. The lights that I will see are manifestations of sambhogakaya. It is all the display of my own mind." Then reestablish your close connection to Buddha Amitabha, who is the embodiment of all enlightened beings, and release yourself into thought-free, naked awareness. Simply by maintaining your mind in this state, you will attain enlightenment the moment you release your body, without having to encounter the illusory tricks of the bardo.

These instructions, as well as those given throughout the *Mountain Retreat*, are related mainly to Trekcho. As we have said, Trekcho is the view and meditation of self-liberation, where we simultaneously abide in pure awareness and allow all sensory experiences to come and go by themselves. It is the supreme method to recognize the infinite openness and purity of our own minds.

His Holiness Dudjom Rinpoche and all the great Dzogchen masters have taught that once we have achieved good stability in Trekcho, we should practice Togal. Actually, these are not two separate practices so much as sequential, ultimately seamless ways to completely access the extraordinary richness of our minds. As I just said, through Trekcho we reveal our mind's infinite openness; through Togal we reveal the infinite power, or creative energy of that openness. In this way Trekcho corresponds to dharmakaya, Togal to sambhogakaya.

Trekcho establishes us in the deep, unshakeable understanding that all experience is personal experience and that the universe is inseparable from ourselves. It anchors us in the great perfection of the here and now and liberates us from all speculation and anxiety regarding the success and failure of our spiritual endeavors. This is needed before beginning Togal practice, otherwise the visionary experiences of Togal will evoke all kinds of intellectual and emotional interference, and our progress will be obstructed, or possibly derailed. This means that when our Trekcho practice is stable, Togal is very easy to accomplish.

The actual practice of Togal begins by cultivating the *Three Relaxing Moods*. These three moods are non-busyness of body, speech, and mind as a way of life. Thus, they should be cultivated not only during formal meditation sessions, but during post-meditation as well. 1) The body mood is to reduce all mundane physical activity. 2) The speech mood is to reduce all unnecessary talk. 3) The mind mood is to reduce all intellectualizing and emoting, and to abide in a state of love, peace, and joy totally blended into space.

Togal practice should take place in a spacious environment. This can be outdoors or indoors, depending on what is most convenient. Begin by arousing devotion and bodhichitta, and then abide for a time in the Trekcho view. The next step is to arrange your body into one of the three special Togal postures: 1) the lion, 2) elephant, or 3) sage. Each posture has a specific gaze, which corresponds to the three kayas. In the lion posture, you look upward. This is known as the dharmakaya gaze. In the elephant posture, you look straight ahead. This is the sambhogakaya gaze. In the sage posture, you look downward, which is the nirmanakaya gaze. Once you have arranged your posture and gaze, remain quiet and still. Breathe gently and naturally, and let your mind rest in utter openness.

Practicing like this, we ignite what the Dzogchen tradition calls the *Four Lamps*. The four lamps are:

1) the *Lamp of Space*
2) the *Lamp of the Long-Distance Lasso that Catches Everything*
3) the *Lamp of Self-Born Awareness*
4) the *Lamp of Empty Spheres and Beams of Light*

1) THE *LAMP OF SPACE* refers to the object of your eyes. Whether you are gazing upward, straight ahead, to the left or right, or downward, do not focus on a solid object, but only into empty space.

2) THE *LAMP OF THE LONG-DISTANCE LASSO THAT CATCHES EVERYTHING* refers to the eyes themselves. Do not move them; keep them focused and alert.

3) THE *LAMP OF SELF-BORN AWARENESS* refers to the Trekcho state—your own pure awareness, free of thoughts and emotions.

4) THE *LAMP OF EMPTY SPHERES AND BEAMS OF LIGHT* refers to visionary experiences, which take the form of circles, triangles, lines, and other shapes which randomly dart about and come and go. Although these visionary experiences appear to be externally existing, you are actually projecting them through your eyes into the space in front of you. They are effortless manifestations of your sambhogakaya mind. As we mentioned earlier, it is very important not to think about or become emotionally attached to these visions, otherwise you will create obstacles for yourself. Simply witness them in a carefree way.

The fourth lamp corresponds to the first of the *Four Visions of*

Togal, known as *Direct Realization of the True Nature*. To progress still further, continue to arouse devotion and bodhichitta at the beginning of each practice session—in particular, pray to the lamas of your lineage with great longing. Then adopt the posture of your choosing, fix your gaze appropriately, and relax in the natural state. If you practice like this, the second and third visions—known respectively as *Increasing Experience* and *Awareness Reaching Full Measure*—will arise. These two visions are the natural, inevitable development of the first one. This means that what you saw earlier becomes increasingly larger and more intricate and stable. In time your entire visual field will be saturated with light. Once again, know that all this light emanates from you. It is you.

Do not cling, but keep practicing, and you will arrive at the fourth and final Togal vision, which is known as *Exhaustion of Phenomena*. At this time, all duality ceases. Dualistic conceptions are totally extinguished. You have reached the state that is beyond hope, fear, and fixation, suffused with infinite compassion. If a thousand buddhas suddenly appeared, you would not be excited. If a thousand enemies appeared, you would not be afraid. The fourth vision is the perfect union of Trekcho and Togal—complete and total enlightenment. At that moment, you become what you have always been.

Lama Chimed Namgyal

CHAPTER 38

EPILOGUE

For one month we have come together in this beautiful retreat center of Padma Samye Ling, studying and practicing the teachings of Buddha Shakyamuni, Guru Padmasambhava, and the great masters. In particular, we have been exploring His Holiness Dudjom Rinpoche's *Mountain Retreat.* If we take His Holiness' instructions to heart and practice them with great enthusiasm, we can realize the true nature of our minds, inseparable from the great perfection of the universe, in this very lifetime.

His Holiness Dudjom Rinpoche was the combined reincarnation of many realized beings. He was the regent of Guru Padmasambhava and the master of masters. One of the greatest scholars, siddhas, and tertons in Tibetan Buddhist history, His Holiness was and is renowned throughout the world. Many people spoke about his amazing powers and they were indeed impressive, but what impressed me most was that he was so profoundly humble and down to earth. Every one of us is deeply connected to this sublime master and can draw upon his blessings at any time.

This place where we have gathered, Padma Samye Ling, is the natural manifestation of the inspiration and blessings of many realized beings—in particular my beloved brother, our great teacher, Khenchen Palden Sherab Rinpoche. I remember how he spent many hours, day after day, in this shrine room, designing and overseeing—down to the finest detail—the creation of all the beautiful mural paintings which now adorn its walls. Khen Rinpoche's spiritual power abides in all of the sacred images at Padma Samye Ling, as well as on the grounds and in the sky, water, and wind. Truly, his love, compassion, and wisdom are everywhere.

My dearest father, Lama Chimed Namgyal, has been a role model and a great source of inspiration for as long as I can remember. His profound humility and devotion always touched my heart. People wanted to serve him as the great lama that he was, but he always preferred a simple life. He made his own soups, sat on the floor, and practiced non-stop. He gave freely to others without any expectation, and when he died he did so in the manner of a great Dzogchen yogi.

I consider myself extremely fortunate to have sat at the feet of His Holiness Dudjom Rinpoche, Khenchen Palden Sherab Rinpoche, and Lama Chimed Namgyal. In their presence and in their honor, from the depths of my heart, I thank you all.

DEDICATION OF MERIT

May the victory banner of the fearless teachings of the Ancient Tradition be raised.
May the victorious drum of the teaching and practice of Dharma resound in the ten directions.
May the lion's roar of reasoning pervade the three places.
May the light of unequalled virtues increase.

May all the temples and monasteries,
All the readings and recitations of the Dharma flourish.
May the Sangha always be in harmony,
And may their aspirations be achieved.

At this very moment, for the peoples and nations of the earth,
May not even the names disease, famine, war, and suffering be heard.
But rather may pure conduct, merit, wealth, and prosperity increase,
And may supreme good fortune and well-being always arise.

APPENDICES

GLOSSARY

The **ABHIDHARMA** is the third of the Three Baskets of the Buddha's teachings, the other two being the Vinaya and Sutras. The Abhidharma includes teachings on Buddhist psychology and logic, descriptions of the universe, the steps on the path to enlightenment, descriptions of the different kinds of beings, and refutations of mistaken beliefs.

ABSOLUTE TRUTH refers to the ultimate nature of the mind and the true nature of all phenomena, the state beyond all conceptual constructs, and beyond arising, dwelling, and ceasing.

ARHAT literally means "foe-destroyer." This term refers to beings who have conquered their "enemies"—the afflictive emotions—by realizing the non-substantiality of the self. By doing so they are free from suffering, but they do not achieve complete buddhahood until they realize the non-substantiality of all phenomena as well.

ASHVAGOSHA (c. 80-150 C.E.) was an Indian Buddhist philosopher and poet. He is considered to be both the father of Sanskrit drama and the greatest poet in India prior to Kalidasa.

The ***AVATAMSAKA SUTRA***, or *Flower Ornament Sutra* is one of the most influential Mahayana texts, particularly in East Asia. It describes the interdependence of all phenomena, the path to enlightenment, and a universe of infinite realms which mutually contain one another.

AWARENESS, when used by masters of Dzogchen, means consciousness devoid of ignorance and dualistic fixation. It is one of the English translations of what is known in Tibetan as rigpa. It refers to the mind that is unfettered by and independent of preconceptions and free from the need to structure experience.

BARDO means intermediate state. Khenpo Tsewang Dongyal Rinpoche says that bardo is synonymous with "dream." There are generally six bardos listed, of which the most commonly referred to is the state between death and the next rebirth. The six bardos are:

1) the ground bardo of the natural condition
2) the meditation bardo of luminosity
3) the dream bardo of deluded experience
4) the death bardo of disturbed elements
5) the dharmata bardo of spontaneous presence
6) the karmic bardo of becoming

BODHICHITTA literally means the "mind of enlightenment." Relative bodhichitta is the wish to attain buddhahood for the sake of all sentient beings by practicing the path of love, compassion, and wisdom. Absolute bodhichitta recognizes that all beings are primordially enlightened; there is no liberator, no liberated, and no action of liberation since nothing ever moves from the absolute space of the dharmadhatu, or rigpa. Resting in this great immovable space is ultimate bodhichitta.

BODHISATTVA literally means "courageous one for enlightenment." A bodhisattva is an advanced Mahayana practitioner who traverses the five paths and ten bodhisattva levels. Such a practitioner is so committed to working for the benefit and welfare of others that he or she chooses to remain in samsara in order to bring all beings to complete enlightenment.

BUDDHA is one who has completely awakened from the fundamental ignorance of the two obscurations and developed unceasing pristine cognition of buddha-nature. Having cultivated every positive quality to its utmost limit, buddhas have traversed the bodhisattva levels and eliminated all obscurations to true knowledge. Thus, they enjoy the five fruitional aspects of a buddha's body, speech, mind, qualities, and activities, or the "five wheels of inexhaustible adornment." Buddha Shakyamuni is the buddha of this era, but innumerable buddhas of the past have shown the way to enlightenment, and innumerable buddhas will teach the way to enlightenment in the future.

CHETSUN SENGE WANGCHUK (eleventh to twelfth centuries) was a great Nyingma yogi and Dzogchen adept who attained the transcendental wisdom rainbow body. His last testament is as follows:

> Amazing that I, madman Senge Wangchuk,

Exhausted karmic winds, while wisdom bloomed.
Freed from the sphere of the five gates of
unknowing,
I have entered the sphere of luminous self-
awareness.
Now that the three doors' illusions have
shattered
How pitiful is all of illusion's game,
And as the knots of confused experience have
been cut,
How tiring is so-called concentration.
Now that illusions dawn as wisdom,
All deceptive phenomena are pure appearances,
And as they have all melted into space,
Nothing whatsoever, yet everything manifests.
Amazing, amazing, the kindness of the Guru.
Amazing, these words at the moment of passing,
the essential state,
Are the heart placed fresh in the palm, nothing else.
May these final words appear at the end of this age.

CLARITY refers to the power of the mind—its wakeful, knowing, and expressive nature.

COMPLETION STAGE DISSOLUTION is one of the "two stages" of Vajrayana practice, the other being the "creation stage." The completion stage focuses primarily on the vajra mind through one of two techniques: 1) the completion stage with characteristics and 2) the completion stage without characteristics. Examples of the first include Tummo, Dream Yoga, Phowa, Bardo, and other practices, also known as "skillful means practices." By visualizing and meditating on the actual, inherent qualities within our body, including our channels, winds, and essence elements, we discover great bliss-emptiness, the absolute Guru Padmasambhava. In all these practices, we hold, visualize, and concentrate on something. In the completion stage without characteristics, we don't concentrate on anything but simply rest in the fresh, present state and behold the panoramic view of outer and inner phenomena without any boundaries. Examples of this include the Dzogchen practices of Trekcho and Togal.

CREATION STAGE VISUALIZATION is one of the "two stages," the other being the "completion stage." The creation stage is related to Mahayoga, in which everything is seen as the indestructible body, speech, and mind of enlightenment, or the "three vajra states." Creation stage practice can be generally divided into 1) visualization and 2) mantra recitation. After we establish the visualization of the deities, we recite their mantra. In Vajrayana, when we visualize our environment and ourselves as enlightened, we're bringing out our inner, self-born awareness wisdom without being disturbed by duality and habitual patterns. We're discovering the splendid qualities of our inner primordial wisdom, which then shines out through our body and speech. Our body becomes primordial wisdom form and our speech becomes primordial wisdom sound.

DEDICATION OF MERIT is the last of the "three excellences" of authentic Dharma practice, in which a practitioner dedicates the merit generated by performing virtuous activities to the complete enlightenment of all sentient beings without partiality. This is the expression of a practitioner's compassion, love, and concern for the welfare of infinite parent beings. The other two excellences include 1) beginning practice by cultivating the vast motivation of bodhichitta, and 2) engaging in practice with one-pointed concentration, free from dualistic fabrications, while abiding in the recognition of the true nature.

DEVOTION is the root of all accomplishment, and practice of the Vajrayana is impossible without it. The three stages of devotion are 1) "initial, interested devotion," 2) "devotion of intense longing," and 3) "final devotion of unshakable certainty." A variation of these three types of devotion or faith is described by Longchenpa: "Generally, three types of faith are discussed in the scholastic tradition: lucid faith, desirous faith, and the faith of conviction. 1) The first entails a lucid frame of mind that arises in reference to the Three Jewels." 2) The second concerns the desire to take up the Three Jewels very closely in the heart and develop a clear sense of the four renunciation thoughts. And 3) "the third involves having conviction in the principle of karmic causality."

DHARMA. The Sanskrit word Dharma has about ten different meanings, but here it refers to the teachings of Buddha Shakyamuni. In general, there are two aspects of the Buddhadharma: 1) transmission, or teachings that are actually given; and 2) the Dharma of realization, or the stages that are attained by applying the teachings. What distinguishes the Dharma as such is the presence of "four seals" or "four marks" that separate worldly teachings from transcendent ones. These are often given as follows: 1) "all compounded things are impermanent," 2) "all afflictive emotions are of the nature of suffering," 3) "all phenomena are empty and devoid of a self-identity," and 4) "nirvana is peace," or "nirvana is beyond extremes."

The ***DIAMOND SUTRA*** is a renowned Mahayana text emphasizing the practice of non-abiding and non-attachment.

DHARMAKAYA is the infinite, open, all-encompassing, all-inclusive, inconceivable nature of the mind, known commonly in Buddhism as "emptiness." It is inseparable from sambhogakaya and nirmanakaya. Sambhogakaya is the knowing capacity of mind, its radiance and power. Nirmanakaya is mind's constant erupting, its ceaseless play, the constant flow of thoughts and emotions.

Khenpo Tsewang Dongyal Rinpoche, in his "Tissue Terma," says,

> "In essence,
> Dharmakaya is primordial emptiness.
> Samoghogakaya is radiant self-luminosity.
> Nirmanakaya is the unceasing radiant activity of mind.
> Whoever relies on this completes the realization of the Primordial Buddha.
> This is the heart essence teaching of Samantabhadra.
> How wonderful."

DHARMAKIRTI (c. sixth to seventh centuries) was one of the greatest philosophers and logicians in Buddhist history. His magnum opus, the *Seven Treasuries of Valid Cognition*, was hugely influential, and continues to be studied to this day.

DUALITY refers to the ordinary perceptual framework of unenlightened beings where mind is seen as "I" and external phenomena are seen as "other." It refers to our strong tendency to name, analyze, judge, and rank what we see, hear, smell, taste, touch, and think and then to live with this as a basis for all of our experiences. In simple terms, duality means believing in and relying on thoughts and emotions.

The ***DUDJOM TERSAR NGONDRO*** is a renowned set of Vajrayana preliminary practices discovered as termas by the great master and crazy wisdom adept Dudjom Lingpa, as well as by his immediate reincarnation, His Holiness Dudjom Rinpoche.

DZOGCHEN, also known as Atiyoga, and translated as Great Perfection or Great Completion, is the body of teachings within the ninth and highest yana of the Nyingma school. Dzogchen teaches how to recognize and abide in the nature of the mind, and that the nature of the mind and the nature of the universe are inseparable. With this understanding one is free from hope and fear, acceptance and rejection.

EMPTINESS refers to the ultimate nature of both mind and external phenomena. All phenomena of the universe—all sights, sounds, smells, tastes, tactile sensations, and thoughts—are open, fluid, and totally beyond the intellect. No matter how hard we try, phenomena can never be qualified or quantified in any ultimate sense.

FABRICATIONS are the stories and fantasies—they can take the form of rules and facts—that we weave about ourselves and our world based on thoughts and emotions.

The **FIRST KHYENTSE**, Jamyang Khyentse Wangpo, Terchen Pema Osel Dongak Lingpa (1820-1892) was an emanation of King Trisong Deutsen, Vimalamitra, and many other masters, as well as being the body reincarnation of Jigme Lingpa. He was a great visionary, siddha, and scholar, the lord of all tertons, as well as their complete embodiment, and a master of masters in whom all the lineages of Tibetan Buddhism found—and continue to find—their confluence. Along with the First Jamgon Kongtrul Rinpoche, he was the co-founder of the Rime non-sectarian movement in the nineteenth century and saved many teaching and practice lineages from extinction. Due to his tremendous realization, he was able to recover many lineages that had been lost over time, and is therefore the father of the nineteenth-century Tibetan renaissance, the lord of the seven entrusted transmissions.

FIVE DHYANI BUDDHAS are Vairochana, Akshobhya-Vajrasattva, Ratnasambhava, Amitabha, and Amoghasiddhi. They represent the five aspects of primordial wisdom: 1) infinite openness and nonduality, 2) clarity and precision, 3) equanimity, 4) perfect discernment, and 5) action that is effortless, spontaneous, and perfect.

GAMPOPA (1079-1153), is equally well known as Dakpo Lhaje, the physician from the Dagpo region of southern Tibet. He was one of Milarepa's most famous students. His brilliant synthesis of Atisha's Kadam teachings, along with Tilopa's Mahamudra, helped catalyze the institutionalization of the Kagyu lineage. Except for the Shangpa Kagyu, all the different Kagyu schools originated from or were transmitted by his disciples.

GRASPING refers to the subjectively-oriented mental process of taking hold of, apprehending, seizing, or clinging to perceptions. In simple terms, grasping means believing that one's thoughts and emotions are true, and then speaking and acting with this as a foundation.

The ***GUHYAGARBHA TANTRA***, or the *Glorious Web of Magical Illusions*, the principal tantra of Mahayoga, is a massive text in twenty-two chapters, which contains teachings on enlightened mind and its infinite manifestations, as well as all that is necessary to reveal it, from the Nyingma Vajrayana perspective.

GURU. Among the "Three Roots" of Vajrayana practice, the guru is the source of blessings. It is often said that one's guru is even kinder than the Buddha, since he or she directly bestows the empowerments, transmissions, and lineage instructions that lead to enlightenment. Guru Yoga is among the most profound techniques of the Secret Mantra, in which a practitioner merges his or her mind with the wisdom mind of the guru.

GURU PADMASAMBHAVA is an emanation of Buddha Amitabha and Avalokiteshvara, born miraculously on a lotus in Dhanakosha Lake (sometimes called Sindu Lake) in the land of Oddiyana, northwest of India. He is the embodiment of all the buddhas of the three times and the ten directions, and was predicted by Buddha Shakyamuni as the great being who would serve as his regent. He is a buddha who attained the transcendental wisdom rainbow body, an ever-youthful immortal body. In the eighth century, Shantarakshita encouraged King Trisong Deutsen to invite him to Tibet in order to subdue the forces that were thwarting the establishment of the Buddhadharma. Out of compassion for future generations, knowing that the oral transmission (kama) of the Buddha's teachings would either become lost or diluted, he hid innumerable Dharma treasures of texts and relics, known as "terma," throughout Tibet, Nepal, Bhutan, and elsewhere to be discovered by destined disciples, known as "tertons," in the centuries to come. Guru Padmasambhava is a living buddha, ever-present and available, manifesting in infinite forms, who at all times and in all places fulfills the temporal and spiritual wishes of all beings.

The ***HEART SUTRA***, otherwise known as the *Heart of Transcendent Wisdom*, is perhaps the most famous of all the Prajnaparamita texts, which teaches the emptiness of all phenomena.

HINAYANA. Literally "Lesser Vehicle," this group of Buddhist teachings is so named because it focuses on individual enlightenment rather than that of all sentient beings. The Hinayana comprises the foundational Buddhist teachings of the Shravakayana and Pratyekabuddhayana. It emphasizes monastic discipline, strict meditation, contemplation of the Four Noble Truths, renunciation of the worldly distractions of samsara, and rigorous study of the twelve links of dependent origination, all of which eventually bring about the realization of the emptiness of self and thereby liberation from cyclic existence, known as arhathood. The principal philosophical views of the Hinayana are expounded in the Vaibhashika and Sautrantika schools.

IMPERMANENCE is one of the essential points of Buddha Shakyamuni's teaching. There are two forms of impermanence: 1) gross impermanence refers to the obvious constant change perceived by the senses, while 2) subtle impermanence reflects the fact that nothing can remain identical to itself even from one moment to the next.

JAMGON KONGTRUL LODRO THAYE (1813-1900) was the reincarnation of Vairochana. A great scholar, siddha, and teacher, as well as a prolific writer, he synthesized the knowledge and experience of many Tibetan Buddhist lineages in his *Five Great Treasures*, and over the course of his long life he authored over one hundred volumes of scripture. He is widely renowned—along with the First Khyentse—for being one of the founders of the Rime, or non-sectarian movement of Tibetan Buddhism.

JIGME GYALWAI NYUGU (1765-1843), along with the first Dodrupchen Jigme Thinley Ozer, was responsible for the spread of the Longchen Nyingthig lineage throughout Tibet, particular in the eastern region. When he first met his root teacher, Jigme Lingpa, he felt such profound devotion that immediate realization of the Dzogchen view dawned in his heart. Considered an embodiment of Avalokiteshvara, he was a beloved teacher and a profound realization being.

JIGME LINGPA (1730-1798) was an emanation of both Vimalamitra and King Trisong Deutsen's grandson, Prince Lhaje. One of the greatest visionaries in Tibetan history, he discovered the Longchen Nyingthig, or the *Heart Essence of Longchenpa*, which is one of the most widely practiced terma cycles. He was also a poet, siddha, and scholar. All of his knowledge was gained through Dzogchen meditation rather than through study. He therefore exemplifies the teachings that assert that once the true nature is discovered and stabilized, all wisdom is spontaneously revealed.

JNANASUTRA was born to a low-caste family in Kamashila, eastern India. He became a scholar and went to Bodhgaya, where he met Vimalamitra. Vajrasattva appeared in the sky to both of them saying, "Oh noble sons, you have been scholars for five hundred lives without reaching your goals. If you want to attain enlightenment and the transcendental wisdom rainbow body in this lifetime, you should go and receive the Dzogchen teachings from Shri Singha." Vimalamitra went to Shri Singha first, received teachings, and returned. Then Jnanasutra went to Shri Singha, and studied with and served him for many years. Shri Singha gave Jnanasutra the complete Dzogchen teachings, including some that he had not given to Vimalamitra. He also gave Jnanasutra his last testament, the *Seven Nails*. Later, Jnanasutra gave all the teachings he received from Shri Singha to Vimalamitra. When Jnanasutra attained the transcendental wisdom rainbow body, he imparted his last testament, the *Four Methods of Contemplation*, to Vimalamitra:

> Homage to the primordially pure emptiness.
>
> How wonderful! If you train in this, joy will naturally arise. If you wish to attain the state of great equanimity, gain experience in these contemplations:
>
> 1) If you wish to be trained in all esoteric activities, maintain all appearances in the directness of natural contemplation.
> 2) If you wish to gain strength in your meditation, remain in the unity of mind and phenomena, through the ocean-like natural contemplation.
> 3) If you wish to attain self-liberation from all views, bring phenomena to cessation through the mountain-like natural contemplation.
> 4) If you wish to attain all the results as they are, liberate all the errors in training with the mountain-like view.

KAGYU means "hearing lineage," and is one of the New Translation schools of Tibetan Buddhism. The Kagyu follows the teachings of Tilopa and Naropa, which were brought to Tibet in the eleventh century by Marpa and transmitted to Milarepa.

KAMA refers to the oral transmission of the Nyingma school, the body of teachings translated during the period when Guru Padmasambhava was in Tibet, which has been transmitted in an uninterrupted and continuous lineage through this day.

KARMA CHAGME (1613-1678), an emanation of Avalokiteshvara and an ardent devotee of Amitabha, was a great Nyingma and Kagyu master. A prolific scholar and author, he was both the teacher and manager of the youngest terton in Nyingma history, Migyur Dorje, the discoverer of the Namcho cycle.

KHENPO NGAKCHUNG (1879-1941), also known as Khenpo Ngawang Palzang, was an emanation of Vimalamitra, a major Longchen Nyingthig lineage holder, and one of the most revered and influential Dzogchen masters of recent times. Many have called him the "Second Longchenpa."

KING TRISONG DEUTSEN (742-810), along with Guru Padmasambhava and Shantarakshita, established Buddhism in Tibet. During his reign, Tibet became perhaps the most powerful nation in central Asia. An emanation of Manjushri and a realized being, his reincarnations include the two terton kings, Nyangral Nyima Ozer and Guru Chowang.

LAMA SHANG RINPOCHE (1123-1189), also known as Shang Yudrakpa Tsandru Dakpa, was the founder of the Shangpa Kagyu school of Tibetan Buddhism and a highly realized siddha of Mahamudra.

LONGCHENPA (1308-1363), known as the "Great Omniscient One" and the "Second Garab Dorje," was a Dzogchen master admired by all schools of Tibetan Buddhism for the majestic scope of his Dzogchen and tantric writings, which reconciled and synthesized many prior traditions. His "Seven Treasures" are a monument of Tibetan religious literature, and his more than 250 treatises on all manner of subjects have informed the doctrinal core of Nyingma monastic learning for five hundred years. It is widely held that no one in history has written on the Dzogchen view as powerfully and eloquently as he. Many masters have said that simply by reading Longchenpa's Dzogchen writings one will directly experience the Dzogchen state.

LORD DRIKUNG (1143-1217), also known as Kyobpa Jigten Sumgon, was the reincarnation of Nagarjuna and the founder of the Drikung Kagyu lineage of Tibetan Buddhism.

MACHIK LABDRON (1055-1143) was a student of Padamapa Sangye and the mother of the practice of Chod, a radical synthesis of the Prajnaparamita and tantric Guru Yoga that "cuts through" the ego.

The **MADHYAMAKA**, or Middle Way school, was founded by Nagarjuna based on the Prajnaparamita sutras taught by the Buddha. It holds that all phenomena are empty of substantial existence because they depend on multiple causes and conditions, and also that all phenomena are encompassed by the two truths, absolute and relative. All phenomena are considered illusory manifestations of the true nature. Even mind—the ground of consciousness—is devoid of substantial existence.

MAHAMUDRA means "Great Seal." It is the most direct practice for the realization of buddha-nature in Vajrayana according to the Kagyu, Sakya, and Gelug schools of Tibetan Buddhism.

MAHASIDDHA means "great accomplished one." It refers to a master of meditation, particularly one who can manifest great spiritual powers.

MAHAYANA. Literally, "Great Vehicle," the Mahayana teachings are characterized by the practice of the six paramitas, the cultivation of the altruistic intention to free all beings from the sufferings of samsara, and the active application of this intention in action or practice. These latter two are respectively known as "aspiring bodhichitta" and "actualizing bodhichitta." Including both sutras and tantras, the Mahayana is generally associated with the second, third, and fourth turnings of the wheel of Dharma, which emphasize the inseparable union of wisdom and compassion.

MAITREYA is the Future Buddha, the fifth buddha of this Fortunate Aeon, and the successor of Buddha Shakyamuni. Maitreya means "loving-kindness." It is also possible to interpret Maitreya as being the potential for enlightenment inherent in each one of us. This remains a "future" attainment until we realize it.

MANJUSHRIMITRA was one of the greatest scholars of his day. When he heard of Garab Dorje's teaching that transcended effort and the laws of cause and effect, he deemed them heretical. He searched for Garab Dorje with the hope of engaging and defeating him in debate. Manjushrimitra lost the debate, became Garab Dorje's student, and studied with him for seventy-five years, becoming his principal disciple and spiritual heir. It was Manjushrimitra who divided the Dzogchen teachings into three sections: 1) Mind, 2) Space, and 3) Pith Instruction. Upon attaining the transcendental wisdom rainbow body, he imparted his last testament, known as the *Six Meditation Experiences*, to his principal disciple, Shri Singha:

> Oh son of good family, if you wish to experience
> the continuity of naked awareness:
> 1) Focus on absolute awareness as the object (the clear sky).
> 2) Press the points of the body (by posture).
> 3) Close the way of coming and going (breathing).
> 4) Focus on the target (ultimate sphere).
> 5) Rely on the unmoving (body, eyes, and awareness).
> 6) Grasp the vast expanse (the nature of awareness itself).

MARPA (1012-1097) was the great Tibetan lay master who inherited Naropa's complete lineage and passed it on to Milarepa.

MINDFULNESS means "alertness," "recollection," "not forgetting," "attentiveness," and "presence of mind."

MIPHAM RINPOCHE (1845-1912) was a renowned Nyingma scholar, master, and terton. Even though he attained the highest realization and was one of the greatest Nyingma masters in history, he was a simple and humble wandering hermitage monk. He is considered to be an emanation of both Manjushri and Nubchen Sangye Yeshe. His root teacher was the First Khyentse, and he also studied with Patrul Rinpoche and many other great masters. He was a major figure in the Rime non-sectarian movement in Tibet. His written works fill thirty-two volumes. He wrote from his own direct knowledge on topics from all ten sciences, and these became the textbooks used in all the Nyingma monastic institutions.

NAROPA was the disciple of Tilopa and the teacher of Marpa. The endurance and devotion he demonstrated as he was tested and trained by Tilopa is legendary. He is famous for his Six Yogas. He is an archetype of the scholar who becomes a siddha by serving a guru. Tilopa's last words to him were, "Do not imagine, think, deliberate, or act, but be at rest. Have no concern for an object."

NAGARJUNA (50 BCE-550 CE) was the great founder of the Madhyamaka school, and the *Root Verses of the Wisdom of the Middle Way* is his most famous work. He discovered the *Prajnaparamita Sutra in One Hundred Thousand Verses*. Among the eight vidyadharas, he is the Lord of Lotus Speech.

The **NINE YANAS** comprise the complete Buddhist path to enlightenment according to the Nyingma school of Tibetan Buddhism. They are:

1) Shravakayana, or "Hearer Vehicle"
2) Pratyekabuddhayana, or "Solitary Realizer Vehicle"
3) Bodhisattvayana, or "Bodhisattva Vehicle"
4) Kriyayogatantra, or "Action Yoga Tantra"
5) Upayogatantra, or "Dual Yoga Tantra"
6) Yogayogatantra, or "Yoga Tantra"
7) Mahayogatantra, or "Great Yoga Tantra"
8) Anuyogatantra, or "Subsequent Yoga Tantra"
9) Atiyogatantra, or "Supreme Yoga Tantra"

According to the Nyingma classification, the first two yanas are known as "Foundational Buddhism," or "Hinayana," and all the rest of the yanas—from the third through the ninth—are known as "Mahayana." The Vajrayana, also known as "Tantrayana," includes everything from Kriyayoga (the fourth yana) up to and including Atiyoga (the ninth). Yanas four through six—Kriyayoga, Upayoga, and Yogayoga—comprise the Outer Tantras, while yanas seven through nine—Mahayoga, Anuyoga, and Atiyoga—make up the Inner Tantras.

NONDUALITY literally means "not two," and is the realization that in absolute truth, there is no "I" and no "other;" that all external phenomena are inseparable from mind. It can also be understood as the mind freed from all conceptual and emotional fixations.

NYINGMA means "ancient tradition." The earliest of the four schools of Tibetan Buddhism, it follows the teachings that Guru Padmasambhava, Shantarakshita, and Vimalamitra first propagated in Tibet in the eighth century during the reign of King Trisong Deutsen. The Sarma, or "New Tradition" schools of Tibetan Buddhism—Kagyu, Sakya, Kadam, and Gelug—are based primarily on translations of Dharma texts that were undertaken when a new wave of Buddhist teachings were introduced from India during the eleventh century. It was after this point that the lineage associated with the early dissemination of Buddhism in Tibet became known as "Ancient." The Nyingma school is transmitted in two principal lineages: 1) the "long or distant lineage of kama" and 2) the "short or close lineage of terma."

NYOSHUL LUNGTOK (1829-1901), also known as Nyoshul Lungtok Tenpe Nyima, was an emanation of Shantarakshita and the greatest realized disciple of Patrul Rinpoche. His last words were: "To be immersed in genuine, unfettered being is to be like the sun rising at dawn. This is the vision of dharmakaya—how marvelous!"

PADAMPA SANGYE (eleventh century) was an Indian mahasiddha who visited Tibet at least three times before eventually settling in Tingri. He is the father of Chod, and his best-known teaching is Shije, or "Pacifying Suffering." His testament to the people of Tingri, called the *Hundred Verses of Advice*, contains one hundred epigrams that encompass the entire Buddhist path, and has been renowned and studied for centuries.

PATRUL RINPOCHE (1808-1887), a great Nyingma scholar, poet, and teacher, was the speech incarnation of Jigme Lingpa. His teaching style was simple, direct, and powerful. It is said he had the ability to uproot the errors of even the most obstinate wrongdoers. He lived as a wandering mendicant, traveling from village to village and inspiring the people to give up hunting and slaughtering animals, and to cultivate love, peace, and harmony. He was also the root teacher to many disciples who themselves became great masters.

POST-MEDITATION. During formal meditation we learn how to rest in profound emptiness, the nongrasping state of nonduality, and during post-meditation we learn how to continuously work with the richness qualities of mind, including love, compassion, and wisdom. This helps us maintain a balance between the absolute and relative aspects of awareness, enabling us to increasingly discover them both.

PRAJNAPARAMITA literally means "transcendent wisdom." The Prajnaparamita sutras contain the Mahayana teachings on emptiness associated with the second turning of the wheel of Dharma, which explain how to transcend fixation on subject, object, and action.

The ***PRAYER OF KUNTUZANGPO*** is a hugely influential Dzogchen teaching discovered as a terma by the great Nyingma master Rigdzin Godemchen (1337-1408). It instructs us to abide relaxedly in the nature of mind, and to let all mental events, particularly emotions, come and go. By doing so, we instantaneously attain enlightenment in the form of the Primordial Buddha Kuntuzangpo, with the power to lead all beings into that same state.

PRIMORDIAL. Timeless, from the beginning, original, beyond time, free from all grasping.

PRIMORDIAL NATURE. Traditionally referred to as buddha-nature, this is the inherent nature of all sentient beings, and the essential teaching of both the Mahayana sutras and the tantras. Although the beautiful, radiating qualities of mind are often obscured by temporary dualistic conceptions, the nature of mind is the unborn, indivisible union of emptiness and compassion, pervading all subjects. In fact, "buddha-nature" is known by many names: it is sometimes called "absolute bodhichitta," "Prajnaparamita," "Mother of All the Buddhas," "Madhyamaka," "Mahamudra," and "rigpa," among others. According to the Mahayana sutras, buddha-nature transcends the four extremes of 1) existence, 2) nonexistence, 3) both, and 4) neither. In the context of the Inner Tantras and Dzogchen in particular, buddha-nature is often called the "inseparable union of primordially pure and spontaneously inherent qualities" of mind, as well as the "self-born luminosity of awareness." Each of these terms points to the inseparability of wisdom and compassion, or emptiness and appearance. Briefly, the emptiness aspect of the nature of mind is known as the absolute equality of emptiness, whereas compassion is the clarity aspect of the nature of mind that radiates out to oneself and others.

RELATIVE TRUTH refers to ordinary, conditioned beliefs about how the world is, which can be unique to one being or shared collectively.

RIGDZIN KUMARADZA (1266-1343) was a great Dzogchen master and teacher, and a major lineage holder of the Vima Nyingthig. A wandering yogi-mendicant, he was renowned for his austere nomadic lifestyle and unconventional approach to teaching. He was a senior disciple of Drupchen Melong Dorje and the root teacher of both Longchenpa and the Third Karmapa Rangjung Dorje.

SARAHA (c. eighth century) was of the greatest yogis in Indian Buddhist history and a founder of the Mahamudra tradition. His life story and his spontaneous songs of realization, known as the *Three Cycles of Doha*, are testaments to his iconoclastic approach to spiritual liberation, as well as to his poetic genius.

The ***SEVEN CHAPTER PRAYER*** was composed by Guru Padmasambhava himself in response to the requests of five of his closest disciples. It is a rich, multi-layered Guru Yoga liturgy that, according to His Holiness Dilgo Khyentse Rinpoche encompasses the entire scope of Nyingma Buddhist theory and practice. It was discovered as a terma by Tulku Zangpo Dragpa and Rigdzin Godemchen in the fourteenth century.

SHANTARAKSHITA, considered to be an emanation of Vajrapani, was the head abbot of Nalanda Monastic University, as well as a world-class logician and philosopher. He is the author of the *Ornament of the Middle Way*, which synthesized the Madhyamaka tradition of Nagarjuna, the Yogachara tradition of Asanga, and the logic and epistemological thought of Dharmakirti. He was the co-founder of Tibetan Buddhism, along with King Trisong Deutsen and Guru Padmasambhava, and ordained the first seven monks in Tibet. While in Tibet, he taught both the sutras and tantras to many disciples, trained the first Tibetan translators, and translated many texts himself. He was renowned for his gentleness and kindness. In Tibet he is called "Khenchen Bodhisattva."

SHANTIDEVA (eighth century) was an Indian Buddhist scholar-monk and adherent of Nagarjuna's Madhyamaka philosophy. He is also counted among the eighty-four mahasiddhas. His *Guide to the Bodhisattva's Way of Life* is esteemed as one of the greatest writings in Buddhist history.

SHRI SINGHA, heeding the prophecies of Avalokiteshvara, went to Manjushrimitra and studied with him for twenty-five years, becoming his principal disciple. Shri Singha received Manjushrimitra's last testament, the *Six Meditation Experiences*, just as Manjushrimitra was entering mahaparanirvana. Shri Singha thus became the third lineage holder of the complete Dzogchen teachings, and later became the first to spread them more widely. When he attained the transcendental wisdom rainbow body, he imparted his last testament, known as the *Seven Nails*, to Jnanasutra:

> Homage to perfect primordial wisdom, the unity of clarity and emptiness, the great self-existing awareness, open and impartial, which pervades and abides in all. Nail the original, unchanging

ground with the seven great nails of the path of nonduality, and unchanging great bliss will arise.

1) Nail samsara and nirvana together with the unobstructed clarity of pure wisdom.
2) Nail the observer and observed together with self-appearing clear light.
3) Nail mind and matter together with spontaneous pure essence.
4) Nail phenomena and the nature of phenomena together with absolute awareness.
5) Nail nihilism and eternalism together with freedom from views.
6) Nail elation and depression together with the liberation of the sense faculties.
7) Nail appearances and emptiness together with the primordially perfect dharmakaya.

The **SIX ORNAMENTS OF INDIA** are the six great commentators on the Buddha's teaching: the Mahayana masters Nagarjuna, Aryadeva, Asanga, Vasubhandu, Dignaga, and Dharmakirti.

SIX PARAMITAS, or the "six perfections" are a bridge we use to cross from samsara's shore of delusion to the other shore of enlightenment, and are thus the principal practices of the bodhisattvas. They are 1) generosity, 2) self-discipline, 3) patience, 4) joyful effort, 5) concentration, and 6) wisdom. We usually do our practice on a cushion, maintaining the mind in its natural state, which is free from concepts. This is the combined practice of the fifth paramita of concentration and the sixth paramita of wisdom, or emptiness meditation. But it is difficult to maintain this kind of practice when engaged in normal, everyday activities. So, in order to help bodhisattvas carry their Dharma practice out into the world to benefit others, the Buddha taught the first three paramitas of generosity, self-discipline, and patience. These are methods of training in actual post-meditation activities rooted in loving-kindness and compassion. The fourth paramita of joyful effort is considered to be an essential support of all the other paramitas, whether related with meditation or post-meditation.

The **SUTRAS** are the second of the Three Baskets. They are original discourses given by Buddha Shakyamuni in response to requests from his students. A sutra always begins with the statement, "Thus have I heard," followed by details of the time and place at which the sutra was taught, the students' questions and the Buddha's answers, and concluding with everyone rejoicing in the teachings. These discourses were compiled and transcribed by his arhat followers during the "First Council" held shortly after the Awakened One's mahaparinirvana, especially with the help of his cousin and long-time attendant Ananda, who possessed the siddhi of perfect recall, as well as arhats Mahakashyapa and Upali. The Sutras are classified as belonging either to the Hinayana or Mahayana, depending on whether they are related with the first, second, or third turnings of the wheel of Dharma.

TERMA are Dharma treasures—teachings, texts, and relics—hidden throughout Tibet, Nepal, Bhutan, and indeed throughout the world during the eighth and ninth century by Guru Padmasambhava, assisted by Yeshe Tsogyal. These treasures are later discovered at the appropriate time by destined disciples, who are all reincarnations of the twenty-five disciples of Guru

Padmasambhava. The treasure-revealers, or tertons, recover these treasures from the sky and earth, from sacred places such as temples, sometimes in the form of pure visions, or even from within their own minds.

TOGAL, one of the two major Dzogchen practices, literally means the "leap-over (or jump) that puts one on top." The practice of Togal unveils the radiance and power of the nature of mind; it also reveals the essences of the five elements—space, wind, fire, water, and earth—that comprise the physical universe. A good foundation in Trekcho is needed for the practice of Togal to fully blossom.

TILOPA is the father of the Kagyu lineage. He is most famous as the powerful and enigmatic guru of Naropa. His songs are essential Mahamudra teachings.

TRANSCENDENTAL WISDOM RAINBOW BODY is the transformation of the gross physical body into a body of pure light that can occur at the time of death for advanced Dzogchen practitioners, if they so choose.

TREKCHO literally means "cutting through." It is the path of effortlessly letting go of all ideas and emotions, of opening oneself up to pure experience ungoverned by grasping. Trekcho is the foundational practice of Dzogchen; it reveals the vast expanse of dharmakaya, while Togal reveals the full splendor of sambhogakaya and nirmanakaya.

TSASUM LINGPA (c. 1697-c.1744), was born in eastern Tibet near the holy mountain Jowo Zegyal, and was an incarnation of Nubchen Sangye Yeshe. He was a great Nyingma master and one of the greatest crazy wisdom yogis in Tibetan Buddhist history. He was also renowned as a revealer of earth termas and for his mastery of wind walking. His terma teachings fill twenty-three volumes.

TURNING THE WHEEL OF DHARMA is a poetic expression that refers to how the Buddha began and continued to teach the sacred Dharma—here the "wheel of Dharma" is an allusion to the "wheel of sharp weapons" said to be held by a universal monarch, or *chakravartin*. Each of the turnings of the wheel of Dharma is known as *dharmachakra* in Sanskrit. According to the Nyingma school, the Buddha turned the wheel of Dharma four times, where the Vajrayana is considered to be the fourth turning. 1) First, he taught the emptiness of self and the Four Noble Truths. 2) Second, he taught the emptiness of both self and other (phenomena) in his Perfection of Wisdom teachings, or Prajnaparamita, characterized by emptiness, signlessness, and aspirationlessness. 3) Third, he taught buddha-nature. 4) Finally, he taught the union of the first three turnings of the wheel of Dharma, the Vajrayana and Dzogchen.

The **TWELVE ASCETIC PRACTICES** are: 1) wearing clothing found in a dust-heap; 2) owning only three robes; 3) wearing felt or woolen clothes; 4) begging for food; 5) eating one's meal in a single sitting; 6) restricting the quantity of food; 7) staying in isolation; 8) sitting under trees; 9) sitting in exposed places; 10) sitting in charnel grounds; 11) sitting even during sleep; 12) and staying wherever one happens to be.

TWO TRUTHS. The two truths include relative truth and absolute truth. Taught by Buddha Shakyamuni principally during the second and third turnings of the wheel of Dharma, the teachings on absolute truth emphasize the nature of all phenomena, or emptiness, whereas teachings on relative truth emphasize the manifest, radiating qualities of the nature, including the inherent, beautiful qualities of buddha-nature. In general, relative truth describes that which accords with conventional, worldly understanding of phenomena; however, when subjected to thorough analysis, the solidity of phenomena dissolves. All phenomena are thus revealed to be dependently arisen mere appearances with the nature of emptiness.

VASUBANDHU (fourth century) was a great Indian Buddhist scholar, logician, and author. Along with his half-brother Asanga, he was one of the main founders of the Yogachara (Mind Only) school of philosophy, and author of the famous book *Abhidharmakosha*, a summary of the entire Hinayana philosophy.

VIMALAMITRA (eighth and ninth centuries), one of the greatest Indian Buddhist scholars and siddhas, was a major Dzogchen lineage holder, and one of the first Dzogchen teachers in Tibet, along with Guru Padmasambhava and Vairochana. His most renowned teaching is called the Vima Nyingthig, or the *Heart Essence of Vimalamitra.* He achieved the transcendental wisdom rainbow body, and is said to be residing in that form at Five-Peaked Mountain in China. According to tradition, an emanation of Vimalamitra appears every century in the human world in order to revitalize the Dzogchen teachings.

The **VINAYA** is the first of the Three Baskets. It includes the Buddha's teachings on ethics in general and on monastic discipline in particular.

YANGOMPA (1213-1287) was one of the great masters of the Drukpa Kagyu school, and a principal disciple of Gotsangpa.

LIST OF FIGURES

All gonpa wall and mural photographs are used with permission.

ABOUT THE AUTHORS

KHENCHEN PALDEN SHERAB RINPOCHE (1938-2010)

Venerable Khenchen Palden Sherab Rinpoche was a renowned scholar and meditation master of Nyingma, the Ancient school of Tibetan Buddhism. He was born on May 10, 1938, in the Dhoshul region of Kham, eastern Tibet, near the sacred mountain Jowo Zegyal. On the morning of his birth a small snow fell with the flakes in the shape of lotus petals. Among his ancestors were many great scholars, practitioners, and tertons.

His family was semi-nomadic, living in the village during the winter and moving with the herds to high mountain pastures, where they lived in yak hair tents during the summers. The monastery for the Dhoshul region is known as Gochen Monastery, founded by the great terton Tsasum Lingpa, and his father's family had the hereditary responsibility for administration of the business affairs of the monastery. His grandfather had been both administrator and chantmaster in charge of the ritual ceremonies.

Khenchen Rinpoche began his education at Gochen Monastery at the age of four. He entered Riwoche Monastery at age fourteen, completing his studies there just before the Chinese invasion of Tibet reached that area. His root teacher was the illustrious Khenchen Tenzin Dragpa (Katok Khenpo Akshu).

In 1959, Rinpoche and his family were forced into exile, escaping to India. After the tumultuous period following their escape, in 1967 he was appointed head of the Nyingma department of the Central Institute of Higher Tibetan Studies in Sarnath by His Holiness Dudjom Rinpoche, the Supreme Head of the Nyingma school of Tibetan Buddhism. He held this position for seventeen years, dedicating all his time and energy to ensure the survival and spread of the Buddha's teachings. Venerable Khenchen Palden Sherab Rinpoche moved to the United States in 1984 to work closely with His Holiness Dudjom Rinpoche. In 1985, he and his brother, Venerable Khenpo Tsewang Dongyal Rinpoche, founded the Dharma Samudra Publishing Company. In 1988, they founded the Padmasambhava Buddhist Center (PBC), which has centers throughout the United States, as well as in Puerto Rico, Russia, and India, among others. The principal center is Padma Samye Ling, located in Delaware County, upstate New York. PBC also includes a traditional Tibetan Buddhist monastery and nunnery at the holy site of Deer Park in Sarnath, and the Miracle Stupa for World Peace at Padma Samye Jetavan, which is in Jetavan Grove, Shravasti, India.

Khenchen Palden Sherab Rinpoche traveled extensively within the United States and throughout the world, giving teachings and empowerments, conducting retreats and seminars, and establishing meditation centers. He authored three volumes of Tibetan works, and co-authored over twenty-five books in English with Khenpo Tsewang Dongyal Rinpoche. His collected Tibetan works include:

Opening the Eyes of Wisdom, a commentary on Sangye Yeshe's *Lamp of the Eye of Contemplation*;

Waves of the Ocean of Devotion, a biography-praise to Nubchen Sangye Yeshe, and *Vajra Rosary*, biographies of his main incarnations;

The Mirror of Mindfulness, an explanation of the six bardos;

Advice from the Ancestral Vidyadhara, a commentary on Padmasambhava's *Stages of the Path, Heap of Jewels*;

Blazing Clouds of Wisdom and Compassion, a commentary on the hundred-syllable mantra of Vajrasattva;

The Ornament of Vairochana's Intention, a commentary on the *Heart Sutra*;

Opening the Door of Blessings, a biography of Machik Labdron;

Lotus Necklace of Devotion, a biography of Khenchen Tenzin Dragpa;

The Essence of Diamond Clear Light, an outline and structural analysis of *The Aspiration Prayer of Samantabhadra*;

The Radiant Light of the Sun and Moon, a commentary on Mipham Rinpoche's *Wisdom Sword*;

The Ornament of Stars at Dawn, an outline and structural analysis of Vasubandhu's *Twenty Verses*;

Pleasure Lake of Nagarjuna's Intention, general summary of Madhyamaka;

Supreme Clear Mirror, an introduction to Buddhist logic;

White Lotus, an explanation of prayers to Guru Rinpoche;

Smiling Red Lotus, a short commentary on a prayer to Yeshe Tsogyal;

Clouds of Blessings; an explanation of prayers to Terchen Tsasum Lingpa; and other learned works, poems, prayers and sadhanas.

The Smile of Sun and Moon: A Commentary on the Praise to the Twenty-One Taras.

KHENPO TSEWANG DONGYAL RINPOCHE (1950-)

Venerable Khenpo Tsewang Dongyal Rinpoche was born in the Dhoshul region of Kham in eastern Tibet on June 10, 1950. On that summer day in the family tent, Rinpoche's birth caused his mother Pema Lhadze no pain. The next day, upon moving the bed where she had delivered the baby, his mother found growing a beautiful and fragrant flower which she plucked and offered to Chenrezig on the family altar. Soon after Khenpo Tsewang was born, three head lamas from Jadchag Monastery came to his home and recognized him as the reincarnation of Khenpo Sherab Khyentse, who had been the former head abbot at Gochen Monastery. Sherab Khyentse was a renowned scholar and practitioner who spent much of his life in retreat.

Khenpo Rinpoche began his formal schooling at the age of five, when he entered Gochen Monastery. However, his first Dharma teacher was his father, Lama Chimed Namgyal Rinpoche.

The Chinese invasion of Tibet interrupted his studies, and he escaped to India with his family on 1959. There his father and brother continued his education until he entered the Nyingmapa Monastic School of northern India, where he studied until 1967. Khenpo Rinpoche then entered the Central Institute of Higher Tibetan Studies, which at the time was then a part of Sanskrit University in Varanasi, where he received his BA degree in 1975. He also attended Nyingmapa University in West Bengal, where he received another BA and an MA in 1977.

In 1978, His Holiness Dudjom Rinpoche enthroned Venerable Khenpo Tsewang Dongyal Rinpoche as the abbot of the Wish-fulfilling Nyingmapa Institute in Boudanath, Nepal, where he taught poetry, grammar, and philosophy. Then, in 1981, His Holiness appointed Khenpo Rinpoche as the abbot of the Dorje Nyingpo center in Paris, France. Finally, in 1982, he asked Khenpo Tsewang to work with him at the Yeshe Nyingpo center in New York. During that time until His Holiness Dudjom Rinpoche's mahaparinirvana in 1987, Khenpo Rinpoche continued to work closely with him, often traveling with His Holiness as his translator and attendant.

In 1988, Khenpo Tsewang Dongyal Rinpoche and his brother, Venerable Khenchen Palden Sherab Rinpoche, founded the Padmasambhava Buddhist Center. Since that time, he has served as a spiritual director at the various Padmasambhava Buddhist Centers throughout the world. He maintains an active traveling and teaching schedule.

Khenpo Tsewang Rinpoche is the author of *Light of Fearless Indestructible Wisdom: The Life and Legacy of His Holiness Dudjom Rinpoche*, published in both Tibetan and English. He has also authored a book of poetry on the life of Guru Rinpoche entitled *Praise to the Lotus Born: A Verse Garland of Waves of Devotion*, and a unique two-volume cultural and religious history of Tibet entitled *Six Sublime Pillars of the Nyingma School*, which details the historical bases of the Dharma in Tibet from the sixth through ninth centuries. At present, this is one of the only books yet written that conveys the Dharma activities of this historical period in such depth, and His Holiness Dudjom Rinpoche encouraged Khenpo Tsewang to complete it, describing the work as an important contribution to the history of the kama lineage.

Along with these, Khenpo Tsewang Dongyal Rinpoche has co-authored over twenty-five Dharma books in English with Venerable Khenchen Palden Sherab Rinpoche.

PADMA SAMYE LING SHEDRA SERIES

The Venerable Khenpo Rinpoches have taught the Dharma in the United States for more than thirty years. In that time, they have given over a decade of shedra teachings. These clear and profound teachings include detailed summaries and commentaries by great Nyingma masters such as Kunkhyen Longchenpa and Mipham Rinpoche. Each of the PSL Shedra Series books distills the essential meaning of the Nyingma Shedra program that the Venerable Rinpoches received in Tibet as the last generation of lamas to be taught in the traditional monastic setting, which had carefully preserved the lineage teachings for centuries.

The PSL Shedra Series is developing into a complete and comprehensive Nyingma shedra curriculum that will serve as the basis for the present and future study of the Buddhadharma in PBC Centers. It is our hope that these books will provide a solid framework for traditional Tibetan Buddhist study by people in the English-speaking world, whose busy lives do not easily allow for more extended periods of retreat and study.

With the PSL Shedra Series, the Venerable Khenpo Rinpoches

are directly sustaining and glorifying the study curriculum that has enabled the Buddhadharma to be successfully carried from generation to generation. By developing intelligent, thorough analysis, practitioners establish a reliable foundation for realizing the path of enlightenment. The PSL Shedra Series currently includes:

(Nine Yanas) *Turning the Wisdom Wheel of the Nine Golden Chariots*

(Vol. 1) *Opening the Clear Vision of the Vaibhashika and Sautrantika Schools*

(Vol. 2) *Opening the Clear Vision of the Mind Only School*

(Vol. 3) *Opening the Wisdom Door of the Madhyamaka School*

(Vol. 4) *Opening the Wisdom Door of the Rangtong & Shentong Views: A Brief Explanation of the One Taste of the Second and Third Turning of the Wheel of Dharma*

(Vol. 5) *Opening the Wisdom Door of the Outer Tantras: Refining Awareness Through Ascetic Ritual and Purification Practice*

(Vol. 6) *Splendid Presence of the Great Guhyagarbha: Opening the Wisdom Door of the King of All Tantras*

(Vol. 7) *Key to Opening the Wisdom Door of Anuyoga: Exploring the One Taste of the Three Mandalas*

OTHER PUBLICATIONS BY THE AUTHORS

The Beauty of Awakened Mind: Dzogchen Lineage of the Great Master Shigpo Dudtsi

The Buddhist Path: A Practical Guide from the Nyingma Tradition of Tibetan Buddhism (formerly titled Opening to Our Primordial Nature)

Ceaseless Echoes of the Great Silence: A Commentary on the Heart Sutra Prajnaparamita

The Dark Red Amulet: Oral Instructions on the Practice of Vajrakilaya

Discovering Infinite Freedom: The Prayer of Kuntuzangpo

Door to Inconceivable Wisdom and Compassion

The Essential Journey of Life and Death
Volume I: Indestructible Nature of Body, Speech, and Mind
Volume II: Using Dream Yoga and Phowa as the Path

Heart Essence of Chetsun: Voice of the Lion (restricted)

Illuminating the Path: Ngondro Instructions According to the Nyingma School of Vajrayana Buddhism

Liberating Duality with Wisdom Display: The Eight Manifestations of Guru Padmasambhava

Light of Fearless Indestructible Wisdom: The Life and Legacy of His Holiness Dudjom Rinpoche

Lion's Gaze: A Commentary on the Tsig Sum Nedek

Pointing Out the Nature of Mind: Dzogchen Pith Instructions of Aro Yeshe Jungne

Prajnaparamita: The Six Perfections

Praise to the Lotus Born: A Verse Garland of Waves of Devotion

The Smile of Sun and Moon: A Commentary on the Praise to the Twenty-One Taras

Supreme Wisdom: Commentary on Yeshe Lama (restricted)

Tara's Enlightened Activity

OPENING THE DOOR OF THE DHARMA TREASURY PRACTICE GUIDES

A series of condensed instructions on some of the main practices of the Padmasambhava Buddhist Center and Nyingma lineage.

Volume 1: *Practice Guide for a Eulogy Praising the Twelve Deeds in the Life of the Buddha*
Volume 2: *Commentary on the Blessing Treasure: A Sadhana of the Buddha Shakyamuni*
Volume 3: *Practice Guide of the Seven Line Prayer of Padmasambhava*
Volume 4: *Practice Guide for the Contemplation of the Four Thoughts That Turn the Mind From Samsara*
Volume 5: *Practice Guide for the Contemplation of Vows and Conduct in the Nyingma Tradition*

More information about these and other works by the Venerable Khenpo Rinpoches can be found online at:
padmasambhava.org/chiso

PADMASAMBHAVA BUDDHIST CENTER

Venerable Khenchen Palden Sherab Rinpoche and Venerable Khenpo Tsewang Dongyal Rinpoche have established Padmasambhava Buddhist Center (PBC) to preserve the authentic message of Buddha Shakyamuni and Guru Padmasambhava in its entirety, and in particular to teach the tradition of Nyingmapa and Vajrayana Buddhism. It is dedicated to world peace and the supreme good fortune and well-being of all. PBC now includes over twenty centers in the United States, Russia, Canada, and Puerto Rico, in addition to monastic institutions in India, Russia, and the United States.

The Samye Translation Group was founded by the Venerable Khenpo Rinpoches to commemorate and preserve the great ancient tradition of translation that was firmly established during the glorious Tibetan Buddhist era of the seventh through tenth centuries. As a reflection of gratitude for the unique activities of these enlightened translators, the Samye Translation Group has published Dharma books that cover all nine yana teachings of the Nyingma school of Tibetan Buddhism, including shedra philosophy books.

For more information about the Venerable Khenpo Rinpoches' activities, the Samye Translation Group, or the Padmasambhava Buddhist Center, please contact:

Padma Samye Ling
618 Buddha Highway
Sidney Center, NY 13839
(607) 865-8068
padmasmabhava.org
jowozegyal@catskill.net

PADMA SAMYE CHÖKHOR LING MONASTERY • SARNATH, INDIA

ORGYEN SAMYE CHÖKHOR LING NUNNERY • SARNATH, INDIA

PADMA SAMYE JETAVAN, MIRACLE STUPA • SHRAVASTI, INDIA

GOCHEN MONASTERY • TIBET

PALM BEACH DHARMA CENTER • WEST PALM BEACH, FLORIDA

PALDEN SHERAB PEMA LING • JUPITER, FLORIDA

PADMA GOCHEN LING • MONTEREY, TENNESSEE

YESHE TSOGYAL HOUSE • NASHVILLE, TENNESSEE

PEMA TSOKYE DORJE LING • SAN JUAN, PUERTO RICO

MAHAKALA

EKAJATI

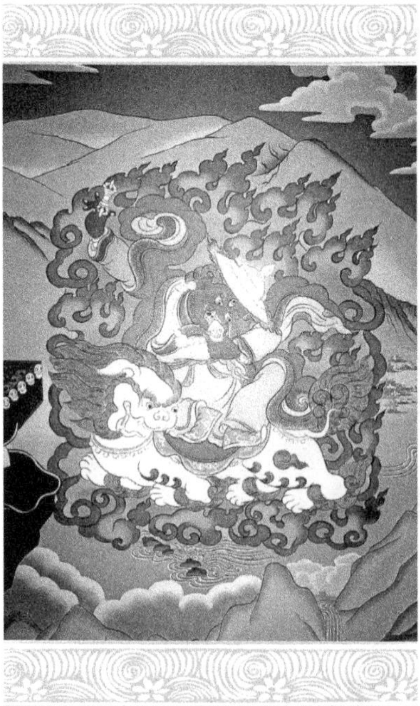

DORJE LEGPA

RAHULA

MANTRA THAT PURIFIES MISHANDLING A DHARMA TEXT

ཡི་གེ་ཉི་ཤུ་རྩ་དྲུག་པ་འདི་དཔེ་ཆའི་ནང་དུ་བཞག་ན་དཔེ་ཆ་དེར་ཅི་འདྲར་
བགོམས་ཀྱང་ཉེས་པ་མི་འབྱུང་བར་འཇམ་དཔལ་རྩ་རྒྱུད་ལས་གསུངས་སོ། །

CPSIA information can be obtained
at www.ICGtesting.com
Printed in the USA
BVHW060848130121
597694BV00002B/4

9 780983 407454